Home Cooking

2005 Recipe Annual

HOUSE of
WHITE
BIRCHES

PUBLISHERS
SINCE 1947

Home Cooking 2005 Recipe Annual

EDITORS	Judy Shaw, Alice Robinson
EDITOR-AT-LARGE	Carol Guthrie Dovell
ASSOCIATE EDITOR	Barb Sprunger
COPY EDITORS	Michelle Beck, Nicki Lehman, Mary O'Donnell, Beverly Richardson
EDITORIAL ASSISTANT	Holly Sprunger
PHOTOGRAPHY	Scott Campbell, Tammy Christian, Carl Clark, Don Clark, Christena Green, Matthew Owen
PHOTO STYLISTS	Martha Coquat, Nancy Sharp, Tammy M. Smith
FOOD TEAM	Joye Gardenour, Marcia VanGelder, Jerry Shaw
ART DIRECTOR	Brad Snow
ASSISTANT ART DIRECTOR	Nick Pierce
PUBLISHING SERVICES MANAGER	Brenda Gallmeyer
GRAPHIC ARTS SUPERVISOR	Ronda Bechinski
GRAPHIC ARTIST	Erin Augsburger
PRODUCTION ASSISTANTS	Cheryl Kempf, Marj Morgan
CHIEF EXECUTIVE OFFICER	John Robinson
PUBLISHING DIRECTOR	David J. McKee
MARKETING DIRECTOR	Dan Fink
EDITORIAL DIRECTOR	Vivian Rothe
PUBLISHING SERVICES DIRECTOR	Brenda R. Wendling

Printed in China
First Printing: 2005
Library of Congress Number: 2005928634
ISBN: 1-59217-091-9

1 2 3 4 5 6 7 8 9

Welcome!

2005 has been the first full year of our redesigned *Home Cooking* magazine. Even though our look has changed, the heart and soul of *Home Cooking* has not. We are still delivering tried-and-true, reader-provided comfort foods—many of which are quick to prepare.

We have introduced regular features to help you easily find some of your favorite kinds of recipes—From My Family Cookbook; Almost Homemade; Make-Ahead Recipes; Cook Quick, Eat Great; Bake Sale Best Sellers; Recipes for a Better You; Savings You'll Savor; Slow Cooker Recipes; and Cooking for Two.

As you leaf through these pages, you'll find all 539 delicious recipes from the issues, most with color pictures. It's been said that we eat first with our eyes, so knowing what something looks like before you make it helps you assemble a meal that is as attractive as it is delicious.

Judy Shaw and Alice Robinson, *Home Cooking,* **Editors.**

To give you a jump-start on meal planning, we have included 30 sample menus.

We have highlighted some of the staff's favorite recipes with our comments on what made them our top picks.

We hope you enjoy having a year's worth of recipes bound together in one convenient package.

Happy cooking,

Editors—Judy & Alice

Contents

January/February

The new year is a time of joy, festivity, and food! Whatever the occasion, we offer delectable selections sure to please: healthful dishes to take the drudgery out of keeping those New Year's resolutions; hearty, zesty snacks to satisfy "the boys" during the big game; hot, comforting soups to take the chill out of long winter evenings; and rich desserts sure to satisfy the most demanding sweet tooth.

March/April

The results are in! Indulge your chocolate cravings with one of our brownie contest winners—or try all four! And if that isn't enough, we have five scrumptious springtime cakes to add the finishing touch to your spring holiday ham or leg of lamb. Speed up your dinner preparations with a variety of make-ahead dishes and easy sautés that are as simple as they are delicious.

May/June

Savor the diversity of our great country with distinctive recipes from several regions. From New England we chose a traditional chowder and boiled dinner; the Midwest gave us farm-fresh pork chops and strawberry shortcake. The South is all about Southern hospitality with Daisy's Fruit Tea and Rose's Coconut Cream Pie. Spice up your menu as you prepare our dishes from the Southwestern corner of the United States. From Classic Grilled Alaska Salmon to The California Sandwich, you'll enjoy these easy-to-prepare dishes that offer natural goodness.

July/August

From tempting grilled fare to cool, creamy desserts, we give you every reason to turn off the stove and enjoy the carefree days of summer. We've provided a bounty of tried-and-true summer grilling recipes—including grilled vegetable and fruit kabobs. Pair these dishes with Connie Moore's colorful garden-fresh salads and scrumptious desserts for a spectacular Fourth of July picnic. Or try one of our cool and fruity beverages—best enjoyed while lounging under your favorite shade tree.

September/October

As farmers are harvesting the bounty of a summer's hard work, you can reap benefit from your own garden's plentiful produce. Use herbs to punch up the flavor of everyday foods—try the Tomato Basil Pita Pizza, or lemony Grecian Chicken. Apples, one of America's favorite fruits, taste great in pies, crisps and after-school snacks. We'll show you how to create delightful dishes to showcase the fruit—or vegetable—of your labor.

November/December

With favorite family recipes from our readers, you are sure to find something new to try at your next gathering. And when you go visiting during the holidays, don't go empty-handed. Craft a basket of homemade treats to take along. As you focus on big family dinners at the holidays, don't forget breakfast, too!

Indexes

Meet Our Staff

This is just some of the Home Cooking Team who has helped us fulfill our dream of a full-color magazine with pictures of all the recipes. We thought you'd like to see who they are.

Pictured left to right: Nancy Sharp, Photo Stylist; Brad Snow, Art Director; Erin Augsburger, Graphic Artist; Matthew Owen, Photographer; Marsha Van Gelder, Home Cooking Food Team; Holly Sprunger, Editorial Assistant; Barb Sprunger, Associate Editor and Joye Gardenour, Home Cooking Food Team. (Not pictured: Carl Clark, Photographer; Don Clark, Photographer.)

Pictured left to right: Scott Campbell, Photographer, and Martha Coquat, Photo Stylist.

Pictures left to right: Alice Robinson, Editor; Carol Dovell, Editor-at-Large and Judy Shaw, Editor.

Highlights from 2005

January/February

In our January/February issue of *Home Cooking* we were continually intrigued by the variety of traditions and food from different regions and ethnic origins for the New Year. We had a good time reading the different ways of celebrating—all of which included eating. We must confess we did not know how many ways there are to use cabbage!

Pasta With Tuna & Olives
Tuna, olives, lemon and capers give this easy—and quick—pasta a Mediterranean flare. Boiling the water for the pasta is the most time-consuming step.

Smoked Salmon & Spinach Quiche
Incredibly rich and luscious is the only way to describe this quiche. The smoky saltiness of the salmon pumps up the flavor of the spinach.

Chocolate Buttermilk Layer Cake
Smooth and chocolaty, this beautiful cake avoids being too sweet with the added tang of buttermilk, both in the layers and in the frosting. As an added bonus, every layer we baked was stable and did not fall.

Broccoli Wild Rice Soup
There is such a thing as a cream soup that is not loaded with fat! Fat-free cream cheese and 1 percent milk give great taste and texture to this healthful soup.

Strawberry Pecan Coffeecake
Using fresh or frozen strawberries in this coffeecake sets it apart from the usual blueberries, although it would be delicious that way, too.

Pigskin Calzones
Oh, the convenience of frozen bread dough! Don't allow the finished calzone to rise before baking, and you'll get a dense, chewy crust without any fuss.

March/April

In March/April it was our privilege to judge the brownie contest. Anytime we were baking a new series of brownie recipes, the other department employees would come from far and wide to see if we needed any additional testers. It was a popular feature.

There were some other wonderful things we tried in March/April for our theme of making dinner as quick and easy as possible—the make-ahead meatballs and the quick sautés were great.

Seven-Layer Dip
This traditional Mexican favorite can be varied to suit your own taste, but it makes for easy entertaining because it can be made ahead and refrigerated until the party.

Pear Waldorf Salad
Firm, ripe pears and sweet bananas combine to provide a refreshing change from the classic apples.

Roast Leg of Lamb
Roasted with savory pockets of garlic slivers, lamb is no more difficult that roasting beef or chicken. It makes a meal a special occasion.

Chicken Piccata
Chicken cutlets, sautéed and served in a tangy sauce containing lemon, butter, capers and spices makes a special meal that's ready in minutes.

Brownies
All of the Brownie Contest Winners were irresistible, but Helen Phillips' Irresistible Brownies were king with their perky chocolate chips on top. Try them all; they are great. The Turtle Brownies are chock-full of nuts for those who think brownies must have nuts, and the Marble Cheese Brownies have a creamy texture with the addition of cream cheese. The Chocomallow Brownies are super-simple because they start with a mix.

May/June

In the May/June issue we loved the regional cooking. We cooked wonderful things from all parts of the country, which demonstrate the diversity we find in comfort food. We were delighted to try the flavors of the West Coast because they brought new things to the cooking mix. It was fun finding figs and trying them with blue cheese and balsamic reduction sauce. Cooking a whole salmon for the Classic Grilled Alaska Salmon was a real treat.

Apricot Chicken Salad
We love pairing chicken with fruit in cold salads. This one is even more special with the yogurt, mayonnaise, apricot preserves and fresh ginger in the dressing.

Classic Grilled Alaska Salmon
The glaze used to brush on the salmon before grilling adds wonderful flavor without being overpowering. The Dijon-style mustard adds just the right amount of zip.

Mesclun & Goat Cheese Salad
Baby greens, dates, goat cheese and walnuts sound like a strange combination, especially if you have not tried goat cheese. Trust us, the sweetness of the dates, the unique flavor of the cheese and the crunch of the walnuts combine beautifully with the dark, flavorful greens.

Citrus Blast Sherbet
Citrus Blast Sherbet is an ice cream contest winner and a real staff favorite for its unique mixture of three citrus flavors—fresh orange, lemon and lime juice. It has an intensely refreshing taste.

Cherry-Berry Pie
This is a quick and easy fruit pie that can be made any season by combining frozen berries with canned pie filling.

Berry Buttermilk Pie
From Pat Eby's Midwest Farm Cooking article, this is a traditional buttermilk pie given the twist of fresh flavor by adding pureed strawberries.

Spinach, Strawberry & Pecan Salad With Orange Vinaigrette Dressing
Take advantage of flavorful, locally grown strawberries and a tangy orange vinaigrette to perk up your next spinach salad.

Tasty Crispy Tacos
This traditional Mexican staple, using prepared taco shells and a pound of ground beef, is so easy it will become a family favorite, especially when time is limited.

July/August

July/August found us loving summer and getting outside to work in the garden and fire up the grill. The recipes for a summer celebration are a mix of make-ahead dishes and things that can be grilled at the last minute. Grilling outside keeps the kitchen cool and adds a wonderful flavor.

Lump Crab Cakes
Even in land-locked, small-town Indiana, we were able to find a fish market in a nearby city for the lump crab. The staff really enjoyed these.

Shrimp-Filled Tomatoes
Marinated shrimp and crunchy vegetables pack a pleasing punch when loaded into a ripe, juicy tomato. Lunch testing was very popular the day we tried these.

Brie in Puff Pastry
Often served at wedding receptions and fancier parties—this treat is easy enough to serve on any occasion and will really impress your friends!

Chocolate Wows
Don't overbake these rich fudgy treats—after you bite one of them, you'll know why we call them wows!

Icebox Turtle Cake
Light, moist and tender, you'll rarely taste a more luscious cake.

Tomato Pie
You know you have a winner when the test cooks take the recipe home as soon as the test is done. This savory pie is colorful, fresh and really delicious.

California Sunburst Salad
Crisp, cool and refreshing—on hot summer days this salad is satisfying enough to be your whole meal.

September/October

September/October brings an abundance of fresh fruits and vegetables to the market. We had a great time gathering the different kinds of squash, potatoes, onions, tomatoes, apples, pears and nuts. We wanted to share ideas about how to spice them up with fresh herbs and preserve them for later use. Tomatoes, especially, seem to ripen at the same time, and using them in a fresh tomato sauce to store in the freezer makes growing those veggies all worthwhile.

Tomato-Basil Pita Pizza
This has become a favorite afternoon snack around the Home Cooking *kitchens. In about five minutes you can have a fresh, light, satisfying treat to share or to eat for a light lunch.*

Pumpkin Patch Bread
Moist and full of flavor, this bread keeps well for days—if it lasts that long.

Pumpkin Custards
These were so good we rationalized that most of the calories in a pumpkin pie are in the crust—something these custards don't have—so we could keep eating.

Cinnamon Roll Pudding
This raises cinnamon rolls and custard to a whole new level. What a great combo!

Jumbo Spinach & Cheese-Stuffed Shells
It's easy to sneak healthy food like spinach into your family's diet with these great shells from Pat Eby.

November/December

The anticipation of the holidays creates a lot of excitement around the *Home Cooking* kitchen. Whether learning to roast the perfect turkey, adding new side dishes to your sentimental favorites or crafting a gift to take to someone special, we couldn't wait for the holidays to come. We hope you and your loved ones enjoy the holidays with plenty of good eating.

Couscous Curry
This spicy, yet slightly sweet side dish will perk up any simple entrée. Couscous is versatile and fast—this can be ready in less than 10 minutes.

Chocolate Chip Cheesecake
Chocolate chip cookies and cheesecake are a double treat. Take this generous dessert to your next carry-in.

Apple-Cranberry Baked French Toast
The aroma of this baking drew people to the test kitchen. Adding apple slices and dried cranberries to the brown sugar and butter that is traditional in baked French toast will make your family feel like they are the honored guests at breakfast.

Swiss Onion Loaf
Adding two easy ingredients, shredded Swiss cheese and minced, dried onion, to a package of roll dough mix creates a mouthwatering loaf of bread. The leftovers didn't last more than a day around the kitchen.

Snowy Weekend Turkey & Bean Soup
Thick and hearty—we used one each of the beans listed when we made this soup. Cozy up to a steaming bowl on a cold winter evening.

Sweet Potato Pone
Fresh grated sweet potato added to a rich custard base might fool you into thinking you're eating dessert! This side dish tends to please even the pickiest eater. ■

January/February 2005

Favorite Family Baking

Cornmeal Yeast Rolls

These rolls are worth the extra time they take. Your family will love them.

> 1 package yeast
> ¼ cup lukewarm water
> ⅓ cup cornmeal
> ½ cup sugar
> 2 cups milk
> 1 teaspoon salt
> ½ cup margarine
> 2 eggs
> 4 cups flour

Preheat oven to 375 degrees. Dissolve yeast in lukewarm water.

In double boiler, cook cornmeal, sugar, milk, salt and margarine until thick. Remove from heat and cool.

Add dissolved yeast and eggs; mix well. Cover and let rise 1 hour.

Add flour to make a soft dough. Knead until smooth. Place in a greased bowl and let rise 1 hour.

Shape into rolls, rolling in cornmeal as they are shaped. Place on greased baking sheet; let rise until doubled in size. Bake 15 minutes or until lightly browned. Makes 2 dozen.

Editor's Note: *The dough can be made the night before and allowed to rise in the refrigerator overnight.*

Butter Pecan Pound Cake

Be prepared to share this recipe with your friends.

> 1 box butter pecan 2-layer
>   cake mix
> 1 (4-serving) box instant coconut
>   cream pudding
> 4 eggs
> 1 cup oil
> 1 cup hot water

Preheat oven to 325 degrees. Mix together cake mix, pudding mix, eggs, oil and hot water; beat at medium speed for 2 minutes.

Pour into well-greased Bundt pan. Bake 45 minutes or until cake tests done in the center. Serves 12. ■

Evelyn M. Lett, Tomball, Texas

New Year's Day Traditions

Increase your chances for wealth and happiness with these hearty and appealing recipes.

By Connie Moore

What do black-eyed peas, soba noodles, sauerkraut, sausage and lentils, vasilopitas, pork roasts, cabbage and collard greens have in common? New Year's Day!

Whether you are a Southerner, Northerner or from another country and culture, no doubt you serve one or more traditional foods on the first day of the new year. The folklore stories behind eating certain foods on this day all tie in with prosperity, wealth, good fortune and abundance during the new year. Some desserts are even baked with a dime or quarter inside for some lucky eater to be assured of an instant start on the fortune. And whether or not you believe in the folktale itself, the foods are delicious enough to carry on the traditions.

In Japan, soba (buckwheat) noodles are eaten without breaking them. Not breaking them is said to bring long life. In Greece, the vasilopita cake has a coin baked in it. In Italy, the cotechino sausage is said to bring abundance while the lentils symbolize money. In the southern United States, collard greens symbolize green money and black-eyed peas bring wealth also.

In my family of German descent, pork and sauerkraut are a must on New Year's Day, served with mashed potatoes, a root vegetable such as carrots, homemade dinner rolls, a fruit dish such as apples and a light dessert such as sponge cake (no coin is baked in ours). My father was always especially happy with this meal and optimistic that he would be able to provide for the family and have enough to share. A good frame of mind to start out the new year!

Whether or not you believe in the folktales, these foods are delicious enough to carry on the traditions. So, come Jan. 1, offer up one dish or an entire menu, and look forward to a whole year of good eating and a wealth of happiness.

Pork & Sauerkraut

This dish simmers while you enjoy your family and friends.

- **2-pound boneless pork roast (or 3-pound bone-in roast)**
- **3 teaspoons pepper**
- **4 cups water**
- **1 (29-ounce) can or 2-pound bag sauerkraut**

Leaving a thin layer of fat on the roast, place in large Dutch oven or kettle with tight-fitting lid. Sprinkle with pepper. Add water, cover and bring to boil. Reduce heat and simmer for 2½ to 3 hours.

Add sauerkraut and more water if necessary and continue to simmer for about 2 more hours or until meat is fork tender and no longer pink. Serve with mashed potatoes. Serves 6.

Beef & Cabbage Rolls

This lucky cabbage dish is a good choice any day of the year.

- **1 medium head cabbage**
- **1 pound ground beef**
- **3 tablespoons chopped onion**
- **3 tablespoons chopped green pepper**
- **3 tablespoons chopped celery**
- **1 tablespoon Worcestershire sauce**
- **½ to ¾ cup uncooked rice**
- **Salt and pepper**
- **Garlic powder, optional**
- **1 (16-ounce) can sauerkraut, undrained**
- **1 cup or more tomato juice or vegetable juice cocktail**

Remove and discard core from cabbage. Place in a pan of simmering water. As leaves begin to wilt, remove them and drain. You will need about 12 large leaves. Remove rest of cabbage and set aside.

In large bowl, mix beef, onion, green pepper, celery, Worcestershire sauce and rice. Add salt and pepper to taste and mix well. Garlic powder to taste may be added, if desired.

Spoon mixture onto leaves and roll up, tucking in sides to make a tight roll. Place rolls seam-side down in large baking dish or Dutch oven. Cover with sauerkraut and tomato juice. The ▶

Shown on this page, clockwise from the top: Black-Eyed Pea Salad (page 14), Quick Buttermilk Corn Bread (page 14), Hoppin' John (page 14), Easy New Year's Day Greens (page 14), "Rich" Sponge Cake (page 14), Pork & Sauerkraut (page 12) and Beef & Cabbage Rolls (page 12).

remaining cabbage may be chopped and added or cooked separately.

Add juice as needed to cover rolls. Cover tightly and bake for 1 hour at 350 degrees.

Check after 45 minutes to make sure enough liquid is in the pot so rolls do not dry out or burn. Serves 6.

Note: *This dish may also be baked at a lower temperature (300 degrees) for longer (2 hours). More sauerkraut may be used, if desired.*

Hoppin' John

Some people believe you receive one dollar sometime in the new year for every black-eyed pea you eat on New Year's Day. Enjoy!

> **2 to 4 slices bacon**
> **1 onion, chopped**
> **1 clove garlic, minced or**
> **1 teaspoon garlic powder**
> **1 (16-ounce) package frozen black-eyed peas**
> **1 (16-ounce) can diced tomatoes with juice**
> **1¾ cups cooked rice**
> **Salt and pepper**

In skillet, fry bacon until crisp. Remove and crumble. In the drippings, fry onion and garlic. Adjust heat to low and add peas, tomatoes and rice.

Simmer until black-eyed peas are cooked through and mixture is bubbly hot. Add salt and pepper to taste.

Serve with bacon over top. Serves 6.

Note: *Some people season this dish with hot pepper sauce.*

Black-Eyed Pea Salad

This chilled, refreshing salad is a vegetarian alternative for eating your way to good luck.

> **2 (15-ounce) cans black-eyed peas, drained**
> **⅓ cup salad oil**
> **⅓ cup wine vinegar**
> **1 clove garlic**
> **¼ cup chopped onion**
> **½ teaspoon salt**
> **Pepper**

In large bowl, combine black-eyed peas, salad oil, wine vinegar, garlic, onion, salt, and pepper to taste. Mix well. Cover and chill at least 24 hours. Remove garlic before serving. Serve with crackers or tortilla chips as an appetizer or as a nice side dish with pork. Makes about 1 quart.

Note: *This salad may be made in advance as it will keep in refrigerator for several days.*

Easy New Year's Day Greens

Serve these typical Southern-style greens with hot corn bread.

> **2 (16-ounce) packages frozen collard, kale, mustard, turnip or spinach greens, thawed**
> **½ cup chopped onion**
> **¼ cup ham bits (leftover ham or fried bacon bits)**
> **Salt and pepper**
> **Water**

In large pan, place greens, onion and ham. Season with salt and pepper to taste and add enough water to barely cover greens. Cover and simmer for about ½ hour. Serve hot with corn bread. Serves 6 to 8.

Quick Buttermilk Corn Bread

This is a savory corn bread. If you prefer yours to be sweeter, feel free to add 2 tablespoons of sugar.

> **2 cups self-rising cornmeal mix**
> **1¾ cups buttermilk**
> **¼ cup melted margarine**

Preheat oven to 450 degrees. Grease 9-inch round baking pan.

Mix together cornmeal mix, buttermilk and margarine until smooth batter forms.

Pour into pan and bake for about 20 minutes or until golden brown. Serves 6.

"Rich" Sponge Cake

Including the wrapped coin adds to the fun of this cake, but it is a marvelous sponge cake to use year-round.

> **6 eggs, separated**
> **½ cup cold water**
> **1 teaspoon lemon zest**
> **1 teaspoon vanilla**
> **1⅓ cups sugar, divided**
> **1¼ cups flour**
> **Dash of salt**
> **1 teaspoon cream of tartar**
> **Clean coin wrapped in foil, optional**

Preheat oven to 325 degrees. In small bowl, beat egg yolks until thick. Add water, lemon zest and vanilla. Beat in ½ cup of the sugar.

Combine flour, salt and ⅓ cup of the sugar. Gradually beat flour mixture into egg mixture.

Using clean beaters, in large mixing bowl, beat egg whites until frothy. Add cream of tartar and beat until soft peaks form. Gradually add the remaining ½ cup sugar and beat until stiff peaks form. Stir 1 cup of egg white mixture into egg yolk mixture.

Using rubber spatula, fold egg mixture into remaining stiff egg whites. Pour batter into ungreased 10-inch tube pan. If using coin, push wrapped coin down into batter.

Bake 50 to 60 minutes or until cake springs back when pressed and tests done with toothpick. Invert pan and cool cake completely. Pan may be inverted onto soup cans or level coffee mugs. When cool, loosen cake gently on sides and around middle tube. Gently tap pan until cake releases. Serves 12. ■

A Bunch of Brunches

Keep these recipes handy for a plan-ahead brunch or light supper.

Strawberry Pecan Coffeecake
Serve a sweet slice with a steaming hot cup of coffee for a real break.

Coffeecake
- 1 cup sliced fresh or thawed frozen strawberries
- 3 tablespoons brown sugar
- ½ cup flour
- ½ cup whole-wheat flour
- ⅓ cup sugar
- ½ teaspoon baking powder
- ¼ teaspoon baking soda
- ⅛ teaspoon salt
- ½ cup low-fat sour cream
- 2 tablespoons butter or margarine, melted
- 1 teaspoon vanilla extract
- 1 egg
- ¼ cup chopped pecans

Icing
- ½ cup confectioners' sugar
- 1½ teaspoons low-fat milk
- ¼ teaspoon vanilla extract

Preheat oven to 350 degrees. Spray 8-inch round cake pan with nonstick cooking spray.

For coffeecake, combine strawberries and brown sugar in bowl.

In large bowl, combine flour, whole-wheat flour, sugar, baking powder, baking soda and salt. In small bowl, combine sour cream, butter, vanilla extract and egg. Mix well. Add to dry ingredients. Stir until just moistened.

Spoon ⅔ of batter into prepared pan. Spread strawberry mixture over batter in pan. Spoon remaining batter over top. Sprinkle pecans on top.

Bake for 40 minutes, or until done. Cool for 10 minutes in pan on a wire rack. Remove from pan to cool completely.

For icing, combine confectioners' ▶

Preheat oven to 425 degrees. Line 9-inch pie pan with bottom pie crust. Sprinkle 1 cup ham over bottom crust. Break eggs over ham in crust, keeping yolks intact. Sprinkle on pepper, hot pepper sauce, cilantro, chives and green onions. Sprinkle remaining 1 cup ham over top.

Sprinkle cheese over ham. Spoon half of soup over cheese in small dots. Cover with top pie crust, sealing edges and cutting slits to vent. Bake for 30 minutes, or until done.

In saucepan, cook remaining soup and milk until heated through. Pour over baked pie. Serves 6.

Rita Kitsteiner, Tucson, Ariz.

Fruit Platter

Use our suggested fruits or substitute to fit your family's tastes and seasonal availability.

3 oranges, pared and cut into slices
2 grapefruit, pared and sectioned
2 kiwi fruit, pared and sliced
1 (17-ounce) jar figs, drained
2 bananas, peeled and chunked
Lettuce leaves (optional)

Arrange oranges, grapefruit, kiwi fruit, figs and bananas on lettuce. Sprinkle bananas with orange or grapefruit juice left from cutting.

Refrigerate up to 3 hours. Serves 6.

Kathy Lausted, Appleton, Wis. ∎

Shown on page 17, clockwise from the top: Zesty Southwestern Breakfast Pie (page 16), Smoked Salmon and Spinach Quiche (page 16), Strawberry Pecan Coffeecake (page 15), Fruit Platter (page 16).

sugar, milk and vanilla extract in bowl. Stir well. Drizzle over coffeecake. Serves 8.

Dorothy Brummer, Albert City, Iowa

Smoked Salmon & Spinach Quiche

This rich brunch favorite is worth the extra calories.

4 cups cream
8 eggs
2 egg yolks
Salt and pepper
Cayenne pepper
Ground nutmeg
2 tablespoons Dijon mustard
¾ pound smoked salmon, crumbled
1 pound frozen chopped spinach, thawed, drained and squeezed dry
1 (9-inch) unbaked pie shell

Preheat oven to 350 degrees. In mixing bowl, mix cream, eggs and egg yolks. Season lightly with salt and pepper, cayenne pepper and nutmeg. Add Dijon mustard, smoked salmon and spinach.

Pour mixture into pie shell. Bake for 45 minutes, or until set. Serves 6.

Note: *Keep in mind that the salmon is salty; do not over season.*

Kit Rollins , Cedarburg, Wis.

Zesty Southwestern Breakfast Pie

A hearty start to any day, this morning pie is good served with seasoned tomato wedges.

Pastry for 9-inch double-crust pie, divided
2 cups diced cooked ham or cooked sausage, divided
6 eggs
⅛ teaspoon pepper
2 tablespoons chopped fresh cilantro or parsley
1 tablespoon chopped fresh chives
1 tablespoon chopped green onions
Dash of hot pepper sauce, to taste
½ cup shredded Monterey Jack, pepper jack or cheddar cheese
1 (10¾-ounce) can cream of mushroom soup, divided
3 tablespoons milk

Soups shown on this page, clockwise from the top: Beef Barley Soup (page 19), Tortilla Soup (page 19), Stuffed Bell Pepper Soup (page 19) and Broccoli Wild Rice Soup (page 19).

Soup for the Soul

Nothing warms your soul on a cold winter's day more than a satisfying bowl of soup.

Tortilla Soup
This light soup makes a great starter for a traditional Tex-Mex meal.

2 to 3 flour tortillas
¼ cup oil
¼ cup water
1 medium tomato, cut into fourths
1 small onion, cut into fourths
1 clove garlic
2 (10¾-ounce) cans condensed chicken broth
1 soup can water
¼ teaspoon dried coriander
¼ teaspoon salt
¼ teaspoon pepper
Dash of hot sauce (optional)
Shredded Monterey Jack cheese

Cut tortillas into ⅓-inch strips. Heat oil in a 10-inch skillet until hot. Fry one-fourth of the strips at a time over medium heat, stirring occasionally, about 3 minutes until crisp and golden. Drain well on paper towels.

Place ¼ cup water, tomato, onion and garlic in blender container. Cover and blend at high speed until smooth. Heat tomato mixture, chicken broth, 1 can water, coriander, salt and pepper in a saucepan. Cook, uncovered, about 5 minutes.

Sprinkle each serving with cheese and tortilla strips. Serves 8.

Eleanor Craycraft, Sequim, Wash.

Beef Barley Soup
Add a crusty bread for a hearty mid-winter supper.

1 pound ground round
2 medium diced onions
4 medium diced tomatoes
2 tablespoons garlic salt
1 tablespoon fresh basil, crushed
12 cups water
1 (16-ounce) bag frozen mixed vegetables
4 bay leaves
1 teaspoon Worcestershire sauce
½ teaspoon pepper
1 (11-ounce) box quick-cooking barley

In large Dutch oven, brown meat. Add the onions, tomatoes, garlic salt and basil; cook 5 minutes.

Add water, mixed vegetables, bay leaves, Worcestershire sauce, pepper and barley; bring to a boil. Reduce heat, cover and simmer 25 minutes. Remove bay leaves before serving. Serves 8.

Alise Sack, Brevard, N.C.

Stuffed Bell Pepper Soup
If you like Stuffed Bell Peppers, you will love this soup. Pass jalapeño hot sauce at the table for diners to add a dash or two, if they like.

2 pounds ground beef
8 cups water
4 cups tomato juice (32-ounce can)
3 bell peppers, diced
1 (12-ounce) jar chili sauce
1 cup uncooked long-grain rice
2 ribs celery, diced
1 large onion, diced
3 cubes chicken bouillon
1 teaspoon minced garlic
Salt and pepper

In large saucepan over medium heat, brown ground beef. Drain.

To saucepan, add water, tomato juice, bell peppers, chili sauce, rice, celery, onion, bouillon, garlic, and salt and pepper to taste. Bring to a boil. Reduce heat and simmer, uncovered, for 1 hour, or until rice is tender. Makes 4 quarts.

Note: *This soup freezes well.*

Bobby Langley, Rocky Mount, N.C.

Broccoli Wild Rice Soup
If you like rich, creamy soup but don't want all the fat, this is a tasty alternative no one will believe is healthful.

5 cups water
1 (6-ounce) package long grain and wild rice, with seasoning
1 (10¾-ounce) can reduced fat, reduced sodium cream of chicken soup
1½ cups 1 percent milk
1 (8-ounce) package fat-free cream cheese, cubed
¼ teaspoon salt
1 (10-ounce) package frozen chopped broccoli, thawed
1 large carrot, shredded
¼ cup sliced almonds, toasted

In large saucepan, combine water, rice and contents of seasoning packet and bring to a boil. Simmer, covered, for 20 minutes.

Add cream of chicken soup, milk, cream cheese and salt. Stir until cheese melts.

Add broccoli and carrots and cook on medium-low for 5 to 6 minutes, or until vegetables are tender.

Garnish with almonds. Serves 6. ■

Arlene Ranney, Eureka, Calif.

Dazzling Desserts

A great dessert is the crowning touch, whether you're having a dinner party or feeding your family.

By Mary Sowers

Chocolate Turtle Cheesecake
As with most cheesecakes, this is a rich dessert that goes a long way.

> 6 tablespoons margarine, melted
> 2 cups vanilla wafer crumbs
> 1 pound caramel candies
> ¾ cup evaporated milk
> 1¼ cups coarsely chopped pecans
> 2 (8-ounce) packages cream cheese, softened
> ½ cup sugar
> 2 eggs
> 4 ounces semisweet chocolate, melted

Preheat oven to 350 degrees. Combine margarine and vanilla wafer crumbs and press into bottom of 9-inch springform pan. Bake 5 minutes. Remove from oven and set aside.

Place candies and milk in saucepan; melt together. Pour into crust. Sprinkle pecans over top. Set aside.

Beat together cream cheese and sugar. Add eggs, one at a time, and mix in melted chocolate. Pour over pecans and smooth out.

Bake for 40 minutes. Remove from oven and let cool on wire rack for 1 to 2 hours. Chill 4 to 6 hours. Serves 12 to 16.

Editor's Note: *You may omit the chocolate altogether or swirl it in as we have shown.*

Mary Sowers, Taft, Texas

White Chocolate & Blueberry Bread Pudding
Traditional bread pudding is enlivened by the addition of white chocolate and blueberries.

> 2 tablespoons unsalted butter, softened, plus 2 tablespoons, melted
> 4 large eggs
> 3 cups heavy cream
> 1 cup milk
> 1 cup packed light brown sugar
> 1 teaspoon pure vanilla extract
> ½ teaspoon ground cinnamon
> 6 cups ½-inch cubes day-old bread
> 6 ounces white chocolate, chopped
> 1 cup fresh blueberries
> ½ cup dried blueberries

Amaretto Cream Sauce
> 1 tablespoon cornstarch
> ¼ cup Amaretto liqueur
> 1½ cups heavy cream
> ¼ cup granulated sugar

Preheat oven to 350 degrees. Butter a 10 x 14-inch baking dish with softened butter. Whisk the eggs in a large bowl. Whisk in the cream, milk, brown sugar, vanilla and cinnamon. Add the bread, chocolate, blueberries and dried blueberries and stir well; mix in the melted butter. Let sit for 30 minutes so the bread will absorb the egg mixture.

Pour into prepared dish. Bake until firm when pressed in the center, about 1 hour. Cool on a wire rack until just warm, about 20 minutes.

In a small bowl, dissolve the cornstarch in the liqueur and whisk until smooth.

In a medium saucepan, scald cream over medium heat. Add the Amaretto mixture to the hot cream; whisking constantly, bring to a boil. Reduce the heat and cook, whisking for 30 seconds.

Remove from heat and add sugar. Whisk until dissolved. Let cool to room temperature before serving with the bread pudding. Serves 6 to 8.

Chocolate Buttermilk Layer Cake
This is a great make-ahead dessert. It keeps very well in the refrigerator for several days.

> 1 cup butter, softened
> 2 cups sugar
> 3 eggs
> 2½ cups cake flour
> ¾ cup firmly packed unsweetened cocoa powder
> 2 teaspoons soda
> 1 teaspoon baking powder
> ½ teaspoon salt
> 1½ cups buttermilk
> **Buttermilk Chocolate Frosting**

Preheat oven to 350 degrees. Grease 2 (9-inch) round layer pans; dust with flour.

In a large bowl, beat together butter and sugar with an electric mixer on medium speed until light and fluffy. Beat in eggs just until combined.

Sift together cake flour, cocoa powder, soda, baking powder and salt. Add to butter mixture alternately with buttermilk, beating just until blended.

Divide batter between prepared pans. Bake 35 to 40 minutes, or until cakes test ▶

Desserts shown on page 21, clockwise from the top: Chocolate Buttermilk Layer Cake (page 20), Prizewinning Lemon Meringue Pie (page 22), Ice Cream Roll (page 22), White Chocolate & Blueberry Bread Pudding (page 20) and Chocolate Turtle Cheesecake (page 20).

done. Let cakes cool 10 minutes in pans, then unmold onto racks and let cool completely. Frost with Buttermilk Chocolate Frosting. Refrigerate until serving time. Serves 12 to 15.

Buttermilk Chocolate Frosting
4 tablespoons butter, softened
½ cup unsweetened cocoa powder
½ cup buttermilk
4 cups powdered sugar

In medium bowl, beat together butter and cocoa powder with an electric mixer on low speed until smooth, 1 to 2 minutes. Add buttermilk and powdered sugar and beat on high speed until smooth and fluffy.

Sue Wadsworth, Lufkin, Texas

Prizewinning Lemon Meringue Pie
Lemon pie is always a refreshing favorite.

Crust
2 cups flour
1 teaspoon salt
⅔ cup butter-flavored shortening
1 egg yolk
4 to 5 tablespoons cold milk
Preheat oven to 400 degrees. Combine flour and salt. Cut in shortening with pastry blender. Mix egg and milk. Stir into flour mixture with a fork. Mix well. Wrap in plastic wrap and chill for 30 minutes. Roll out to fit 9-inch pie plate. Flute edges and prick the dough with a fork.

Bake for 10 minutes. Reduce heat to 375 degrees and bake an additional 13 minutes or until crust is golden brown. Makes 1 crust.

Lemon Filling
1½ cups sugar
1½ cups hot water
4 tablespoons cornstarch
4 tablespoons flour
¾ teaspoon salt
3 egg yolks, beaten
⅓ cup plus 1 tablespoon lemon juice
Grated lemon peel
2 tablespoons butter

Combine sugar, water, cornstarch, flour and salt in a saucepan. Over medium heat, stir constantly for 8 minutes Remove from heat. Add beaten egg yolks. Bring mixture to a second boil and cook an additional 4 minutes. Slowly add the lemon juice, lemon peel and butter. Mix well. Add filling to baked pie crust.

Meringue
⅛ cup sugar
½ cup water
1 tablespoon cornstarch
4 egg whites
4 tablespoons sugar
½ teaspoon vanilla

Preheat oven to 375 degrees. Mix 2 tablespoons sugar, water and cornstarch; cook until clear. Cool.

Beat egg whites until frothy. Gradually add 4 tablespoons sugar. Add cooked mixture and vanilla. Beat until stiff peaks form.

Spoon onto pie. Bake 12 to 15 minutes, or until golden brown. Serves 6 to 8.

Donna Rooney, Pt. Pleasant, N.J.

Ice Cream Roll
This elegant-looking cake is simpler to make than it looks.

4 large eggs (at room temperature)
1 cup sugar
⅓ cup water
1 teaspoon vanilla
¼ cup unsweetened cocoa powder
¾ cup all-purpose flour
1 teaspoon baking powder
¼ teaspoon salt
Confectioners' sugar
2 to 3 cups ice cream

Preheat oven to 350 degrees. Line 15½ x 10½ x 1-inch jelly roll pan with cooking parchment paper; generously grease paper with shortening, being very careful to not get any grease on the sides of the pan.

Beat eggs until very thick and lemon colored (5 minutes or more). Gradually beat in sugar. Beat in water and vanilla on low speed. Sift cocoa powder, flour, baking powder and salt and add gradually, beating on low speed just until batter is smooth. Pour into pan, spreading to corners.

Bake 12 to 15 minutes until the cake springs back when lightly tapped in the center. Immediately loosen cake from edges of pan and turn upside down onto towel generously sprinkled with Confectioners' sugar. Carefully remove paper. Trim off stiff edges of cake if necessary. While cake is hot, carefully roll cake and towel from narrow end. Cool on wire rack at least 30 minutes.

Unroll cake and remove towel. Spread with slightly softened ice cream. Roll up cake, wrap in plastic and freeze 4 hours, or until firm. Dust surface with cocoa powder. Serve with Hot Fudge Sauce if desired. Serves 6 to 8.

Hot Fudge Sauce
1 (12-ounce) can evaporated milk
2 cups (12 ounces) semisweet chocolate chips
½ cup sugar
1 tablespoon butter
1 teaspoon vanilla

Heat milk, chocolate chips and sugar to boiling in 2-quart saucepan over medium heat, stirring constantly; remove from heat.

Stir in butter and vanilla until mixture is smooth and creamy. Cool about 30 minutes or until sauce begins to thicken. Serve warm. Store remaining sauce covered in refrigerator up to 4 weeks. Sauce becomes firm when refrigerated; heat slightly before serving (sauce will become thin if overheated). ■

Jerry Shaw, Bluffton, Ind.

Make mealtime easier by planning ahead.

Do-Ahead Company Fare

Make-Ahead Artichoke & Rice Salad

For a pretty buffet offering, scatter sliced black olives across the top of this salad served in a lettuce-lined bowl.

1 (6.9-ounce) package chicken-flavored rice mix
½ cup mayonnaise
1 tablespoon Worcestershire sauce
1 tablespoon lemon juice
1 teaspoon curry powder
1 to 2 drops hot pepper sauce
2 (6-ounce) jars marinated artichoke hearts, drained and finely chopped (reserve marinade)
6 to 8 green onions, finely chopped
1 to 2 ribs celery with leaves, finely chopped
½ green bell pepper, finely chopped

Prepare rice mix according to package directions, omitting butter. Chill.

In small bowl, stir together mayonnaise, Worcestershire sauce, lemon juice, curry powder, hot pepper sauce and reserved marinade. Blend thoroughly.

In large bowl, combine green onions, celery, green bell pepper and artichoke hearts. Add rice and mayonnaise mixture. Stir well. Cover and chill overnight to blend flavors.

Stir again before serving. Serves 6 to 8.

Eleanor Craycraft, Sequim, Wash.

Orange Pecan French Toast

Serve this make-ahead breakfast to your overnight guests for a fuss-free morning.

4 eggs
⅔ cup fresh orange juice
⅓ cup milk
¼ cup sugar
½ teaspoon vanilla extract
¼ teaspoon ground nutmeg
8 (½-inch-thick) slices hearty, country-style bread
¼ cup butter
½ cup chopped pecans

In mixing bowl, beat eggs, orange juice, milk, sugar, vanilla extract and nutmeg. Arrange bread slices in single layer in casserole dish. Pour egg mixture over top. Chill for at least 2 hours or overnight.

Preheat oven to 350 degrees. Melt butter in 15 x 10 x 2-inch baking pan. Arrange bread slices over butter. Bake for 20 minutes. Sprinkle pecans on top. Bake for an additional 10 minutes, or until done. Serves 4. ■

Kit Rollins, Cedarburg, Wis.

Our Most Requested Recipe

We received many letters requesting our easy and oh-so-scrumptious Peanut Butter Brownie Torte recipe in the May/June 2004 issue of Home Cooking *magazine. So many, we decided to feature it again just for you!*

Peanut Butter Brownie Torte
This dish makes a great carry-in dessert for cookouts and potlucks.

- 1 (21-ounce) package family-size brownie mix
- 1 (10-ounce) package peanut butter chips
- 24 regular-size peanut butter cups, divided
- 2 (4-serving-size) packages instant vanilla pudding mix
- 3 cups milk
- ½ cup creamy peanut butter
- 2 teaspoons vanilla
- 1 (12-ounce) container frozen whipped topping, thawed, divided

Preheat oven according to brownie mix package directions. Line 13 x 9 x 2-inch baking pan with foil, extending ends over sides.

Prepare brownie mix according to package directions. Stir in peanut butter chips. Pour into prepared pan. Bake according to package directions. Cool completely on a wire rack.

Lift foil out of pan. Invert onto cutting board. Remove foil. Cut brownies into ¾-inch pieces with a sharp knife.

Coarsely chop 20 peanut butter cups, reserving 4 for garnish.

Combine pudding mix and milk in large mixing bowl. Beat on low speed for 2 minutes, or until thickened. Add peanut butter and vanilla. Beat until smooth. Gently fold in 2 cups whipped topping.

Place half of brownies in bottom of trifle bowl or large glass bowl. Top with half of chopped peanut butter cups. Spoon on half of pudding mixture. Repeat layering. Top with remaining whipped topping. Slice each of remaining 4 peanut butter cups into 4 long pieces. Arrange on whipped topping to garnish. Chill. Serves 16. ■

Carol Faith, Brockton, Mass.

Planning Great Meals

Here's our all-new collection of recipes! Plus we're offering these menu suggestions to help you plan great meals.

Special Occasion
Shrimp Kabobs, 41
Brown rice
Sweet Onion-Zucchini
Stir-Fry, 30
Chunky Applesauce, 49

Speedy Weeknight Supper
Pasta With Tuna & Olives, 28
French bread
Prizewinning Lemon
Meringue Pie, 22

Easy Entertaining
Fish Santa Fe, 42
Zesty Tomato Risotto, 34
Green beans
Chocolate Banana Parfaits, 28

Homey Feast
Mix-&-Fix Meat Loaf, 27
Mashed Potato Timbales, 35
Marinated Garden Salad, 30
White Chocolate & Blueberry
Bread Pudding, 20

Hearty Dinner
Chicken Reuben Casserole, 27
Potato & Squash Bake, 31
Special Spinach Salad, 45
The Whistle Stop Sugar Cream Pie, 29

Recipes From Our Readers

Home cooks share their favorite recipes—quick-to-prepare comfort foods, good for family, friends and special occasions.

Chocolate Cheese Fudge

Ruth McClendon, Waukegan, Ill.

> 2 pounds confectioners' sugar
> ½ cup cocoa powder
> 1 cup butter
> 8 ounces processed cheese
> 1½ teaspoons vanilla
> ½ cup chopped pecans

Mix sugar and cocoa powder together; set aside. Melt butter and cheese over low heat, stirring constantly. Remove from heat. Stir in vanilla. Pour over sugar-and-cocoa mixture. Mix quickly.

Spread in a buttered 13 x 9 x 2-inch pan. Sprinkle pecans over top and press in lightly. Let stand two hours. Cut into squares. Makes 117 (1-inch) pieces.

Microwave Fudge

> ½ cup cocoa powder
> 1 pound confectioners' sugar
> ½ cup margarine
> ¼ cup milk
> 1 teaspoon vanilla
> 1 cup chopped nuts

Mix cocoa powder and confectioners' sugar in microwave pan. Slice margarine on top. Pour on milk but do not mix. Cover and cook in microwave for 2 minutes at full power.

Add vanilla and nuts; stir to mix

well. Pour into greased 8 x 8 x 2-inch pan. Chill 1 hour. Cut into squares. Makes 64 pieces.

Chocolate Toffee Candy

Shirley Ann Weimann, Woodstock, Conn.

> ½ cup coarsely chopped pecans
> ½ cup butter
> ¾ cup brown sugar, packed
> ½ cup semisweet chocolate chips

Sprinkle pecans in the bottom of a buttered 8 x 8 x 2-inch pan. Combine

butter and brown sugar in a 2-quart saucepan; cook over medium heat, stirring constantly, until mixture comes to a boil. Continue cooking, stirring until mixture reaches hard crack stage (295 degrees) on a candy thermometer.

Immediately pour hot mixture over pecans, spreading evenly.

Sprinkle with chocolate chips; let set 5 minutes. Spread melted chocolate evenly over all. When chocolate is set, break into bite-size pieces. Store in a covered container. Makes ¾ pound.

Mom's Cream Cheese Mints

> 4 ounces cream cheese, softened
> Confectioners' sugar (enough to make mints smooth and doughy)
> ¼ teaspoon peppermint extract
> ¼ teaspoon wintergreen extract
> Green food coloring
> Red food coloring
> Sugar

Mix cream cheese and confectioner's sugar by hand until smooth and doughy. Divide mixture in half; add a few drops of peppermint extract to one half and a few drops of wintergreen extract to the other half. Taste and adjust flavoring.

Blend green food coloring (several drops at a time) into wintergreen mixture until soft green. Blend red food coloring (several drops at a time) into peppermint mixture until pastel pink.

Pinch off small pieces of dough; roll into balls and dip into sugar. Makes 2 to 3 dozen mints.

Grilled Apricot Ham

Galelah Dowell, Fair and, Okla.

¼ cup apricot spreadable fruit
2 teaspoons Dijon mustard
2 teaspoons cider vinegar
1 (16-ounce) low-sodium ham
   steak

Combine apricot spread, mustard and vinegar.

Grill ham steak over high heat, brushing occasionally with sauce until browned on both sides, about 8 to 10 minutes. Serves 4.

Mix-&-Fix Meat Loaf

Anneliese Deising, Plymouth, Mich.
This mix-and-fix recipe is simple to prepare. Plus, it's delicious hot or cold.

2 pounds ground round
1 (6-ounce) package stuffing mix
   (any flavor)
1 envelope onion soup mix
2 eggs, slightly beaten
1½ cups shredded cheddar
   cheese
2 cups water

Preheat oven to 350 degrees. In bowl, combine ground round, stuffing mix, onion soup mix, eggs, cheese and water. Mix well.

Press mixture into large nonstick loaf pan. Bake for 1½ hours, or until top is golden brown and a bit crunchy. Serves 8.

Chicken Reuben Casserole

Cecelia Rooney, Pt. Pleasant, N.J.

8 boneless, skinless chicken
   breast halves
¼ teaspoon salt
⅛ teaspoon pepper
1 (16-ounce) can or package
   sauerkraut, well drained
4 (6 x 4-inch) slices Swiss cheese
1¼ cups Thousand Island salad
   dressing

Preheat oven to 325 degrees. Place chicken in a single layer in greased 13 x 9 x 2-inch baking pan; sprinkle with salt and pepper.

Press excess liquid from sauerkraut and spoon over chicken. Arrange cheese slices over sauerkraut. Pour dressing evenly over the top.

Cover pan with aluminum foil. Bake 90 minutes or until chicken is tender. Serves 6 to 8.

Pasta With Tuna & Olives

Kit Rollins, Cedarburg, Wis.

2 (7-ounce) cans tuna packed in
    oil, well drained
    and flaked
½ cup olive oil
3 tablespoons fresh lemon juice
2 tablespoons parsley
4 ounces olives (mixed green and
    black), sliced
3 tablespoons capers, drained
    and rinsed
1 large garlic clove, finely
    chopped
Black pepper to taste
1 pound linguine
Grated Parmesan cheese

In serving bowl, combine tuna, olive oil, lemon juice, parsley, olives, capers, garlic and pepper. Toss well to coat.

Prepare linguine according to directions. Add to tuna mixture and toss to coat.

Serve topped with Parmesan cheese. Serves 4 to 6.

Banana-Rum Pudding

Gwen Campbell, Sterling, Va.

6 ripe bananas
2 tablespoons rum or rum extract
1 large egg, beaten
2½ tablespoons butter, divided

¼ teaspoon cinnamon
¼ teaspoon nutmeg
⅛ teaspoon ground cloves
2 tablespoons flour
1 teaspoon baking powder
sugar for dusting

Preheat oven to 325 degrees. Peel bananas, mash and place in bowl.

Combine rum extract, egg, 1 tablespoon butter, cinnamon, nutmeg, cloves, flour and baking powder. Add to mashed bananas.

Pour mixture into a shallow, 1-quart casserole. Dot with remaining butter and dust top with sugar.

Bake 1 hour. Chill pudding and serve with whipped cream and a cherry, if desired. Serves 4 to 6.

Chocolate Banana Parfaits

Galelah Dowell, Fairland, Okla.

2 cups cold, fat-free milk
1 (4-serving) package fat-free,
    sugar-free reduced-calorie
    instant chocolate pudding and
    pie filling
2 medium bananas, sliced
¾ cup lite frozen whipped top-
    ping, thawed

Pour milk into medium bowl; add pudding mix and beat with wire whisk 2 minutes.

Spoon half of the pudding evenly into four dessert glasses. Layer with banana slices, ½ cup whipped topping and remaining pudding.

Garnish with remaining whipped topping. Refrigerate until ready to serve. Serves 4.

Raspberry Almond Bars

Cecelia Rooney, Pt. Pleasant, N.J.

½ cup butter or margarine
1 (10 to 12 ounce) bag white or
    vanilla chips, divided
2 eggs
½ cup sugar
1 teaspoon almond extract
1 cup flour
½ teaspoon salt

½ cup seedless raspberry jam
¼ cup sliced almonds

Preheat oven to 325 degrees. Grease 9 x 9 x 2-inch baking pan.

In a saucepan, melt butter, remove from heat and, without stirring, add 1 cup chips.

In a small mixing bowl, beat eggs until foamy; gradually add sugar. Stir in chip mixture and almond extract.

Combine flour and salt and add to egg mixture, stirring just until combined. Spread half the batter in prepared pan. Bake for 15 to 20 minutes, or until golden brown.

Over low heat, melt jam and spread over warm crust. Stir remaining chips into second half of the batter; drop by teaspoonfuls over the jam. Sprinkle with almonds.

Bake 30 to 35 minutes longer or until it tests done with a toothpick.

Cool completely and cut into bars. Makes 25 bars.

The Whistle Stop Sugar Cream Pie

Timothy Fennell, Birmingham, Ala.
This is the recipe for the locally famous and loved sugar cream pie baked and served at The Whistle Stop restaurant in Glendale, Ky.

1½ cups brown sugar (do not pack)
6 tablespoons flour
Unbaked deep-dish pie crust
1 cup half-and-half
1 cup heavy whipping cream
Pinch of salt
1 teaspoon vanilla

1 tablespoon butter
1 teaspoon cinnamon

Preheat oven to 450 degrees. Mix together brown sugar and flour; put in unbaked deep-dish pie crust.

Mix half-and-half, whipping cream, salt and vanilla; slowly pour mixture over the top of brown sugar mixture. Do not stir. Dot with slices of butter, and sprinkle with cinnamon.

Bake 10 minutes. Reduce heat to 350 degrees and bake for 50 minutes. Serve slightly warm. Serves 8.

Note: *A glass baking dish is recommended for best results.*

Light & Lively Lentil Salad

Gwen Campbell, Sterling, Va.

4 cups tomato juice or vegetable juice cocktail
¼ teaspoon salt
2 large bay leaves
2 cups dried lentils
2 cucumbers, peeled, seeded, chopped
1 cup celery, finely chopped
1 onion, cut into rings
¾ cup fresh orange juice
2 tablespoons red wine vinegar
1½ tablespoons Dijon mustard
1 large tomato, chopped
¾ cup crumbled feta cheese

Combine tomato juice, salt, bay leaves and lentils in a large saucepan. Bring to a boil, cover and simmer 20 minutes until lentils are tender.

Drain, discard bay leaves.

Combine lentils, cucumber, celery and onion in a large salad bowl.

Whisk together orange juice, vinegar and Dijon mustard. Add to lentil mixture along with tomato. Chill one hour.

Garnish each serving with feta cheese. Serves 4 to 6. ▶

Restaurant-Style Coleslaw

Teresa Librock, Beamsville, Ontario

Slaw

- 6 cups shredded cabbage
- 1 cup shredded carrots
- 3 tablespoons sugar
- 1 teaspoon salt
- ¼ teaspoon red pepper
- ¼ cup milk
- ¼ cup vinegar

Dressing

- 1 teaspoon dry minced onion
- ½ cup buttermilk
- ½ teaspoon celery seed
- 1 cup mayonnaise or salad dressing
- 2 to 3 drops hot sauce

Combine cabbage, carrots, sugar, salt, red pepper, milk and vinegar; set aside.

Combine onion, buttermilk, celery seed, mayonnaise and hot sauce. Refrigerate 2 hours, then combine with cabbage mixture. Drain part of the dressing if salad is too juicy. Serves 10 to 12.

Black Bean Salad

Jo Ann Ervin, Glasgow, Ky.

- 1 red bell pepper, diced
- 1 green pepper, diced
- 1 yellow pepper, diced
- ½ cup red onion, diced
- 1 (15-ounce) can corn, drained
- 1 clove garlic, minced
- 1 teaspoon cilantro
- ¼ cup olive oil
- ¼ cup red wine vinegar
- 1 teaspoon lime juice
- Salt and pepper
- 1 (15-ounce) can black beans, drained
- Tortilla chips

In a small bowl, combine peppers, onion, corn, garlic and cilantro. Add olive oil, vinegar, lime juice, salt and pepper to taste and black beans. Toss well and serve with tortilla chips. Serves 4 to 6.

Marinated Garden Salad

Jo Ann Ervin, Glasgow, Ky.

- ½ cup sliced celery
- ½ cup sliced cucumber
- ½ cup sliced carrots
- ½ cup radishes
- ½ cup fat-free Italian salad dressing.
- 5 cups salad greens

In a large bowl, combine the celery, cucumber, carrots, radishes and salad dressing.

Refrigerate one hour. Toss with salad greens just before serving. Serves 4 to 6.

Sweet Onion-Zucchini Stir-Fry

Mary Stowell, Pahrump, Nev.
A quickie favorite.

- 1 sweet onion
- 1 medium-size zucchini
- 1 to 2 tablespoons olive oil
- ½ to 1 tablespoon sesame seeds
- Soy sauce, pepper and garlic powder (optional)

Peel onions and slice into strips. Cut zucchini lengthwise, then ¼ inch thick. Sauté in olive oil.

Add sesame seeds. Season with soy sauce, pepper and garlic powder as desired. Serves 4.

Potato & Squash Bake
Judy Ervin, Glasgow, Ky.

- 1¼ pounds potatoes, scrubbed and cut into 1½-inch pieces
- 2 yellow squash, cut into 1½-inch pieces
- 2 zucchini, cut into 1-inch pieces
- ½ red bell pepper, cut into 1-inch pieces
- 3 cloves garlic, minced
- 2 teaspoons paprika
- ⅓ cup chopped fresh parsley
- 1 tablespoon wine vinegar
- 1 tablespoon olive oil
- ⅛ teaspoon salt
- Pepper
- 4 tablespoons grated Parmesan cheese

Preheat oven to 375 degrees. Lightly oil a 13 x 9 x 2-inch baking dish.

Boil potatoes in salted water until tender. Drain and place in baking dish. Add yellow squash, zucchini, bell pepper, garlic, paprika and parsley; mix well. Sprinkle with vinegar, oil, salt, and pepper to taste.

Cover with foil. Bake 40 minutes. Uncover. Sprinkle with Parmesan cheese and bake an additional 15 minutes or until browned. Serve immediately. Serves 6.

Baked Onion Rings
Arlene Ranney, Eureka, Calif.
If you love onion rings but not the fat from frying them, try baking them. The crisp rings round out lunch or make a scrumptious snack.

- 2 large sweet onions
- 2 eggs
- 1½ cups crushed cornflakes
- 2 teaspoons sugar
- 1 teaspoon paprika
- ¼ teaspoon garlic salt
- ¼ teaspoon seasoned salt

Preheat oven to 375 degrees. Cut onion into ½-inch-thick slices and separate into rings.

In shallow dish, whisk eggs. In another shallow dish, combine crushed cornflakes, sugar, paprika, garlic salt and seasoned salt.

Dip onion rings into eggs, then coat with cornflake mixture.

Arrange rings in a single layer on greased baking sheet. Bake 20 to 25 minutes or until tender. Serves 6 to 8.

Sesame Broccoli
Margy Mann, St. Louis, Mo.

- 1 (10-ounce) package frozen broccoli, or 1 head fresh broccoli cut into florets
- 1 tablespoon canola oil
- 1 tablespoon soy sauce
- 1 tablespoon sugar
- 2 teaspoons white vinegar
- 2 teaspoons toasted sesame seeds

Cook frozen broccoli according to package directions. If using fresh broccoli, cook for 2 to 3 minutes in boiling water.

In small saucepan, combine canola oil, soy sauce, sugar and vinegar. Heat over medium heat until sugar is dissolved and mixture is hot.

Drain broccoli. Place in serving bowl. Drizzle with soy sauce mixture and sprinkle with sesame seeds. Serves 4. ▶

Nutty Stuffed Mushrooms

Mary Stowell, Pahrump, Nev.
There is never any left.

 10 large fresh mushrooms
 1 small onion, chopped
 3 tablespoons butter
 ¼ cup dry bread crumbs
 ¼ cup finely chopped pecans
 3 tablespoons Parmesan cheese
 ¼ teaspoon salt
 ¼ teaspoon dried basil
 Dash of cayenne pepper

Preheat oven to 400 degrees.
Remove mushroom stems and chop. Brown onions and chopped stems in butter for approximately 5 minutes; set aside.
In bowl, combine bread crumbs, pecans, cheese, salt, basid and pepper. Add mushroom stems and onions. Stuff into mushroom caps. Place on greased baking dish. Bake uncovered 15 to 18 minutes. Makes 10.

Chilies Con Queso

Eleanor Craycraft, Sequim, Wash.
Chilies with cheese—a Mexican dip.

 1 small onion, finely chopped
 1 clove garlic, crushed (optional)

 2 tablespoons butter or margarine
 1 cup drained solid-pack tomatoes
 1 (4-ounce) can peeled green chilies, seeded and chopped
 ½ teaspoon salt
 Dash of pepper
 ½ pound Monterey Jack cheese
 ¾ cup half-and-half, or evaporated milk
 Corn chips or tortilla chips for dipping

Cook and stir onion and garlic in butter in 10-inch skillet until tender, about 5 minutes. Stir in tomatoes, chilies, salt and pepper. Simmer uncovered 15 minutes.

Cut cheese into ½-inch cubes; stir into tomato mixture. Stir in half-and-half when cheese begins to melt. Cook and stir until cheese is melted. Continue to cook uncovered on low heat for 10 minutes. Serve with corn or tortilla chips. Makes about 3 cups.
 Note: *Leftovers make a good omelet.*

Marinated Shrimp Relish

Louise Krieger, Youngtown, Ariz.
You may serve this mélange on lettuce or as a cocktail.

 3 pounds cleaned, cooked shrimp
 2 cups minced onions
 2 cups snipped fresh parsley
 1⅓ cups extra-virgin olive oil
 ⅔ cup vinegar
 2 cloves garlic, minced
 1 tablespoon salt
 Pinch of pepper

In large bowl, combine shrimp, onions and parsley. In mixing bowl, combine olive oil, vinegar, garlic, salt and pepper. Beat well. Pour over shrimp mixture. Chill for at least 1 hour before serving or overnight. Serves 8.

Zippy Hot Pepper Spread

Helen Harlos, Ethel, Miss.
This taste-bud-tingling appetizer is embarrassingly simple, yet so delicious. Serve it with an assortment of crackers.

 1 (8-ounce) jar medium-hot green-pepper jelly or jalapeño jelly
 1 (8-ounce) package cream cheese, softened

Spread jelly over cream cheese block. Serves 8 to 10.

Classic Corn Muffins

Margy Mann, St. Louis, Mo.

You'll enjoy the taste and texture of these traditional corn muffins.

1 cup yellow cornmeal
1 cup flour
¼ cup sugar
1 tablespoon baking powder
½ teaspoon salt
1 (15¼-ounce) can whole-kernel gold and white corn, drained
1 (14¾-ounce) can cream-style white corn
½ cup butter or margarine, melted
¼ cup milk
2 eggs, beaten

Preheat oven to 400 degrees. Grease 12-cup muffin tin.

In large bowl, combine cornmeal, flour, sugar, baking powder and salt. Mix well.

In another bowl, combine corns, butter, milk and eggs. Pour into dry ingredients. Stir just until blended.

Pour batter into prepared cups. Bake for 15 to 20 minutes, or until golden brown. Makes 1 dozen.

Variation: You may bake this corn bread in a greased 8 x 8 x 2-inch baking pan. Bake for 25 to 30 minutes, or until done.

Golden Carrot Muffins

Gwen Campbell, Sterling, Va.

1 cup grated carrots
1½ cups all-purpose flour
2 teaspoons baking powder
1 teaspoon baking soda
½ cup light brown sugar, firmly packed
½ teaspoon cinnamon
¼ teaspoon nutmeg
¼ teaspoon ground ginger
¼ teaspoon salt
1 egg plus 1 egg yolk, beaten
1 cup buttermilk
¼ cup oil

Preheat oven to 350 degrees.

Liberally grease muffin tins.

In a bowl, combine carrots, flour, baking powder, baking soda, brown sugar, cinnamon, nutmeg, ginger and salt.

In another bowl, combine beaten egg and egg yolk, buttermilk and oil. Add egg mixture to flour mixture, mixing only until combined. Fill muffin cups ⅔ full.

Bake 35 minutes or until muffins test done in the center. Cool muffins in tins on wire rack 5 minutes before removing. Makes 1 dozen.

Sweet Maple Biscuits

Jennifer Eveland-Kupp, Reading, Pa.

Bake up better biscuits with just a few special ingredients.

½ cup maple syrup
2 tablespoons butter
1 (8-ounce) container refrigerated biscuit dough
2 tablespoons orange juice
½ cup finely chopped nuts

Preheat oven to 400 degrees. Blend together maple syrup and butter. Pour into ungreased 8 x 8 x 2-inch baking pan. Place pan in preheating oven until butter melts.

Separate biscuits. Dip into orange juice. Roll in nuts. Arrange in pan over maple syrup mixture. Bake for 15 to 20 minutes, or until done. Makes 8.

Apple Spice Muffins

Margy Mann, St. Louis, Mo.

> 2 cups whole-wheat flour or
>   wheat-blend flour
> ⅓ cup sugar
> 3 teaspoons baking powder
> 1 teaspoon salt
> 1 teaspoon cinnamon
> ½ to 1 teaspoon nutmeg
> 1 cup skim milk
> ¼ cup oil
> 1 egg, beaten
> 1½ cups finely diced apples,
>   unpeeled

Preheat oven to 400 degrees. Coat bottoms of muffin cups with nonstick cooking spray.

In medium bowl, mix flour, sugar, baking powder, salt, cinnamon and nutmeg.

In second bowl, mix milk, oil and egg. Combine with flour mixture, mixing just until moistened. Batter will be lumpy. Fold in apples.

Fill muffin tins ⅔ full. Bake 18 to 20 minutes until golden brown, or toothpick inserted in center of muffin comes out clean. Makes 1 dozen.

Parmesan Potato Rounds

Shirley Ann Weimann, Woodstock, Conn.

> 4 medium red potatoes, thinly
>   sliced
> 1 small onion, thinly sliced and
>   separated into rings
> 3 tablespoons butter, melted
> ¼ cup grated Parmesan cheese
> ¼ teaspoon salt
> ⅛ teaspoon pepper
> ⅛ teaspoon garlic powder

Preheat oven to 450 degrees. Grease an 11 x 7-inch baking dish, or a 2-quart casserole.

Place ½ of the potatoes in prepared dish. Top with onion and remaining potatoes. Drizzle with butter. Sprinkle with cheese, salt, pepper and garlic powder.

Bake, uncovered, 25 to 30 minutes. Serves 4.

Zesty Tomato Risotto

Gwen Campbell, Sterling, Va.

> 1 cup sliced green onions
> 1 cup chopped red, green or yel-
>   low bell pepper
> 1 cup chopped celery
> 1 (2-ounce) can sliced mush-
>   rooms, drained
> 3 tablespoons butter
> 1½ cups uncooked Arborio rice,
>   or medium-grain white rice
> 1 (14.5-ounce) can chicken broth
> 1 (14.5-ounce) can chopped
>   tomatoes
> ½ teaspoon salt
> ¼ teaspoon pepper
> 1 cup grated sharp Cheddar
>   cheese
> ¼ teaspoon coriander

In large skillet, lightly sauté onions, bell pepper, celery and mushrooms in butter until tender. Stir in rice. Cook 3 minutes. Add chicken broth, tomatoes, salt and pepper.

Bring to a boil. Cover tightly, reduce heat and simmer 20 to 25 minutes. Remove lid and simmer an additional 5 minutes, stirring occasionally.

Remove from heat. Stir in sharp cheese. Sprinkle coriander across top. May be served hot or at room temperature. Serves 6.

Mashed Potato Timbales

Arlene Ranney, Eureka, Calif.

- **2½ pounds potatoes, peeled and cubed**
- **1 tablespoon butter or margarine**
- **1 tablespoon grated onion**
- **1 (8-ounce) carton reduced-fat ricotta cheese**
- **1 cup (8 ounces) sour cream**
- **1 teaspoon garlic powder**
- **½ teaspoon dried rosemary, crushed**
- **1 teaspoon salt**
- **¼ teaspoon pepper**
- **2 egg whites**
- **2 tablespoons dried bread crumbs**

Preheat oven to 425 degrees. Generously coat muffin cups with non-stick cooking spray.

Place potatoes in saucepan and cover with water. Bring to a boil. Reduce heat, cover and cook 20 to 25 minutes or until tender. Drain. Mash potatoes with butter and onion until small lumps of potato remain. Set aside.

In mixing bowl, beat ricotta cheese, sour cream, garlic powder, rosemary, salt and pepper until smooth. In small bowl, beat egg whites until frothy; fold into cheese mixture. Fold into potatoes.

Sprinkle prepared muffin cups evenly with bread crumbs. Fill with potato mixture and smooth tops. Bake 27 to 30 minutes, or until edges of potatoes are lightly browned. Cool 15 minutes.

Loosen timbales from sides of muffin cups and invert on baking sheet to remove. Makes 1 dozen.

Rice & Green Chili Casserole

Eleanor Craycraft, Sequim, Wash.

- **1 cup sour cream**
- **1 (4-ounce) can peeled, seeded, chopped green chilies, drained**
- **3 cups cooked rice**
- **¾ pound Monterey Jack cheese, cut into strips**
- **½ cup shredded Cheddar cheese**

Preheat oven to 325 degrees. Mix sour cream and chilies. Layer 1 cup of the rice, half the sour cream mixture and half the cheese strips in a greased 1½-quart casserole; repeat. Cover with remaining rice.

Cook, uncovered, 30 minutes or until bubbly. Sprinkle with Cheddar cheese and return to oven until cheese melts. Serves 6. ∎

Good Friends, Good Times— Super Bowl Party

A great excuse for gathering friends together for a mid-winter party.

By Vicki Steensma

Super Bowl is a big event regardless of your team choice, or, for that matter, sport choice. It is a great time to gather friends and family for a mid-winter party and have a lot of fun in the process!

This year the big game is in Jacksonville, Fla., on Feb. 6, and though it may be the smallest market to host a Super Bowl, NFL Commissioner Paul Tagliabue says the 2005 game will be unique. That is because it will have fans living on cruise ships and others being ferried to the stadium by river taxis.

Don't be shy, you can pull off a memorable party—even if you are not a sports fan—if you keep these tips in mind and follow the pre-game prep. Remember, if you want to watch the game, you'll need to keep it simple and easy by doing most everything in advance.

Heat-Wave Jalapeño Poppers
Don't be afraid to try these, they are fun and tasty.

> **Jalapeño peppers (12 to 15, depending on size)**
> **1 (8-ounce) package cream cheese**
> **1 (8-ounce) package shredded cheddar cheese**
> **1 egg, beaten**
> **1 cup milk**
> **1 cup flour**

1 cup dry bread crumbs
Oil for frying

Wash, halve and seed the jalapeños. (Wear gloves to protect your hands. Throw them away and thoroughly wash your hands before touching your eyes.) For the filling, mix cream cheese with the shredded cheddar cheese. Stuff the pepper halves with the filling.

In a small bowl, combine egg and milk. Put flour in a second bowl. Dip the stuffed peppers in the milk mixture, then in the flour. Lay them on a wax-paper-lined tray to dry for about 10 to 15 minutes. Put dry bread crumbs in a bowl. Dip the peppers in the milk/egg wash again, then in the bread crumbs. Let them dry for another 10 to 15 minutes. Repeat the last step one more time, then deep-fry in hot oil (365 to 375 degrees) about 3 or 4 minutes each, or until they're browned the way you like them. Drain on paper towels. Makes 24 to 30.

Note: *Jalapeños are hard to coat, plus they are stuffed, so they really need the triple coating. This also works well for other fried veggies, shrimp, mozzarella cheese sticks, etc. Instead of plain bread crumbs, you can also use seasoned bread crumbs, cornmeal, cracker meal or corn-flake crumbs.*

Florida Crabby Dip
Serve this zippy dip with the crackers of your choice.

> **2 (8-ounce) packages cream cheese, softened**
> **½ cup chopped green olives**
> **3 tablespoons milk**
> **2 green onions, finely chopped**
> **2 tablespoons prepared horseradish**
> **2 (6-ounce) cans crabmeat, drained and flaked**

In a medium bowl, blend cream cheese, olives, milk, green onions and prepared horseradish. Gradually mix in crabmeat. Chill in the refrigerator until serving. Makes 3 cups.

Super Bowl Party dishes shown on this page, clockwise from the top: Pigskin Calzones (page 38), Quarterback Cheese Dip (page 38), Heat-Wave Jalapeño Poppers (page 36), Super Bowl Party Sandwiches (page 39), Goalpost Dessert Pizza (page 39) and Florida Crabby Dip (page 36).

Quarterback Cheese Dip

This tasty, make-ahead dip is sure to be a crowd pleaser.

- 2 (8-ounce) packages cream cheese, softened
- 2 (8-ounce) packages shredded Cheddar cheese
- 1 teaspoon garlic powder
- ½ cup beer, regular or non-alcoholic
- 1 (1-pound) loaf round bread

Place cream cheese, Cheddar cheese, garlic powder and beer in a large bowl. Using an electric mixer, blend until smooth.

Remove and reserve top of round bread. Hollow out the loaf, reserving removed bread pieces. Spoon cream cheese mixture into the hollowed loaf (or if you have a small plastic bowl that fits in, you may use that). Replace bread top until ready to serve. Use the reserved bread pieces for dipping. Makes about 3 cups.

Pigskin Calzones

Choose your favorite of the two fillings or use two frozen loaves and make them both.

Calzone Dough

- 1 (16-ounce) loaf frozen Italian or white bread dough

Vegetarian Spinach Filling

- 1 (10-ounce) package frozen, chopped spinach, thawed and drained
- 1½ cups finely shredded Cheddar cheese
- 1 small red onion, chopped
- 1 teaspoon dried basil
- ½ teaspoon dried oregano
- ¼ teaspoon garlic powder
- Salt and pepper

Combine well-drained spinach, cheese, onion, basil, oregano, garlic powder, and salt and pepper to taste in medium-sized bowl. Set aside until ready to use.

Hearty Italian Sausage Filling

- ½ pound Italian sausage
- ½ cup shredded Mozzarella cheese
- ¾ cup pizza sauce
- 3 tablespoons grated Parmesan cheese
- 2 tablespoons chopped parsley
- ½ teaspoon garlic powder
- ½ teaspoon dried basil
- ¼ teaspoon dried oregano

Remove sausage from casing. Crumble and cook until no longer pink. Drain well and cool. Toss with Mozzarella cheese, pizza sauce, Parmesan cheese, parsley, garlic powder, basil and oregano. Set aside until ready to use.

A football-shaped pan is fun to use, if available, otherwise use a large, rectangular pan. Preheat oven to 350 degrees. Thaw frozen bread dough according to package directions, until at room temperature. Roll dough into a 12 x 7-inch rectangle. Spray your pan with non-stick cooking spray; place dough in prepared pan.

Place either spinach or sausage filling in center of dough. Gather dough over filling, pinching edges to seal. Brush with water to be sure it is sealed firmly. Allow calzone to rise in warm place 1 to 1½ hours or until doubled in size.

To make calzone flat on bottom, place cookie sheet on top of pan and weigh down using heavy pan with heatproof handle. Bake 20 minutes.

Remove weight and bake additional 5 to 10 minutes or until browned. Bread should sound hollow when tapped with finger. Cool 5 minutes; remove calzone from the pan. Place on cooling rack. Serve hot. Serves 8.

Super Bowl Party Sandwiches

Whether you call them subs, hoagies or heroes, these sandwiches are sure to score with your guests.

> 2 long loaves crusty French bread (about 20 to 22 inches long, each)
> Italian salad dressing
> 12 ounces thin-sliced ham
> 12 ounces thin-sliced hard salami
> 8 ounces thin-sliced pepperoni
> Sweet pepper and onion relish; available in most stores or homemade
> 12 ounces thin-sliced provolone cheese
> 1 small jar green or black olives, or both, if you like
> Cellophane-topped or plastic sandwich picks

About 1½ hours before serving, slice bread loaves lengthwise, in half. Lightly brush both inside tops and bottoms with Italian dressing. Place slices of ham, hard salami and pepperoni on bottom halves. Spread a generous layer of sweet pepper and onion relish over meats. Add slices of provolone. Cover

with top halves of bread. Tightly wrap each loaf in plastic wrap and refrigerate for about 1 hour.

Cut sandwiches diagonally into slices about 3 inches wide. For each sandwich slice, place an olive on a sandwich pick; insert picks and arrange on a serving tray. Serves 6 to 8.

Goalpost Dessert Pizza

This scrumptious dessert pizza will not last long at the party.

> ¾ cup butter, softened
> 1¾ cups flour, divided
> ½ cup sugar
> ½ cup light brown sugar
> 1 egg
> 1 teaspoon vanilla
> 1 (12-ounce) bag milk chocolate chips
> 2 cups mini marshmallows
> 1½ cups chopped pecans
> ½ cup caramel ice cream topping, at room temperature

Preheat oven to 350 degrees. Spray a 14-inch, rimmed-edge pizza pan with non-stick cooking spray; set aside.

In a large bowl, beat butter until light and fluffy, using an electric mixer at medium speed for about 1 minute. Add 1 cup of the flour, sugar, brown sugar, egg and vanilla. Beat mixture until thoroughly blended. Beat in the remaining ¾ cup flour to make a soft dough.

Spread dough onto the bottom of the prepared pan. Bake at 350 degrees for 20 to 25 minutes or until top of dough is a light golden brown.

Remove from oven and reduce oven temperature to 325 degrees. Top with chocolate chips, mini marshmallows and pecans. Return to oven for 6 to 8 minutes or until edges of marshmallows are light golden brown. Cool completely on a wire rack. Drizzle with caramel topping. Slice into 16 wedges for serving. ■

Super Bowl Party Tips

- Decorate your house in your team's colors or both if your guests are divided.
- Plan for more than you think will attend. It is better to have too much—leftovers are welcome.
- Warming trays on a table near where you plan to watch the game can be very helpful.
- Keep paper towels and a wet rag handy.
- There is usually a person or two that has no interest in football. Enlist their help to get more food from the kitchen, clear off plates, etc.
- Record the game to catch the parts you might miss. After the game, you can all catch your favorite highlights and those super-expensive, but hilarious commercials.

Shown on this page, clockwise from the top: Shrimp Kabobs (page 41), Tex-Mex Stuffed Peppers (page 41), Chicken Stir-Fry (page 42), California Chicken Salad (page 42), Fish Santa Fe (page 42) and Strawberry Dream (page 41).

Keep Your New Year's Resolution!

A well-balanced diet with an emphasis on wholesome and delicious dishes will help you keep your promise to eat better this year.

By Deborah J. Myers

Many people resolve every January 1 that this is the year they will lose weight and keep it off. Plenty of marketers are willing to help them out, too. Type "diet" into your Internet search engine and thousands of sites will pop up, featuring diet pills, tips, potions and strategies. Meal-replacement diets, cereal diets, cabbage soup diets, grapefruit diets, fat-free diets, no-carbohydrate diets. Who can admit to never trying at least one of these fad diets? Over the years, the methods may change, but the reasoning is the same: people want to trick their bodies into losing weight quickly and easily.

Literally, a diet is what you eat every day. Of course, in the context of health, as in "going on a diet," the term refers to eating differently than you normally do for the purpose of reducing your body weight and improving your health.

Sticking with a contrived diet of foods you don't normally eat or with odd exclusions may help jump-start weight loss, but won't work for the long run. Real life doesn't work that way. You get busy. You're invited to parties where "forbidden" food is served. Buying premade shakes and entrees becomes expensive. You just plain get sick of eating a limited number of foods.

Although some people enjoy short-term results, using weight-loss pills proves to be ineffective as a long-term solution to maintaining a healthy weight.

To really lose weight and keep it off, you need to exercise sufficiently and

change how you eat in a positive way for the rest of your life. It's as simple as that. It took a long time to put on the weight, and, depending upon how much weight you want to lose, it will take a while to get it off.

Most nutrition experts agree that eating a well-balanced diet that focuses on wholesome foods, such as fruits, vegetables, whole grains, lean sources of protein and heart-friendly fat is the most livable diet. Focus on eating delicious, healthful food in moderation for your health's sake, not the number on the scale. The following recipes hold to that ideal.

Shrimp Kabobs

For easier removal, lightly spray skewers with nonstick cooking spray.

- **1 pound medium shrimp, de-veined and de-tailed**
- **1 green bell pepper, cut into 1-inch pieces**
- **24 cherry tomatoes**
- **12 pearl onions**
- **1 clove garlic, crushed**
- **¼ cup olive oil**

Skewer shrimp, pepper pieces, tomatoes and onions, alternating items. In small bowl, combine garlic and oil. Brush onto skewers and grill or broil until pepper pieces are tender-crisp. Delicious served on brown rice or whole-grain noodles. Serves 4.

Per serving: 255 Cal.; 19.8g Protein; 14.9g Fat; 11.5g Carb.; 204.3mg Sodium; 168.1mg Chol.; 2.3g Fiber.

Strawberry Dream

Cool and light, but not too sweet, this dessert is sure to please.

- **2 pasteurized egg whites**
- **1 tablespoon sugar**
- **1 cup fat-free, light vanilla yogurt**
- **1 tablespoon orange juice concentrate, thawed**
- **5 cups frozen strawberries, thawed and well-drained, divided**

Beat the egg whites until stiff peaks form. Gradually beat in sugar. Fold in the yogurt and thawed juice concentrate. In separate bowl, mash one cup of berries. Fold into egg white mixture. Alternate remaining strawberries with egg white mixture in parfait glasses, reserving enough berries to cover the top. Serve immediately. Serves 4.

Per serving: 154.2 Cal.; 4.8g Protein; .3g Fat; 35.5g Carb.; 65.5mg Sodium; 1.2mg Chol.; 5.8g Fiber.

Tex-Mex Stuffed Peppers

Healthful red kidney beans make this dish stick-to-your-ribs satisfying.

- **Nonstick cooking spray**
- **1 pound 90 percent lean ground beef**
- **¾ cup minced onion**

½ teaspoon granulated garlic
1 teaspoon cumin
¼ teaspoon chili powder
½ teaspoon ground cayenne pepper
Salt and pepper
32 ounces unseasoned tomato sauce
1 cup prepared brown rice
1 cup canned red kidney beans,
    drained and rinsed
4 large green bell peppers
4 tablespoons fat-free cheddar
    cheese

Preheat oven to 350 degrees. Lightly coat bottom of oven-safe pan with non-stick cooking spray. In medium saucepan, brown beef and onion with garlic, cumin, chili powder, cayenne pepper, and salt and pepper to taste. Add tomato sauce, rice and beans and heat through. Meanwhile, cut tops off green peppers and remove the seeds. Spoon mixture into peppers and place in oven-safe pan. Bake for 30 minutes. Divide cheese among peppers and sprinkle on top. Bake an additional 5 minutes until cheese melts. Serves 4.

Per serving: 435.9 Cal.; 31.7g Protein; 10.7g Fat; 50.2g Carb.; 432.5mg Sodium; 74.4mg Chol.; 10.6g Fiber.

California Chicken Salad

This light lunch can be made heartier by stuffing the salad into a whole-grain pita pocket.

2 large boneless, skinless
    chicken breasts
¼ cup orange juice
2 tablespoons lemon juice
Dash lime juice
3 tablespoons minced onion
Salt and pepper
3 cups torn romaine lettuce
1 cup iceberg lettuce
2 cups torn fresh spinach

1 medium tomato, chopped
3 tablespoons bean sprouts
3 tablespoons grated carrot
1 green pepper, sliced
¼ cup mandarin orange
    segments, drained
Your favorite light dressing

Cut chicken in thin strips and brown with orange juice, lemon juice, lime juice, onion, and salt and pepper to taste in a skillet over medium heat. Meanwhile, place lettuces, spinach, tomato, bean sprouts, carrot and green pepper in large bowl. When chicken is browned, top the salad with it and garnish with mandarin orange segments. Serve immediately with dressing on the side. Serves 4.

Per serving (without dressing): 171.8 Cal.; 25.1g Protein; 3g Fat; 11.7g Carb.; 88.8mg Sodium; 62.7mg Chol.; 3.3g Fiber.

Fish Santa Fe

This dish is fancy enough for company but so easy to make that you'll prepare it for weeknight meals.

½ cup fat-free salad dressing
½ cup plain, fat-free yogurt
1 tablespoon Dijon mustard
1 teaspoon lemon juice
⅛ teaspoon cayenne pepper
4 white fish fillets, such as Orange
    Roughy, Tilapia, etc. (defrost
    and drain well if frozen)
½ cup shredded fat-free Monterey
    Jack or Co-Jack cheese
2 tablespoons parsley flakes
1 small tomato, diced

Combine dressing, yogurt, mustard, lemon juice and pepper in a bowl. Place fish in one layer in a glass microwave-safe dish. Spread mixture over fish and microwave on high for 7 minutes or until fish flakes easily. Since the size and thickness of fish fillets vary, cooking time may not be the full 7 minutes. Top with cheese and microwave 30 seconds or until cheese melts. Garnish with parsley and tomato. Serves 4.

Per serving: 195.7 Cal.; 32.9g Protein; 2.7g Fat; 8.4g Carb.; 805mg Sodium; 98.4mg Chol.; .7g Fiber.

Chicken Stir-Fry

Authentic Asian cooking tends to use meat as a seasoning and focus on rice and vegetables.

2 boneless, skinless chicken
    breasts cut in 1-inch pieces
¼ cup low-sodium chicken stock
2 cups frozen broccoli
1 red pepper, cut julienne style
1 green pepper, cut julienne style
½ cup water chestnut slices
¼ cup bamboo shoots, cut julienne
    style
½ cup chopped onion
1 teaspoon granulated garlic
2 teaspoons ground ginger
1 tablespoon low-sodium soy
    sauce
4 cups hot cooked rice

Prepare broccoli, red pepper, green pepper, water chestnuts, bamboo shoots and onion and set aside. In large frying pan or wok, brown chicken in chicken stock over medium heat. Increase heat to high and add prepared vegetables, garlic, ginger and soy sauce. Stir continuously until vegetables are tender-crisp. Serve on bed of rice. Serves 4.

Per serving: 296.8 Cal.; 20.6g Protein; 2.4g Fat; 48.3g Carb.; 217.7mg Sodium; 36.8mg Chol.; 5.6g Fiber. ■

Soup & Salad for Lunch

Velvety White Bean Soup
Prepare these elegant bowls when you need a speedy soup.

- 2 (15-ounce) cans cannellini beans or white kidney beans, rinsed and drained, divided
- 1 (14½-ounce) can chicken broth
- 2 tablespoons lemon juice
- 1 tablespoon olive oil
- ¼ teaspoon chopped fresh thyme
- ⅛ teaspoon pepper
- 2 tablespoons chopped fresh parsley or basil
- 4 Kalamata olives, pitted and diced
- 4 sun-dried tomatoes in oil, diced

In blender, purée 1 can beans with chicken broth. Pour into saucepan. Add remaining beans. Bring to a boil. Stir in lemon juice, olive oil, thyme and pepper. Heat through.

To serve, garnish individual servings with parsley, olives and sun-dried tomatoes. Serves 4.

Galelah Dowell, Fairland, Okla.

Editor's Note: Make this vegetarian-friendly lunch heartier by adding chicken—leftover, canned or deli—to the soup.

Prep your salad while the soup heats to have this on the table in a hurry.

Greek Salad Pita Pockets
Combine the tastes of the Mediterranean in a tangy sandwich.

- ¼ cup olive oil
- 2 tablespoons balsamic vinegar or red wine vinegar
- Small red onion, thinly sliced (about 1 cup)
- 1 (14-ounce) can quartered artichoke hearts, drained and coarsely chopped
- 1 (10-ounce) can pitted Kalamata olives, drained (about 1½ cups)
- 1 cup crumbled feta cheese (4 ounces)
- 2 large or 4 small pitas

In large bowl, combine olive oil and balsamic vinegar. Rinse red onion slices under cold running water; drain well. Add red onion, artichoke hearts, olives and cheese to olive oil mixture. Toss to combine.

To serve, cut each pita in half, opening to form a pocket. Spoon salad into pitas. Serve immediately. Serves 4. ■

Kit Rollins, Cedarburg, Wis.

Romantic Valentine Dinner

Easy-to-prepare, healthful and just for two—this dinner will come out just right for any occasion.

By JoAnna M. Lund

Picture this—you've prepared a romantic dinner for just the two of you. You've set the table beautifully. The flickering of the candles just seems to add to the ambiance. The evening is slipping away into magical Romantic Land with your "sweetie" mightily impressed by everything you've prepared. But just as he finishes his last sip of Party "Champagne" you're brought back into the real world. After all, your kitchen is a mess and you have so many leftovers they hardly fit into your fridge.

How many times have you read other "cooking for two" articles only to discover that most of the recipes serve closer to an army than only two people!! I remember just such an article. The headline promised two-serving dishes, but when I started looking the recipes over, I discovered side dishes that served four and even desserts with eight servings! Who did they think they were kidding? No matter how wonderful something tastes, after you've eaten it for the second time in a row, it's still just leftovers.

That will not happen when you serve this menu. Each of my recipes not only are created with only two

servings, they are also healthier, easy to prepare, tasty and call for small-town ingredients. Who could ask for more? Well, maybe a kiss for the cook *and* help with the dishes would be nice.

Green Beans With Mushrooms
Perk up those bland green beans for a special occasion.

- ¼ cup chopped onion
- 1 (8-ounce) can cut green beans, rinsed and drained
- 1 (2-ounce) jar chopped pimento, drained
- 1 (2.5-ounce) jar sliced mushrooms, drained
- 1 teaspoon dried parsley flakes
- ⅛ teaspoon black pepper
- 2 tablespoons no-fat sour cream

In a medium skillet sprayed with butter-flavored cooking spray, sauté onion for 5 minutes or until tender

Add green beans, pimento, mushrooms, parsley flakes, and black pepper. Mix well to combine. Stir in sour cream.

Continue cooking for 3 to 4 minutes or until mixture is heated through, stirring often. Serves 2.

Party "Champagne"
A fun, non-alcoholic drink.

- 1 cup cold unsweetened apple juice
- ½ cup cold club soda
- 2 maraschino cherries

In a 4-cup glass measuring cup, combine apple juice and club soda. Pour into champagne glasses. Serves 2.

Note: *Cut slit in bottom of cherries. Place a cherry on the rim of each glass. Serve at once.*

Special Spinach Salad
These colorful greens perk up a mid-winter meal.

- 2 cups torn fresh spinach
- ½ cup chopped fresh mushrooms
- 2 tablespoons slivered almonds
- ¼ cup reduced-fat raspberry vinaigrette dressing

In a medium bowl, combine spinach, mushrooms and almonds. Add dressing. Toss well to coat. For each serving, place 1 cup of salad on a salad plate. Serve at once. Serves 2.

Dishes shown on page 44, clockwise from the top: Party "Champagne" (page 45), Green Beans With Mushrooms (page 45), South Seas Chicken Over Rice (page 46), Special Spinach Salad (page 45) and Festive Dessert Meringue Cups (page 46).

Preheat oven to 350 degrees. In a medium bowl, beat egg whites and cream of tartar with an electric mixer until soft peaks form. Add coconut extract and sugar substitute. Continue beating until stiff peaks form. Cover a baking sheet with aluminum foil or parchment paper. Spoon the meringue mixture into two even mounds on prepared baking sheet, making sure sides are higher than center.

Bake for 20 minutes. Turn oven off, open oven door 1 inch and let baking sheet sit in oven for 1 hour. For each serving, place a cooled meringue cup on a dessert plate, spoon ⅓ cup ice cream in center, drizzle 1 tablespoon chocolate syrup over ice cream and sprinkle 1 teaspoon coconut and 4 cherry pieces over top. Serve at once. Serves 2. ■

About the Author

JoAnna M. Lund is a cookbook author specializing in common-folk, healthful recipes, which are shared in her various Healthy Exchanges cookbooks and newsletter. These recipes are from her cookbook Dinner For Two, *featuring 60 recipes created with only two at the table! For more information about JoAnna or her recipes, visit her Web site at www.healthyexchanges.com or write to her at Healthy Exchanges, P.O. Box 80, DeWitt, IA 52742.*

South Seas Chicken Over Rice
A nutritious, satisfying entrée.

- 8 ounces skinned and boned uncooked chicken breast, cut into bite-size pieces
- ½ cup chopped onion
- ½ cup unsweetened orange juice
- 1 tablespoon orange marmalade spreadable fruit
- 1½ cups frozen sliced carrots, thawed
- 2 teaspoons reduced-calorie margarine
- ½ teaspoon dried rosemary
- 1 cup hot cooked rice

In a large skillet sprayed with butter-flavored cooking spray, brown chicken and onion for 5 minutes. Stir in orange juice, spreadable fruit, carrots, margarine and rosemary. Lower heat and simmer for 10 minutes or until chicken and carrots are tender, stirring often. For each serving, place ½ cup rice on a plate and spoon about 1 cup chicken mixture over top. Serves 2.

Hints Usually ⅔ cup uncooked instant rice or ½ cup uncooked regular rice cooks to about 1 cup. Thaw carrots by placing in a colander and rinsing under hot water for 1 minute.

Festive Dessert Meringue Cups
A light and airy ending to a satisfying meal.

- 2 egg whites (at room temperature)
- ¼ teaspoon cream of tartar
- ¼ teaspoon coconut extract
- Sugar substitute suitable for baking, equal to ½ cup
- ⅔ cup sugar- and fat-free chocolate ice cream
- 2 tablespoons reduced-calorie chocolate syrup
- 2 teaspoons flaked coconut
- 2 maraschino cherries, quartered

Flavorful Baked Doughnuts

Give these fun, baked doughnuts a try.

If you have ever been reluctant to attempt frying in a hot pan of oil, maybe you wondered about baking doughnuts instead of deep-frying them. In recent years many of us have tried to avoid too much fried food in our diet, so when Billie Wesolowski from Stratford, Conn. asked for baked doughnut recipes in our Reader Swap feature, we were really interested in trying them. We sifted through a variety of baked doughnut recipes and we are giving you the results of some of the recipes.

A certain amount of flavor is lost from baking rather than deep frying, but it can be overcome by a glaze or by rolling the doughnuts in sugar and cinnamon, or by adding nuts or sprinkles.

Tip Locating nonstick doughnut pans takes a little searching. We ordered them from a mail-order catalog we found on the Web: www.bakerscatalogue.com. They come in two sizes and we baked some of the recipes in each of them. Some readers recommended baking the doughnuts in muffin tins, but that just doesn't seem like a doughnut.

Chocolate Cake Doughnuts

These little chocolate doughnuts are a tasty treat, especially when they are topped with glaze.

- **1½ cups flour**
- **⅓ cup unsweetened cocoa powder**
- **1 teaspoon baking powder**
- **⅛ teaspoon salt**
- **2 eggs**
- **⅔ cup sugar**
- **1 teaspoon vanilla**
- **½ cup milk**
- **2 tablespoons butter, melted**

Preheat oven to 325 degrees.

Lightly coat nonstick petite doughnut pan with cooking spray.

Combine flour, cocoa powder, baking powder and salt.

In separate bowl, mix eggs, sugar and vanilla until thick.

Combine milk and butter. Alternately combine egg mixture and milk mixture with flour mixture and mix until smooth and soft.

Fill each doughnut hole ⅔ full with batter. Bake 8 minutes. Cool. Carefully remove doughnuts from pan and dip into glaze.

Repeat with rest of batter. Makes one dozen large doughnuts.

Glaze

6 tablespoons whipping cream
6 tablespoons light corn syrup
8 ounces semisweet chocolate, chopped

Bring cream and corn syrup to a boil in heavy pan on medium heat. Reduce heat to low. Add chocolate; whisk until smooth. Remove from heat. Let cool until glaze thickens slightly, but can still be poured, about 25 minutes.

Cake Doughnuts
Glaze

1 cup confectioners' sugar
2 tablespoons hot water

Doughnuts

2 cups flour
¾ cup sugar
2 teaspoons baking powder
1 teaspoon salt
1 tablespoon butter, melted
2 eggs, beaten
¾ cup milk
1 teaspoon vanilla
¼ teaspoon nutmeg
¼ teaspoon cinnamon

Preheat oven to 325 degrees.

Lightly coat nonstick petite doughnut pan with cooking spray.

Mix confectioners' sugar and hot water. Set glaze aside.

In bowl, mix together flour, sugar, baking powder and salt. Add butter, eggs, milk, vanilla, nutmeg and cinnamon. Beat until well blended.

Fill each doughnut hole ⅔ full. Bake 8 minutes, or until tops spring back when lightly touched. Cool. Remove from pan and dip into glaze. Repeat with remaining batter. Makes approximately 36 mini doughnuts.

Note: *Doughnuts may be decorated with sprinkles, nuts, shaved chocolate or coconut. If desired, dip doughnuts in cinnamon and sugar instead of glaze.*

Baked Apple Doughnuts
They have a muffinlike texture and would be satisfying as a breakfast treat.

1½ cups flour
1¾ teaspoons baking powder
½ teaspoon salt
½ teaspoon nutmeg
½ cup sugar
⅓ cup shortening
1 egg, beaten
¼ cup milk
½ cup grated apple
½ cup raisins (optional)
½ cup melted butter
⅓ cup sugar
1 teaspoon cinnamon

Preheat oven to 350 degrees. Coat doughnut pan with cooking spray.

Sift flour, baking powder, salt and nutmeg with ½ cup sugar. Cut in shortening until mixture is fine and crumbly.

Mix egg, milk and apple. Add to dry ingredients. Mix thoroughly. Add raisins if desired.

Fill doughnut pan ⅔ full. Bake 20 to 25 minutes. Cool slightly. Roll in melted butter, then in sugar-and-cinnamon mixture. Makes 1 dozen large doughnuts.

Raised Baked Doughnuts
Heartier than a deep-fried yeast dough- nut, they have a wonderful flavor. The shape benefits from being baked in a doughnut pan.

1½ cups milk
⅓ cup shortening
½ cup sugar
2 teaspoons nutmeg
½ teaspoon cinnamon
1 teaspoon cardamom
½ teaspoon mace
2 packages yeast, or 2 cakes
¼ cup lukewarm water
3¾ cups sifted flour
2 eggs
2 teaspoons salt
Melted butter, or oil

Preheat oven to 425 degrees.

Scald milk. Add shortening, sugar, salt, nutmeg, cinnamon, cardamom and mace. Cool.

Soften yeast in lukewarm water. Add to shortening/sugar mixture with flour, eggs and salt. Cover; let rise 1 hour.

Knead several times. Roll ½ inch thick; cut with doughnut cutter. Place on cookie sheet. Brush with melted butter or a little oil. Let rise 20 minutes.

Bake 8 to 10 minutes. Brush again with melted butter, then roll in sugar or put on glaze. Makes 2½ to 3 dozen. ■

Plan ahead and dinner is ready when you are.

Hassle-Free Teen Pleasers

Slow Cooker White Chili

1 pound Great Northern beans, soaked
2 pounds boneless chicken breasts
1 medium onion, chopped
3 cloves garlic, minced
2 (4-ounce) cans green chilies
2 teaspoons ground cumin
1 teaspoon oregano
1 to 1½ teaspoons cayenne pepper, to taste
½ teaspoon salt
1 (14½-ounce) can reduced-sodium chicken broth
1 cup water

Put beans in medium pan and cover with water. Bring to boil; reduce heat and simmer 20 minutes. Discard water.

Skin chicken breasts and cut into 1-inch pieces. Brown, if desired.

Put beans, chicken, onion, garlic, green chilies, cumin, oregano, cayenne pepper, salt, broth and 1 cup water in slow cooker. Stir to mix thoroughly.

Cover and cook on low 10 to 12 hours (5 to 6 hours on high). Serves 6 to 8.

Hazel Hullinger, Decatur, Ill.

Note: *You may not find parboiling the beans to be a necessary step. We had good results without.*

Slow Cooker Pizza Casserole

While not really a pizza, you'll nonetheless be greeted with the smells of freshly delivered pizza as soon as you lift the lid.

1 to 1½ pounds hamburger
1 small onion
2 (4-ounce) cans black olives
2 (15-ounce) cans pizza sauce
8 ounces rotini noodles, cooked
1 (7-ounce) can mushrooms
1 (3-ounce) package pepperoni
12 ounces shredded Mozzarella cheese
12 ounces shredded Cheddar cheese

Brown hamburger and onion together in skillet; drain. Put half in bottom of slow cooker. Layer with half the olives, pizza sauce, rotini noodles, mushrooms, pepperoni and cheeses. Repeat with remaining ingredients.

Cover and cook on high 1 hour. Turn heat to low and cook an additional 3 to 4 hours. Serves 6 to 8.

LuAnn Fulton, Huntington, Ind.

Chunky Applesauce

Nothing beats the taste of homemade applesauce and fixing it in the slow cooker couldn't be easier. Serve it alone or spooned over warm gingerbread.

½ to 1 cup sugar
8 to 10 large cooking apples, peeled, cored and sliced
½ to 1 cup water
1 teaspoon cinnamon

Place apples, water, cinnamon and sugar in slow cooker. Cook on low 8 to 10 hours, or on high 3 to 4 hours. Serves 6 to 8. ■

March/April 2005

Family Secrets Make a Meal

Spinach Lasagna

This recipe was given to me by my grandmother. She loved to make dinner for her family. This was one of her favorites and ours as well.

- 1 pound ricotta cheese
- 2 cups shredded mozzarella cheese, divided
- 1 egg
- 1 package frozen chopped spinach, thawed and drained
- ½ teaspoon salt
- 1 teaspoon oregano
- Dash pepper
- 32 ounces spaghetti sauce
- 9 or 12 lasagna noodles or enough to fill pan in layers, uncooked
- 1 cup water

Preheat oven to 350 degrees. Grease 9 x 13-inch pan.

In large bowl, mix ricotta cheese, 1 cup mozzarella cheese, egg, spinach, salt, oregano and pepper. In greased pan, layer 1 cup sauce, 3 or 4 noodles and half of cheese mixture. Repeat. Top with remaining noodles and sauce.

Sprinkle with remaining 1 cup mozzarella cheese. Pour water around edges of pan. Cover tightly with foil and bake for 1 hour and 15 minutes. Let stand for 15 minutes before serving. Serves 6 to 8.

Susan L. Weiner, Spring Hill, Fla.

Crunch-Top Applesauce Bars

1940s recipe from my mother's cooking notebook.

- 1¼ cups sugar, divided
- 1 cup unsweetened applesauce
- ½ cup shortening
- 2 cups flour
- 1 teaspoon baking soda
- 1½ teaspoons cinnamon
- 1 teaspoon grated nutmeg
- Dash cloves
- ¼ teaspoon salt
- 1 cup raisins
- ¾ cup coarsely chopped walnuts, divided
- 1 teaspoon vanilla
- ⅔ cup crushed cornflakes
- 2 tablespoons butter or margarine

Preheat oven to 350 degrees. Grease a 15½ x 10½ x 1-inch jelly-roll pan.

In large bowl, combine 1 cup sugar with applesauce. Add shortening; blend.

Sift together flour, baking soda, cinnamon, nutmeg, cloves and salt on a piece of waxed paper. Add to applesauce mixture and stir until smooth. Stir in raisins, ½ cup walnuts and vanilla. Spread batter in jelly-roll pan.

Combine cornflakes, ¼ cup sugar, ¼ cup walnuts and butter; sprinkle over top of batter in pan. Bake about 30 minutes or until batter pulls away from sides of pan. Cool and cut into bars. Makes about 32 bars. ■

Eleanor Craycraft, Sequim, Wash.

Meatless Italian Meal

Eggplant With Marinara Sauce
Delicious when served with buttered pasta!

- **1 (6-ounce) can tomato paste**
- **1 medium tomato, peeled and chopped**
- **2 tablespoons chopped fresh mushrooms**
- **1 tablespoon minced green pepper**
- **1 teaspoon lemon juice**
- **1 teaspoon minced onion**
- **¼ teaspoon basil**
- **Dash each: garlic powder, cayenne pepper, salt and pepper**
- **1 medium eggplant**
- **Oil**

In small pan, combine tomato paste, tomato, mushrooms, green pepper, lemon juice, onion, basil, garlic powder, cayenne pepper, salt and pepper. Bring to a boil. Reduce heat and simmer 10 minutes, stirring frequently. Set aside and keep warm.

Rinse eggplant under cool water and pat dry. Slice unpeeled eggplant into ½-inch-thick slices. Brush slices lightly with oil.

Place on grill over medium heat (or in oven under broiler on oiled broiler rack) for about 2 minutes on each side, or until tender.

Transfer to serving platter and top with marinara sauce. Serves 6.

Editor's Note: *We used a preheated, cast aluminum grill pan and it worked very well.*

Kit Rollins, Cedarburg, Wis.

Lettuce With Spring Garden Dressing
Perk up your plain, bottled dressing.

- **½ small carrot**
- **8 radishes**
- **2 green onions**
- **2 tablespoons mayonnaise**
- **¼ cup bottled French dressing**
- **1 small head lettuce, washed and broken in pieces**

Shred or finely chop carrot, radishes and green onions (include some of green tops). Mix with mayonnaise and French dressing in small bowl.

Pour over lettuce in salad bowl and toss until well coated. Serves 4. ■

Hazel Hullinger, Decatur, Ill.

Spring Holiday Entertaining

Celebrate spring with the warmth of gathering together with family and friends for an Easter or Passover meal.

Baked Ham With Raisin Sauce
Adding the simple glaze dresses up an ordinary ham.

1 (12-pound) fully cooked ham
Cloves (optional)

Glaze
1 cup brown sugar
1 tablespoon dry mustard

Raisin Sauce
½ cup brown sugar
1 teaspoon dry mustard
1 tablespoon cornstarch
1½ cups water
¼ cup vinegar
½ cup raisins
1 tablespoon butter

Preheat oven to 325 degrees. Place ham, fat side up, on rack in a shallow roasting pan. Insert meat thermometer. Bake until internal temperature reaches 130 degrees—about 20 minutes per pound.

Pull ham out of oven 30 minutes before end of baking time. Pour drippings off and remove any skin. Cut fat into diamond shapes. Insert cloves, if desired.

Mix 1 cup brown sugar and 1 tablespoon dry mustard and cover ham with glaze. Return ham to oven for 30 minutes. Remove ham from oven and allow to sit for 15 to 20 minutes for easier cutting. Serves 10 to 12.

For raisin sauce, mix ½ cup brown sugar, 1 teaspoon dry mustard and

cornstarch in medium saucepan. Add water, vinegar and raisins. Cook and stir until thick. Add butter and blend. Makes 2 cups.

Kit Rollins, Cedarburg, Wis.

Roasted Root Vegetables

Roasting concentrates the sweetness and flavor of these vegetables, and it will be one of your favorites when you see how quick and easy it is.

- **1 pound carrots, peeled**
- **1 pound parsnips, peeled**
- **2 small sweet potatoes**
- **2 white potatoes**
- **1 onion**
- **3 tablespoons olive oil**
- **1½ teaspoons salt**
- **½ teaspoon ground black pepper**
- **2 tablespoons chopped parsley**

Preheat oven to 425 degrees. Cut carrots, parsnips, sweet potatoes, white potatoes and onion into 1- to 1½-inch cubes or rounds, being careful not to cut them too small to allow for shrinkage when baking.

Put vegetables into a large bowl and sprinkle with olive oil. Toss until they are thoroughly covered. Spread in an even layer on a 15 x 10 x 1-inch jelly-roll pan and sprinkle generously with salt and pepper.

Bake for 25 to 35 minutes, or until vegetables are tender. Turn once midway through baking.

Sprinkle with parsley and adjust seasonings to taste. Serve hot. Serves 8.

Roast Leg of Lamb

Lamb is a flavorful stand-in for beef or chicken and it's easier to cook than you might think.

- **1 (8-pound) whole leg of lamb or 1 (4-pound) shank or sirloin end**
- **Oil**
- **3 to 6 garlic cloves**
- **Salt and pepper**

Preheat oven to 325 degrees. Wash and pat dry whole leg of lamb. Rub entire roast with oil. Make slots or pockets in fat side and insert garlic slivers. Apply a generous amount of salt and pepper to entire roast.

Roast in oven until meat thermometer registers 180 degrees (30 to 35 minutes per pound). Serves 6 to 8. **Note:** *Use rack in pan. Thermometer should not touch bone.*

Lemon-Butter Asparagus

Lemon and asparagus are a natural pair. Asparagus is at its peak from February through June.

- **3 pounds fresh asparagus, trimmed**
- **¼ cup fresh lemon juice**
- **¼ cup butter**
- **Salt**
- **Freshly ground pepper**

Trim asparagus by snapping off the tough ends. Steam 5 minutes or until tender. Arrange asparagus on a platter.

Bring lemon juice to a simmer in a heavy medium saucepan over low heat. Gradually whisk in butter.

Season asparagus with salt and pepper; pour lemon butter sauce over asparagus. Serve immediately. Serves 6 to 8.

Strawberry Salad

A pretty make-ahead that can double as a light dessert.

- **2 (6-ounce) packages strawberry gelatin**
- **2 cups boiling water, divided**
- **1 (8-ounce) package cream cheese, softened**
- **1 cup sugar**
- **2 cups whipped cream**
- **2 (10-ounce) boxes frozen strawberries, divided**

Dissolve 1 box of gelatin in 1 cup boiling water. Add one package of frozen strawberries and stir until berries are thawed. Pour into a 9 x 13-inch glass dish. Chill until firm in refrigerator.

Blend softened cream cheese and sugar; mix well. Fold in whipped cream and spread over gelatin layer in dish.

Dissolve 1 box gelatin in 1 cup boiling water. Add remaining frozen strawberries. Stir until thawed. Set in refrigerator for 10 minutes. Pour over cream cheese layer and refrigerate at least 4 hours, or until firm. Serves 12. ■

Nancy Foust, Stoneboro, Pa.

Shown on this page, clockwise from the top, Roast Leg of Lamb with Roasted Root Vegetables (page 54), Strawberry Salad (page 54) and Lemon-Butter Asparagus (page 54).

Eggs, Eggs, Eggs

Once Easter has come and gone, what do you do with the all the eggs you've boiled and colored with the kids?

Egg salad, creamed eggs over toast and hiding them as a surprise in your next meatloaf are all favorite options. Stuffed eggs, also commonly known as "deviled" eggs, are another classic way to put them to good use. We're including a basic deviled egg recipe, but try some of the other variations.

If you're looking for a main dish idea, try the ham and egg casserole.

Basic Deviled Eggs

6 hard-cooked eggs
3 to 4 tablespoons mayonnaise
Salt and pepper to taste
1 to 2 teaspoons mustard

Shell hard-cooked eggs and cut in half. Mash the yolks and moisten with melted butter or mayonnaise. Season to taste with salt and pepper. To season more highly, add lemon juice or vinegar, mustard, cayenne or other seasoning. Fill the whites with the seasoned yolks and smooth the top neatly. Garnish if you like with paprika or a tiny leaf of parsley.

Deviled Eggs: Season highly. If you like, add 1 teaspoon grated cheese or minced pickles or olives for each egg.

Anchovy Eggs: Omit the mustard. Add anchovy paste to taste.

Bacon Stuffed Eggs: Add crumbled crisp bacon to the yolks.

Chicken, Ham or Veal Stuffed Eggs: Add chopped cooked chicken, ham or veal to the mashed yolks. Season to taste.

Eggs Baked in a Casserole: Arrange the cooked, halved eggs in a baking dish. Cover with cheese, tomato or mushroom sauce or undiluted canned tomato or cream of chicken, celery or mushroom soup. Sprinkle with grated cheese or buttered crumbs. Bake at 350 degrees until brown.

Ham & Egg Casserole

This recipe is a great way to use leftover ham and hard-boiled eggs from your Easter dinner.

1 cup macaroni
1 cup cubed ham
1 cup grated American cheese
1 tablespoon chopped onion
1 (10½-ounce) can cream of mushroom soup
3 sliced hard-boiled eggs
1¼ cups milk

Preheat oven to 350 degrees. Grease 1½-quart casserole.

Cook 1 cup macaroni in boiling

water. Drain. Mix soup and milk together in mixing bowl and add macaroni, ham, cheese, onion and eggs; pour into casserole dish.

Bake for 1 hour or until bubbling nicely. Serves 4 to 6. ■

Lorraine McKean, Berne, Ind.

How to Boil an Egg

For the best flavor and texture, the eggs are not actually boiled. They are brought to a boil, set off the burner and allowed to continue cooking in the hot water for a period of time.

Start with eggs that are one or two days old. They are at their best for poaching or boiling because the yolks are certain to keep their shape.

Put the eggs in a pan of cold water with enough water to cover them.

Slowly bring them to the boiling point.

For very soft eggs, take them from the water as soon as it reaches the boiling point.

For soft-cooked eggs, leave them in the water for 3 to 5 minutes.

For hard-cooked eggs, leave them in the water, with the lid on, for 12 to 15 minutes.

Lovely Springtime Cakes

Angel food, chiffon and sponge cakes beckon the sunny days of spring. Enjoy them with family and friends.

By Connie L. Moore

With winter winds and loaded holiday tables gone, the sunny days of spring call for light and lovely cakes. Angel food, chiffon and sponge cakes fit the bill for weekend entertaining, Easter dinners, luncheons and showers.

Perhaps you can recall your grandmother or mother beating egg whites till billowy mounds of soft peaks formed in a mixing bowl. Folding the dry ingredients into the batter was a little more difficult, but the results were tall cakes turned upside down with such names as Sunshine, Daffodil, and Gold and Feather Cake.

In earlier times, women used forks or flat wire whisks to beat the ingredients on large plates for up to an hour, counting strokes and building muscles. Spongy-sweet, "foam" or "sponge" cakes rise from air trapped in the batter. Today our electric mixers do the work, cut the time and ensure a successful cake.

Moist, tender slices can be served plain or embellished with fruits, sauces or whipped toppings. Slices can be sandwiched together with ice cream and then frozen for cool treats. Bake one of these delicious cakes and enjoy springtime with family and friends.

Angel Food Cake With Orange Coconut Frosting

Cake
- 1 cup (8–10) egg whites, room temperature
- 1 teaspoon cream of tartar
- 1¼ cups sugar
- 1 cup cake flour
- ¼ teaspoon salt
- 1 teaspoon vanilla
- ¼ teaspoon almond extract

Preheat oven to 350 degrees.

In large bowl, beat egg whites and add cream of tartar. Continue to beat until stiff. Beat in sugar.

Sift flour and salt together and sift into egg whites. Fold together gently. Fold in vanilla and almond extract.

Spoon mixture into ungreased 9- or 10-inch tube pan. Bake about 55 minutes or until top of cake springs back when pressed. Sides of cake should just be starting to pull away from pan.

Invert pan on soup cans or coffee mugs, using at least 3 for stability. Cook cake completely.

Using thin knife or spatula, loosen cake and release from pan. Serve bottom up plain or frosted. Serves 12.

Orange Coconut Frosting
- 1½ cups sugar
- 2 egg whites
- 5 tablespoons orange juice
- Dash of salt
- ½ cup shredded coconut

Place sugar, egg whites, orange juice and salt in top of double boiler or saucepan that can be placed over larger pan of boiling water.

Bring water to a boil. Using electric mixer, beat egg-white mixture until stiff peaks form. This will take at least 7 minutes.

Remove top pan from heat and continue to beat until mixture is thick

---

Cakes shown on page 59, clockwise from the top: Angel Food Cake With Orange Coconut Frosting (page 58), Easy Spice Sponge Cake (page 60), Marble Chiffon Cake (page 60) and Blackberry Jam Cake With Ice Cream (page 60).

Cake Tips

Sponge cakes rise from the air beaten into eggs. Always beat eggs until thick (yolks) or stiff peaks form (whites). Use large eggs at room temperature. Use clean beaters for the whites. Cream of tartar aids in egg-white structure and uniform air pockets.

Use cake flour if possible. If using all-purpose flour, use 2 tablespoons less per cup than called for. Sifting flour numerous times incorporates air and lightens the texture.

Sifted ingredients are gently folded in to reduce escape of air. Using rubber spatula or flat spoon, cut down through batter to bottom of bowl. Lift spatula up with batter and over, turning bowl frequently.

Most recipes call for ungreased pans, enabling batter to cling to pan sides and rise.

Cakes should cool in inverted pans, cutting down on shrinkage.

Sponge cakes can be frozen and need little thawing time. Also, leftover egg whites or yolks can be frozen in small quantities and used later for puddings, breakfast dishes or other baking.

enough to spread. Fold in coconut or sprinkle it over cake after frosting.

Editor's Note: *This delicious marsh-mallow-like frosting sets up quickly. You'll want to have your cake ready.*

Marble Chiffon Cake

⅓ cup cocoa powder
1 cup hot water, divided
1¾ cups sugar, divided
¼ teaspoon baking soda
2 cups cake flour
3 teaspoons baking powder
1 teaspoon salt
½ cup oil
7 egg yolks, room temperature
2 teaspoons vanilla
7 egg whites, room temperature
1 teaspoon cream of tartar
Whipped topping (optional)

Preheat oven to 325 degrees. In small bowl, mix cocoa powder, ¼ cup hot water, ¼ cup sugar and baking soda until smooth. Set aside.

In large bowl, sift together 1½ cups sugar, flour, baking powder and salt. Form a well in middle of dry ingredients.

Add oil, egg yolks, ¾ cup water and vanilla. Beat until smooth. In another bowl, with clean beaters, beat egg whites and cream of tartar until stiff peaks form. Do not under beat.

Pour egg yolk mixture over egg whites and fold in gently. Divide batter in half. Fold chocolate mixture into half.

Pour plain batter into ungreased tube pan. Gently swirl chocolate batter into plain. Do not stir.

Bake 50 minutes. Increase oven temperature to 350 degrees and bake about 10 minutes longer. Cake should spring back when pressed.

Invert pan on rack, soup cans or coffee mugs. Cool completely. Gently remove cake from pan and serve bottom up glazed, plain or with whipped topping. Serves 12.

Easy Spice Sponge Cake

5 eggs, room temperature, separated
1 cup sugar
1 teaspoon vanilla

1 cup self-rising flour
2 teaspoons pumpkin or apple pie spice
Canned peaches, or confectioners' sugar and cinnamon

Preheat oven to 250 degrees. In large bowl, beat egg whites until stiff.

In another bowl, beat egg yolks and sugar until well blended and deep yellow. Add vanilla.

Fold egg whites and yolk mixture together. Sift flour and spice over batter. Fold in gently.

Bake in ungreased tube pan for about 45 minutes or until cake is golden and springs back when pressed.

Invert pan on rack or soup cans. Cool completely. Serve with canned peaches, or plain with confectioners' sugar and cinnamon sifted on top. Serves 12.

Blackberry Jam Cake With Ice Cream

3 eggs, room temperature
Dash of salt
¾ teaspoon baking powder
¾ cup sugar
¾ cup cake flour
¾ teaspoon vanilla
Confectioners' sugar
1½ cups seedless blackberry jam
Vanilla ice cream
Shredded coconut

Quick Tip This cake may be baked in a lightly greased (bottom only) 13 x 9-inch pan for about 25 minutes and served in squares with fruit on top with a dollop of whipped topping.

Preheat oven to 350 degrees. Line a 15 x 10 x ½-inch jelly-roll pan with waxed paper. Lightly grease paper.

In mixing bowl, beat eggs, salt and baking powder. Gradually add sugar; continue to beat until very thick.

Gently sift and fold in flour. Fold in vanilla. Spread batter in pan and bake about 10 minutes or just until cake springs back when pressed.

Immediately invert cake onto tea towel which is covered with confectioners' sugar. Remove waxed paper.

Cool flat. Remove crisp edges if necessary. Cut cake in half lengthwise. Cut each half into 3 equal sections. Place a section on plate. Spread with some jam. Repeat with all layers and jam. Let cake stand until serving time.

To serve, slice cake into 6 portions. Lay slices on plates and top with large scoop of vanilla ice cream. Sprinkle coconut on top. Serves 6.

Chocolate Angel Tea Cake

6 egg whites, room temperature
1 teaspoon vanilla
½ teaspoon cream of tartar
½ teaspoon salt
½ cup sugar
½ cup cake flour
¼ cup cocoa powder
⅓ cup sugar
Confectioners' sugar, whipped topping, chocolate curls or ice cream

Preheat oven to 375 degrees. Line bottom only of ungreased 9 x 5 x 3-inch loaf pan with parchment paper.

In large mixing bowl, beat egg whites, vanilla, cream of tartar and salt until soft peaks form. Beat in ½ cup sugar until stiff peaks form.

Sift together flour, cocoa powder and ⅓ cup sugar.

Sift half of flour mixture over egg whites and fold in gently. Fold in remaining flour mixture and pour into loaf pan.

Bake about 25 minutes or until cake springs back when pressed. Invert pan and rest edges on a number of soup cans. Cool completely.

Serve slices with confectioners' sugar, whipped topping, chocolate curls or ice cream. Serves 8. ■

Quick Tamales & Yummy Cake

Quick & Tasty Tamales

- 1 dozen tamales (wrappers removed)
- 1 (15-ounce) can chili
- 1 cup chopped onions
- 1¼ cups grated cheddar cheese

Preheat oven to 350 degrees. Place tamales in greased casserole, top with chili and sprinkle with onions and cheese. Bake for 30 minutes. Serves 4.

Toasted Pecan Chocolate Cake

Cake

- 1 (18¼-ounce) package fudge cake mix
- 1 (4-serving-size) package instant French vanilla pudding mix
- 3 eggs
- ¾ cup oil
- 1½ cups milk

Frosting

- ¾ cup margarine
- 1 (8-ounce) package cream cheese
- 1 (3-ounce) package cream cheese
- 5 to 6 cups confectioners' sugar
- 2 teaspoons vanilla
- 2 cups pecans (chopped and toasted)
- 1 to 2 squares baking chocolate, melted

Preheat oven to 350 degrees. Mix cake mix, instant pudding mix, eggs, oil and milk together until smooth. Bake in 3 (9-inch round) cake pans for about 20 to 25 minutes. Cool.

For frosting, beat margarine and cream cheese together until smooth. Beat in confectioners' sugar and vanilla. Set aside ⅓ of this mixture.

To remaining ⅔, add pecans. Spread between layers and on top.

Add melted baking chocolate to remaining ⅓ frosting. Spread on outside of cake. Serves 10 to 12. ∎

Sue Wadsworth, Lufkin, Texas

Plan ahead and dinner is ready when you are.

Versatile Slow-Cooked Dishes

Hungarian Goulash

This has a really nice flavor and slow cooking makes the meat fork-tender.

- **1 pound stew meat, cut into bite-size pieces**
- **2 tablespoons oil**
- **½ cup diced onion**
- **1 clove garlic, minced**
- **⅓ cup ketchup**
- **2 to 4 tablespoons Worcestershire sauce**
- **1 teaspoon salt**
- **½ teaspoon dry mustard**
- **1½ cups water**
- **½ teaspoon vinegar**
- **1¼ teaspoons paprika**
- **Dash red pepper**
- **1 tablespoon flour**
- **2 tablespoons water**
- **Hot cooked noodles**

In skillet, brown meat in oil. Add onion and garlic and cook until onion is tender.

Combine beef mixture, ketchup, Worcestershire sauce, salt, dry mustard, 1½ cups water, vinegar, paprika and red pepper; place in slow cooker. Cover and cook on low for 6 to 8 hours.

Combine flour and 2 tablespoons water; stir into meat mixture. Turn slow cooker to high and cook 5 minutes until thickened.

Serve over hot noodles. Serves 4.

Helen Harlos, Ethel, Miss.

Apple Cobbler

This healthful dessert cooks in the back-ground, leaving you time for other things.

**8 medium tart apples, cored,
peeled and sliced**
½ cup sugar
Juice and grated zest of 1 lemon
¼ cup butter, melted
**2 cups mixed cereal with fruit
and nuts**

Place apples in slow cooker. Combine sugar, lemon juice and zest, butter and cereal; mix with apples. Cook 7 to 9 hours on low or 2 to 3 hours on high. Serves 4 to 6.

Turkey Chowder

These sometimes overlooked vegetables combine to make a hearty, flavorful chowder.

1 pound lean ground turkey
**2 sweet potatoes, peeled
and diced**
1 parsnip, peeled and sliced
**1 large sweet onion, peeled and
sliced**
3 zucchini, sliced
1 (46-ounce) can tomato juice

1 teaspoon dried basil
½ teaspoon ginger
Sour cream (optional)

Set slow cooker temperature to high. Add ground turkey. Cook and stir until crumbly.

Add sweet potatoes, parsnip onion, zucchini, tomato juice, basil and ginger. Decrease temperature to low. Cover and cook on low for 8 to 9 hours.

Garnish with collop of sour cream, if desired. Serves 6.

Variation: You may brown ground turkey in skillet on stove top, if desired.

Sweet & Sour Chicken

Skip the rotisserie chicken, this satisfying bird is waiting for you at home.

**1 (3- to 4-pound) whole roasting
chicken**
1 teaspoon salt
¼ teaspoon garlic powder
2 teaspoons soy sauce
**1 (17-ounce) can chunky mixed
fruit, drained, room temperature**
**1 (10-ounce) jar sweet and sour
sauce, room temperature**
2 tablespoons cold water
2 tablespoons cornstarch
Hot cooked rice

Sprinkle cavity of chicken with salt and garlic powder; place in slow cooker. Brush surface with soy sauce. Cook on low for 8 to 10 hours or on high for 4 to 5 hours.

Remove all but enough chicken broth to cover bottom of slow cooker. Spoon fruit over chicken. Pour sweet and sour sauce over all. Mix together water and cornstarch; add to fruit and sauce in slow cooker. Turn slow cooker to high; cook for 1 hour or until thickened. Serve over rice. Serves 4 to 5. ■

Savory, Sassy Sautés

Learning to sauté brings out the chef in all of us. It's also quick and easy.

By Adrienne Hinds

In French, the word sauté means to jump. When cooking, technically it means that you keep the food moving inside the pan, often with the flick of the wrist. In actuality, the following recipes use pan frying as the cooking method. Cooking with hot oil in a skillet created brown and crispy (and delicious) end results.

Successful sautéing or pan frying requires a few things. First, a heavy-bottomed skillet is mandatory. Using a thin skillet will create both burned and undercooked spots, not appetizing to look at or to eat. Next, the foods to be cooked need to be of a uniform size and thickness. Uneven thickness creates uneven cooking. Finally, a successful sauté mandates that you not crowd the pan to allow the oil to cook and bubble up around the food. Overcrowding the pan creates a steaming effect. If you don't get a nice golden brown and crispy result, crowding could be the problem.

Another component of successful sautéing is seasoning. You'll see that all of the recipes call for generous amounts of salt and pepper. Although not listed, it is highly recommended that you use kosher salt and freshly ground pepper. When pan frying, one is looking to develop a nice flavorful crust. Because of its distinct texture, kosher salt or coarse salt enhances that crunchy sensation. As for your pepper, freshly ground, cracked pepper releases "pepper oils" which are delicious to smell and to taste. By the time you use your preground pepper, all the oils have evaporated. Often this results in just the burning sensation and not the pepper flavor. If you don't currently use freshly ground pepper, you should give it a try and taste the difference.

The thing about sauté recipes is this: You have to be the judge of certain things, such as the amount of oil, the amount of seasoning and the true cooking time. Each pan, stove and cook combination is different, so the recipes as listed are given as guidelines. Sautéing brings out the chef in all of us—enjoy that sensation and create your own sassy sautés.

Chicken Piccata

- **4 skinless, boneless chicken breast halves or 4 skinless, boneless chicken thighs**
- **Salt and pepper**
- **3 tablespoon unsalted butter, divided**
- **2 tablespoons olive oil**
- **2 tablespoons lemon juice**
- **2 tablespoons vermouth or other dry white wine or chicken stock**
- **2 tablespoons capers, drained (optional)**

Place 1 chicken piece at a time in plastic bag. Using flat side of a meat mallet, rolling pin or heavy saucepan, pound chicken pieces until ¼ inch thick.

Generously season both sides of chicken with salt and pepper.

Heat heavy skillet over medium heat. Add 2 tablespoons butter and olive oil. When butter is hot but not yet

brown, place chicken in skillet, making sure not to crowd the pan.

Cook chicken approximately 1 minute, until brown. Using tongs or a spatula, carefully turn chicken to other side and cook about another minute, just until done. Be careful not to overcook. The meat will still have some give and be slightly springy to the touch. Remove from pan and place in oven to keep warm.

Once chicken is cooked, pour off remaining butter and oil. Using same skillet, turn heat to medium and melt 1 tablespoon of butter. Add lemon juice and vermouth. Swirl pan to blend. Add capers, if desired. Pour sauce over cooked chicken. Serves 4.

> **Quick Tip** Chicken Piccata makes an elegant company dinner. Carefully trim all fat and connective tissue from the chicken breasts. Cut into serving-sized pieces and pound as directed in the recipe.

Steak Diane
2 (12-ounce) New York strip steaks
Salt and pepper
¾ cup beef stock, divided
1 tablespoon dijon mustard
2 tablespoons butter, divided
2 tablespoons vegetable oil, divided
2 tablespoons chopped shallots
Worcestershire sauce
Lemon juice
Cognac

Trim steaks of visible fat. Butterfly each by cutting in half horizontally. Between two sheets of plastic wrap, lay split steak open. Using the flat side of a meat mallet, rolling pin or heavy saucepan, pound each piece until ¼ inch thick. Season with salt and pepper.

Mix together ½ cup beef stock and dijon mustard. Set aside.

Place a skillet over high heat. When hot, add 1 tablespoon butter and

1 tablespoon oil, swirling pan to cover bottom.

Add steaks, making sure not to crowd pan. Cook about 1 minute without moving to allow a thorough browning. Using tongs, carefully turn steaks and cook another minute on other side. Remove steaks from pan and place in warm, turned-off oven.

Using same pan with heat off, add remaining butter and oil and shallots. Pan will be very hot, so keep shallots moving to prevent burning. Sauté about 30 seconds or until shallots are softened.

Turn heat to medium. Add remaining ¼ cup beef stock and mustard mixture to shallots, mixing vigorously to scrape up any bits.

Taste sauce and adjust flavor by adding Worcestershire sauce, lemon juice and cognac as desired. Bring sauce to a light simmer, then return steaks to pan. Cook steaks another minute or so, coating both sides, until heated through. Serves 4.

Rosemary Scallop Skewers
4 long sprigs fresh rosemary
12 large sea scallops (about 1 pound)
Salt and pepper
2 tablespoons olive oil

Remove all leaves from rosemary branches, leaving a clean branch. Set aside both branches and leaves.

Place scallops in a dry skillet over moderate low heat for 2 to 3 minutes to allow liquid to escape. Watch carefully so scallops don't cook. You just want to eliminate some excess water. Once liquid is exuded, remove scallops from pan and pour off water.

Using rosemary branches as skewers, place 3 scallops on each branch. Finely chop rosemary leaves. Sprinkle scallops with salt, pepper and rosemary.

Heat skillet until hot; add olive oil. Place scallop skewers in pan, cook about 30 seconds on each side, just until cooked through. Serves 4.

Salmon With Spinach

4 (6-ounce) salmon fillets, skinned
Salt and pepper
2 (10-ounce) packages baby spinach
2 tablespoons olive oil
2 tablespoons unsalted butter
1 tablespoon fresh tarragon, chopped, or 1 teaspoon dried tarragon

Thoroughly salt and pepper both sides of salmon fillets.

Wash and dry spinach. Set aside.

Heat skillet and add olive oil. Place salmon in skillet, making sure not to overcrowd. Cook on first side for 4 minutes, until golden brown. Using a spatula, carefully turn fillets over to cook for an additional 2 minutes. Be careful not to overcook.

Remove salmon from skillet and place on plate tented with aluminum foil.

Drain oil from pan. Melt butter in same skillet. If using dried tarragon, add to butter and cook until just fragrant, about 30 seconds.

Add as much spinach as manageable to the skillet and cook down, adding more fresh spinach as space becomes available. The spinach volume will decrease quite noticeably. Sauté spinach until nicely wilted. Add fresh tarragon and combine.

Divide spinach among 4 plates and place 1 salmon fillet on top of each. Serves 4.

Variation: For an extra-rich addition, add 2 tablespoons heavy cream to reduced spinach. Cook until cream has boiled down to a nice, rich coating.

Spring Vegetable Sauté

6 stalks fresh asparagus
½ pound baby carrots
1 pound English peas in pods
2 cups water
Pinch sugar
4 tablespoons butter
1 shallot, chopped
Up to 1 teaspoon sugar, to taste
Lemon juice (optional)
1 tablespoon fresh mint, chopped
Salt and pepper

Bend asparagus until it snaps. Parboil tips in salted water 2 minutes for thin stalks and up to 4 minutes for thick stalks. Drain and cool. Set aside.

Boil carrots for approximately 3 minutes. Do not overcook. Drain.

Shell peas. Cook until just tender in 2 cups water with a pinch of sugar. Drain.

Over medium heat, melt butter in sauté pan, add and toss chopped shallot. Turn heat to low and add all the prepared vegetables, sugar and lemon juice, if using.

Sprinkle on mint and continue to toss about 2 minutes, thoroughly coating all vegetables with butter sauce. Season with salt and pepper as desired. Serves 4.

Sautéed Potatoes (Crispy Home Fries)

4 large potatoes (yellow, Yukon Gold, Red Bliss)
Salt
2 tablespoons butter
2 tablespoons peanut oil
Pepper

Place potatoes in large saucepan. Cover with cold water. Add 1 teaspoon salt for every quart of water. Bring water slowly to a boil and cook for about 15 minutes, just until tender, not mushy. Drain and allow to cool.

When cool enough to handle, peel potatoes and dice into ¾-inch cubes. Heat butter and peanut oil in skillet over medium-high heat. Add potatoes. It is critical not to overcrowd the pan to ensure a crispy coating and to allow the butter and oil to bubble around the potatoes. Thoroughly season potatoes with salt and pepper. Allow potatoes to remain untouched about 10 minutes.

Using either a spatula or tongs, turn potatoes to opposite side. Sprinkle again with salt and pepper. Allow to cook untouched an additional 5 minutes.

Serve immediately. Serves 4. ■

Planning Great Meals

Here's our all-new collection of recipes! Plus we're offering these menu suggestions to help you plan great meals.

Kid-Friendly Lunch
Baked Tuna Foldovers, 77
Carrot and celery sticks
Congo Bars, 76

Brunch
Breakfast Potato Casserole, 84
Turkey Sausage Patties, 83
Maple Bacon Muffins, 72
Pear Waldorf Salad, 70

Tex-Mex
Shameless Canned
Enchilada Casserole, 74
Steamed rice
Pinto beans
Seven-Layer Dip, 75

Do-Ahead Dinner With Friends
Sweet & Sour Chicken, 63
Hash Brown Casserole, 72
Lemon-Butter Asparagus, 54
Chocolate Angel Tea Cake, 60

Vegetarian Supper
No-Boil Baked Ziti, 76
Spring Vegetable Sauté, 66
Your favorite garlic bread

Recipe Contest Winners

Our first contest was a huge success. Irresistible Brownies, shown at left, were the grand prize winning treats. We're also featuring the recipe runners-up: Chocomallow Brownies, Turtle Brownies and Marble Cheese Brownies.

Irresistible Brownies

Helen Phillips, Greensburg, Ind.

- ¾ cup butter
- 2 cups sugar
- 1½ cups flour
- ½ cup cocoa powder
- ½ teaspoon baking powder
- ¼ teaspoon salt
- 4 eggs
- 2 teaspoons vanilla
- 2 cups semisweet chocolate chips, divided
- ½ cup chopped nuts, optional

Preheat oven to 350 degrees. Grease a 13 x 9 x 2-inch baking pan.

In a medium saucepan over low heat, melt butter. Remove from heat and add sugar, flour, cocoa powder, baking powder, salt, eggs and vanilla. Stir until well blended and smooth.

Stir in 1½ cups chocolate chips; add the nuts, if desired. Spread in prepared pan. Sprinkle with ½ cup chocolate chips.

Bake 30 to 35 minutes. Do not overbake. Cool on wire rack. Cut into 2-inch squares. Makes 24 brownies.

Chocomallow Brownies

Karen Gentry, Somerset, Ky.

- 1 (19-ounce) box brownie mix
- ¼ cup butter
- 3 tablespoons cocoa powder
- 2 cups confectioners' sugar
- 1 teaspoon vanilla
- ¼ cup milk
- 2 cups mini marshmallows

Preheat oven to 350 degrees. Grease and flour a 13 x 9 x 2-inch baking pan.

Prepare brownie mix as directed on box and pour into pan. Bake as directed.

While brownies are baking, make frosting. In medium saucepan, melt butter and cocoa powder. Remove from heat, add confectioners' sugar and vanilla, and slowly add milk, stirring until smooth.

Top baked brownies with mini marshmallows and return to oven just until marshmallows are slightly puffed. Remove from oven and pour chocolate frosting on hot brownies, spreading evenly. Cool before cutting. Makes 24 brownies.

Turtle Brownies

Nancy O'Mary, Rock Island, Ill.

- 4 (1-ounce) squares unsweetened chocolate
- ¾ cup butter
- 2 cups sugar
- 4 eggs
- 1 cup flour
- 1 (14-ounce) package caramels, unwrapped
- ⅓ cup heavy cream
- 2 cups pecans, divided
- 1 (12-ounce) package semisweet chocolate chips

Preheat oven to 350 degrees. Grease a foil-lined 13 x 9 x 2-inch baking pan.

Melt chocolate squares and butter in a medium saucepan or in the microwave. Add sugar and eggs; mix well. Stir in flour.

Spread half of batter in prepared pan. Bake 25 minutes or until firm to touch.

Meanwhile, microwave caramels and cream on high for 3 minutes or until caramels start to melt. Whisk until smooth. Stir in 1 cup pecans.

Gently spread caramel and cream mixture over brownie batter in pan. Sprinkle with chocolate chips. Pour remaining unbaked batter evenly over caramel mixture; sprinkle with 1 cup pecans.

Bake an additional 30 minutes. Cool in pan. Lift out of pan with foil. Makes 24 bars.

Marble Cheese Brownies

Sharon Crider, Lebanon, Mo.

- 1 (3-ounce) package cream cheese
- ⅓ cup butter, divided
- 1 cup sugar, divided
- 3 eggs, divided
- ½ cup plus 1 tablespoon flour
- 2 teaspoons vanilla, divided
- 1 (4-ounce) package sweet chocolate
- ½ teaspoon baking powder
- ¼ teaspoon salt
- ½ cup chopped nuts, optional

Preheat oven to 350 degrees. Grease an 8 x 8 x 2-inch baking pan.

Cream the cream cheese and half of the butter together. Gradually add ¼ cup sugar; cream until fluffy. Add 1 egg, 1 tablespoon flour and ½ teaspoon vanilla; mix well.

Melt chocolate with remaining butter; cool.

Beat 2 eggs until thick; gradually add ¾ cup sugar and 1½ teaspoons vanilla, beating well. Combine and add ½ cup flour, baking powder and salt; mix. Stir in nuts, if desired.

Spread about ¾ of batter in prepared pan. Spread cheese mixture over top; drop remaining chocolate batter over cheese, swirling to give marbled effect. Bake for 35 minutes. Makes 16 brownies. ■

Recipes From Our Readers

Home cooks share their favorite recipes, quick-to-prepare comfort foods, good for family, friends and special occasions.

Salmon Couscous Salad

Arlene Ranney, Eureka, Calif.

- 1 cup plus 2 tablespoons water, divided
- 1 cup couscous
- 2 cups cooked, flaked salmon
- 2 green onions, chopped
- ⅔ cup roasted, chopped red bell peppers
- 20 ripe olives, chopped
- ½ cup chopped fresh cilantro
- ¼ cup lemon juice
- 2 tablespoons olive oil
- 1 teaspoon ground cumin
- ½ teaspoon salt
- ¼ teaspoon freshly ground pepper

Bring 1 cup of water to boil in a medium saucepan. Add couscous; cover and remove from heat. Let stand 5 minutes; fluff with fork.

In a large bowl, stir together couscous, salmon, onions, bell peppers, olives and cilantro.

In a small bowl, whisk together lemon juice, olive oil, remaining water, cumin, salt and pepper. Pour over couscous salad and toss. Serves 4 to 6. ▶

Avocado Salsa

More like a salad than a condiment, this colorful, mild salsa makes a great side dish.

> **2 ripe avocados**
> **2 medium tomatoes**
> **¼ cup chopped onion**
> **½ cup chopped cilantro or parsley**
> **⅛ teaspoon salt**
> **¼ teaspoon pepper**
> **3 tablespoons lemon or lime juice**

Dice avocados and tomatoes into ½-inch cubes. **Note:** *Do not mash avocado.* Add the chopped onion and cilantro or parsley. Sprinkle with salt, pepper and lemon juice. Toss gently. Makes 2½ cups.

Pear Waldorf Salad

Hazel Hullinger, Decatur, Fla.
A delightful twist on a classic.

> **4 fresh pears, cored and diced**
> **4 bananas, peeled and sliced**
> **1 cup sliced celery**
> **½ cup broken walnuts**
> **4 tablespoons salad dressing**
> **4 tablespoons sour cream**
> **2 tablespoons sugar**
> **¼ teaspoon ginger**

Place pears, bananas, celery and walnuts in salad bowl. Combine salad dressing, sour cream, sugar and ginger in a small bowl and mix well. Pour over fruit. Toss lightly, coating well. Serves 8.

Orange Avocado Salad

Edith Muldoon, Baldwin, N.Y.
Adding fruit is an easy, healthful way to perk up a green salad.

> **Romaine lettuce**
> **3 large navel oranges, peeled and sectioned**
> **1 large ripe avocado**
> **¼ cup lemon juice**
> **⅛ teaspoon pepper**

> **¼ teaspoon dry mustard**
> **¼ teaspoon salt**
> **¼ teaspoon sugar**
> **½ cup oil**

Fill a large salad bowl with bite-size pieces of Romaine lettuce. Fill a small bowl with peeled and sectioned oranges. Refrigerate both bowls.

Just before serving, peel, pit and slice avocado. Mix sliced oranges and avocado with salad.

Mix lemon juice, pepper, dry mustard, salt, sugar and oil together and drizzle ⅓ to ½ cup of dressing on top of salad. Serves 4 to 6.

Sugared Pecans

Dottie Luttrell, Enid, Miss.
Sprinkled on a salad or eaten as a snack, these simple nuts are delicious.

> **1 egg white**
> **1 tablespoon water**
> **1 cup sugar**
> **1 teaspoon salt**
> **1 teaspoon cinnamon**
> **1 pound halved pecans**

Preheat oven to 300 degrees. Beat egg white with water until frothy.

In a large, zip-locked plastic bag, combine sugar, salt and cinnamon. Dip pecans into the egg white. Place coated pecans into the bag and shake, coating them well.

Place pecans on a well-greased, shallow baking sheet. Bake for 40

minutes or until egg white is dry. Stir every 10 minutes. Cool on waxed paper. Makes 1 pound.

Speedy Peanut Butter Chocolate Sauce

Galelah Dowell, Fairland, Okla.
You'll want to double or triple this recipe, as it's sure to be popular!

> **3 (1-ounce) squares semisweet chocolate, broken up, or ¼ cup semisweet chocolate chips**
> **⅓ cup heavy cream**
> **½ cup corn syrup**
> **⅓ cup smooth peanut butter**
> **1 teaspoon vanilla extract**

In a microwavable bowl, combine chocolate and heavy cream. Microwave on high for 30 seconds. Stir and microwave an additional 30 seconds. Stir until smooth.

Add corn syrup, peanut butter and vanilla extract. Stir until smooth. Microwave an additional minute or until heated throughout.

Serve immediately or refrigerate. Heat briefly before serving. Makes 1 cup.

Microwave Peanut Brittle

Sue Wadsworth, Lufkin, Texas
An easy treat any time of year.

> **1 cup sugar**
> **½ cup light corn syrup**
> **1 cup raw peanuts**
> **⅛ teaspoon salt**
> **1 tablespoon butter**
> **1 teaspoon vanilla**
> **1 teaspoon baking soda**

In a 2-quart microwavable bowl, combine sugar, corn syrup, peanuts and salt. Microwave on high for 8 minutes, stirring after 4 minutes. Add butter. Microwave on high for 2 minutes.

Stir in vanilla and baking soda until light and foamy. Spread on a buttered baking sheet as thinly as possible. Cool and break into pieces. Makes 1 pound.

No-Bake Date Balls

Sue Wadsworth, Lufkin, Texas
Get the kids to help with these chocolaty nuggets.

> **½ cup butter**
> **4 cups mini marshmallows**
> **¼ cup milk**
> **2 cups milk chocolate coating**
> **4 cups crisp rice cereal**
> **1 (8-ounce) package chopped dates**
> **1 cup chopped pecans**

In a large saucepan, melt butter over low heat. Add marshmallows and milk. Heat until melted, stirring constantly. Stir in chocolate coating and heat until melted.

Remove from heat. Cool until mixture thickens. Blend in rice cereal, dates and pecans. Roll into 1-inch balls.

Store in refrigerator.

Makes 70 to 80 balls.

Vegetable Casserole

Cecelia Rooney, Pt. Pleasant, N.J.
Using California blend makes this a really pretty dish.

3 cups frozen vegetables
1 onion, diced
1 cup biscuit mix
4 eggs
½ cup grated cheese
½ cup oil
Pepper
Parsley
Garlic powder

Preheat oven to 350 degrees. Combine vegetables, onion, biscuit mix, eggs, cheese, oil, pepper, parsley and garlic powder in one bowl. Spoon into a 9 x 5 x 3-inch greased pan. Bake for 45 minutes. Serves 4.

Hash Brown Casserole

Flo Snodderly, North Vernon, Ind.
A popular carry-in dish.

½ cup melted butter
1 teaspoon salt
½ teaspoon pepper
½ cup diced onion
1 can cream of chicken soup

2 cups grated cheese
2 pounds shredded hash browns, thawed

Preheat oven to 350 degrees. In a large bowl, combine butter, salt, pepper, onion, soup and cheese. Gently mix in hash browns. Place in a greased 13 x 9-inch pan. Bake uncovered for 35 minutes. Serves 6.

Maple Bacon Muffins

Arlene Ranney, Eureka, Calif.
Serve this flavorful muffin at a special brunch or any meal.

2 cups flour
8 bacon strips, cooked and crumbled

3 teaspoons baking powder
¼ teaspoon salt
1 egg
½ cup milk
½ cup oil
⅔ cup maple syrup

Preheat oven to 400 degrees. Grease muffin cups or line with paper baking liners.

In a large bowl, combine flour, bacon, baking powder and salt. In another bowl, whisk together egg, milk, oil and maple syrup. Combine ingredients and stir until dry ingredients are moistened.

Fill muffin cups ⅔ full. Bake 20 to 25 minutes or until toothpick comes out clean. Cool 5 minutes before removing from pan. Refrigerate leftovers. Makes 1 dozen.

Rise & Shine Biscuits

Karen Farr, Kansas City, Mo.
Quick, easy and delicious.

⅓ cup club soda
⅓ cup sour cream
1½ tablespoons sugar
2 cups biscuit mix

Preheat oven to 425 degrees. Mix together club soda, sour cream and sugar. Add biscuit mix, stirring with a fork.

Lay dough out onto a lightly floured surface and knead lightly 10 to 12 times. Shape dough into 6 (1-inch-thick) biscuits. Place biscuits into a greased 8-inch round pan. Bake for 12 to 14 minutes. Makes 6 biscuits.

Hot Chicken Salad

Denise Hansen, Jackson, Minn.

- **2 cups cooked and cubed chicken**
- **2 cups thinly sliced celery**
- **½ cup toasted almonds or almond slivers**
- **½ teaspoon salt**
- **2 teaspoons grated onion**
- **1 cup mayonnaise with 2 tablespoons lemon juice added**
- **½ cup grated cheddar cheese**
- **1 cup potato chips**

Preheat oven to 450 degrees. In a large mixing bowl, combine chicken, celery, almonds, salt, onion, mayonnaise and cheese. Spoon into a 1-quart baking dish and cover with potato chips. Bake for 15 minutes. Serves 4.

Creamy Chicken Broccoli Bake

Margy Mann, St. Louis, Mo.

- **4 boneless, skinless chicken breast halves, cubed**
- **1½ cups uncooked quick-cooking white rice**
- **1¼ cups milk**
- **1 (10-ounce) package frozen chopped broccoli, thawed and drained**
- **½ pound processed cheese, cubed**
- **½ cup regular or reduced-fat salad dressing**

Preheat oven to 375 degrees. In a large bowl, combine chicken breast, rice, milk, broccoli, cheese and salad dressing. Spoon into a 12 x 8-inch baking dish. Bake for 30 minutes or until chicken is done. Serves 6.

Easy Chicken

Kit Rollins, Cedarburg, Wis.

This chicken lives up to its name and is just as good leftover as it was straight from the oven.

- **4 boneless, skinless chicken breast halves**
- **4 slices Swiss cheese**
- **1 can cream of chicken soup**
- **½ cup dry sherry or apple juice**
- **2 cups uncooked herb stuffing**
- **½ cup melted butter**

Preheat oven to 350 degrees. Place chicken breasts in a 9 x 13-inch baking pan and cover each with a slice of Swiss cheese. Dilute cream of chicken soup with sherry and pour over chicken. Cover with stuffing and drizzle melted butter on top. Bake for 60 minutes or until done. Serves 4. ▶

Preheat oven to 375 degrees. Brown ground beef in a large nonstick skillet over medium heat for 8 to 10 minutes or until beef is thoroughly cooked. Stir frequently. Drain beef. Add corn, enchilada sauce and green chiles. Mix well.

Spoon ¼ of beef mixture into a 2-quart baking dish coated with nonstick cooking spray. Top with ⅓ of tortilla strips. Repeat layers twice, ending with beef mixture. Cover with foil.

Bake for 40 minutes. Uncover and sprinkle with shredded cheese. Bake an additional 5 minutes or until cheese is melted. Serves 6.

Can-Can Casserole

Dorothy Brummer, Albert City, Iowa
This is very quick and easy to make as well as being very tasty.

- 1 (5-ounce) can evaporated milk
- 1 (10¾-ounce) can chicken and rice soup
- 1 (10¾-ounce) can cream of chicken soup
- 1 (5-ounce) can boned chicken
- 1 (4-ounce) can chow mein noodles
- 1 (4-ounce) can mushrooms, drained
- Crushed cornflakes or potato chips
- Grated cheese

Preheat oven to 350 degrees. Combine milk and both cans of soup. Fold in chicken, noodles and mushrooms. Pour into a greased, 2-quart casserole dish. Top with crushed cornflakes or potato chips and grated cheese. Bake for 30 to 45 minutes. Serves 4.

Beef Enchilada Bake

Linda Nichols, Steubenville, Ohio

- 1 pound lean ground beef
- 1½ cups frozen whole-kernel corn
- 1 (19-ounce) or 2 (10-ounce) cans enchilada sauce
- 1 (4½-ounce) can chopped green chiles
- 1 (6-ounce) package corn tortillas, cut into ½-inch strips
- ½ cup finely shredded cheddar cheese

Shameless Canned Enchilada Casserole

Karen Farr, Warsaw, Mo.
Keep these ingredients on hand—this casserole is a crowd-pleaser.

- 4 (5-ounce) cans boned chicken
- 1 (10-ounce) can enchilada sauce
- 1 (10-ounce) can cream of mushroom soup
- 2 tablespoons instant minced onion
- ½ teaspoon garlic powder
- 1 (10-ounce) package corn or tortilla chips, divided
- 1½ cups shredded sharp cheddar cheese
- 2 chicken bouillon cubes
- 1 cup boiling water
- Parsley flakes
- Paprika

Preheat oven to 350 degrees. In a large mixing bowl, combine chicken, enchilada sauce, mushroom soup, onion and garlic powder.

Line a greased 12 x 8-inch baking dish with ⅔ of corn chips. Pour chicken mixture over chips. Sprinkle with cheese and cover with remaining corn chips.

In a small saucepan, combine bouillon cubes and boiling water; stir until dissolved. Pour over mixture in dish. Sprinkle with parsley flakes and paprika. Bake for 30 minutes. Serves 6.

Beef & Bean Roundup

Margy Mann, St. Louis, Mo.
Make this spicy or sweet with the barbecue sauce you prefer.

- 1½ pounds ground beef
- ¼ cup chopped onion
- 1 cup barbecue sauce
- 1 tablespoon brown sugar
- 1 (16-ounce) can baked beans
- 1 (10-ounce) tube refrigerated biscuits
- ½ cup shredded cheddar cheese

Preheat oven to 375 degrees. In a skillet, brown ground beef and onion. Drain beef and onion. Stir in barbecue sauce, brown sugar and baked beans. Heat until bubbly. Pour into a 2½-quart casserole dish.

Separate biscuit dough into 10 biscuits and cut each biscuit in half diagonally. Place biscuits, cut side down, over hot meat mixture around edge of dish. Sprinkle cheese over biscuits.

Bake for 22 to 27 minutes or until biscuits are golden brown. Serves 6 to 8.

Seven-Layer Dip

Helen Harlos, Ethel, Miss.
A perennial party favorite.

- 1 large ripe avocado
- 1 (9-ounce) container jalapeño bean dip
- 2 tablespoons lemon juice
- ½ teaspoon garlic salt
- ¼ cup sour cream
- ¼ cup mayonnaise
- 1 (1.25 ounce) package taco seasoning

- 2 large tomatoes, finely chopped
- ½ cup sliced black olives
- 1 (9-ounce) container cheddar and jalapeño dip
- ½ cup chopped green onions

Peel and chop avocado. Spread jalapeño bean dip into a shallow 2-quart dish. Arrange chopped avocado on top of dip. Sprinkle with lemon juice and garlic salt.

Combine sour cream, mayonnaise and taco seasoning. Spread over avocados. Top with tomatoes and black olives. Spread cheddar and jalapeño dip over all and top with green onions. Chill well. Serves 6 to 8.

Cornmeal Cookies

JoAnn Ervin, Glasgow, Ky.
Cornmeal adds an interesting flavor to these simple cookies.

- ¾ cup butter
- ¾ cup sugar
- 1 egg
- 1½ cups flour
- ½ cup cornmeal
- 1 teaspoon baking powder
- ¼ teaspoon salt
- 1 teaspoon vanilla
- ½ cup raisins (optional)

Preheat oven to 350 degrees. In a large mixing bowl, combine butter and sugar. Add egg and beat well. Add flour, cornmeal, baking powder, salt, vanilla and raisins, if desired; mix well.

Drop dough by teaspoonfuls onto a greased baking sheet. Bake for 15 minutes or until lightly brown. Makes 3 dozen. ▶

Creamier & Chewier Oat Cookies

Arlene Ranney, Eureka, Calif.

1¼ cups flour
1 teaspoon baking soda
1 cup softened butter or margarine
¼ cup sugar
¾ cup light brown sugar
1 (4-ounce) package instant vanilla
   pudding mix
2 eggs
3½ cups quick-cooking oats
1 cup raisins (optional)

Preheat oven to 375 degrees. Mix flour with baking soda. Combine butter, sugar, brown sugar and pudding mix in a large mixing bowl. Beat until smooth and creamy.

Beat in eggs. Gradually add the flour mixture and stir in oats and raisins, batter will be stiff.

Drop dough by teaspoonfuls onto an ungreased baking sheet approximately 2 inches apart. Bake for 10 to 12 minutes. Makes 5 dozen.

Congo Bars

Dorothy Brummer, Albert City, Iowa

½ cup margarine
2¾ cups brown sugar
4 eggs

2½ teaspoons baking powder
1 teaspoon salt
2¾ cups flour
1 to 2 cups chocolate chips

Preheat oven to 350 degrees. Melt margarine and combine with brown sugar. Add eggs one at a time to the mixture, beating well after each egg.

Add baking powder, salt and flour. Spread mixture in a greased 11 x 15-inch pan. Sprinkle chocolate chips on top. Bake for 20 to 25 minutes. Makes 2 dozen.

Note: *If desired, add chopped nuts when stirring in the dry ingredients.*

Nutjammer Cookies

Cecelia Rooney, Point Pleasant, N.J.
Be sure to stuff these little pockets full of the preserve mixture—to get their sweet goodness.

1 cup butter
1 (8-ounce) package cream
   cheese
2 cups flour
½ teaspoon baking powder
1 (10-ounce) jar apricot or peach
   preserves
2 cups finely chopped walnuts
3 teaspoons sugar
⅓ cup confectioners' sugar

Preheat oven to 350 degrees. Cream butter and cream cheese together. Sift flour and baking powder and add to creamed mixture. Chill dough.

Mix preserves, walnuts and sugar together. Divide dough into 4 equal parts. Roll out dough ¹⁄₁₆ inch thick onto a lightly floured cloth-covered board. Cut into 2-inch squares.

Place 1 teaspoon of nut mixture in the center of each square. Top with another square of dough. Press edges together with a fork.

Bake for 15 to 20 minutes or until lightly brown. Cool and sprinkle with confectioners' sugar. Makes 2 dozen.

No-Boil Baked Ziti

Margy Mann, St. Louis, Mo.
This dish will satisfy your meat eaters as well as the vegetarians in your house.

1 (26-ounce) jar pasta sauce
1½ cups water
1 (15-ounce) carton ricotta cheese
2 cups shredded mozzarella
   cheese, divided
¼ cup grated Parmesan cheese
8 ounces uncooked ziti pasta

Preheat oven to 350 degrees. Combine pasta sauce and water. Stir in ricotta cheese, 1 cup mozzarella cheese and Parmesan cheese. Stir in uncooked pasta.

Spoon mixture into a 13 x 9-inch baking dish. Cover with aluminum foil. Bake for 55 minutes.

Remove foil and sprinkle with remaining mozzarella cheese. Bake an additional 5 minutes. Serves 8.

Baked Tuna Foldovers

Gwen Campbell, Sterling, Va.

- 1 (10-ounce) tube refrigerated biscuits
- 1 (6½- or 7-ounce) can tuna in water, drained
- 1 cup diced cheddar or American cheese
- 3 tablespoons mayonnaise
- ¼ teaspoon prepared mustard
- Paprika

Preheat oven to 375 degrees. Remove biscuits from tube. Pat each biscuit into a thin 3½-inch oval. Arrange half of the

biscuits on a greased cookie sheet.

Mix tuna, cheese, mayonnaise and mustard together. Spread mixture on biscuits. Top with remaining biscuits, pressing edges together with fingertips or a fork. Sprinkle paprika on top of biscuits.

Bake for 20 minutes or until done. Serves 5.

Note: *A side dish of cold, crisp coleslaw would be a nice accompaniment.*

Cheesy Ground Beef & Pasta

Galelah Dowell, Fairland, Okla.

- 1 pound ground beef
- 1¼ cups water
- ¾ cup milk
- ⅓ cup ketchup
- 1 (12-ounce) package pasta with cheese sauce
- 1 tomato, chopped (optional)
- ¼ cup sliced green onions (optional)

Brown ground beef in a skillet and drain. Stir in water, milk and ketchup. Bring to a boil.

Stir in pasta and return to a boil. Reduce heat to medium-low and cover. Simmer 10 minutes or until pasta is tender.

Add cheese sauce, tomato and onions. Stir until well mixed. Serves 4.

Biscuit Mix Cheeseburger Pie

Edna Askins, Greenville, Texas
It makes its own crust!

- 1 pound ground beef
- 1 cup chopped onion
- ½ teaspoon salt
- 1 cup shredded cheddar cheese
- 2 eggs
- ½ cup biscuit mix
- 1 cup milk

Preheat oven to 400 degrees. Spray a 9-inch pie plate with nonstick cooking spray.

Cook ground beef and onion until beef is brown. Drain beef and onion.

Spread mixture in pie plate. Sprinkle with salt and cheese. Stir in eggs, biscuit mix and milk. Bake 25 minutes. Serves 6. ■

Make It With Meatballs!

Who doesn't love the versatile meatball? Make them ahead and put them in your freezer for convenient last-minute meals.

By Suzanne Caithamer

Most of us, faced with a pound or two of ground beef and a looming dinner hour, might think to fashion the meat mixture into a tired loaf or the ubiquitous hamburger patties. But there is a shape more enjoyable, faster to cook and even more versatile: the meatball.

Who doesn't love a meatball? Instead of bringing over the typical fare (such as lasagna) to an ailing friend or new mom, why not a dish of sweet and sour meatballs with rice or a few freezer containers of meatballs with marinara sauce? The whole family will appreciate this underrated entrée. Children love meatballs because they are fun to eat and just the right size for a small mouth.

Meatballs freeze well, thaw quickly and can be used in a variety of ways. Keeping them small—about 1 inch in diameter—also means they cook in no time. One easy way to get meatballs of equal size is to pat the meat mixture into a rectangular shape and then use a sharp knife to cut it into cubes. Keep a bowl of water next to your work station while you roll the cubes into balls—keeping your hands wet will prevent the meat from sticking to your fingers.

Make a large batch of meatballs and freeze them in separate containers (about 30 per container) so you can quickly and easily plan a recipe around them. Most of the ingredients in these recipes you likely already have on hand, so a meal can be on the table without an extra trip to the store. Add a green salad and some crusty bread, and you'll have a wonderful dinner in no time at all.

If you'd rather not make your own, grocers' freezer sections offer premade meatballs, usually in 1-, 2- or 5-pound bags. They are easily thawed and heated in the microwave and can be added to the following recipes. Keeping meatballs on hand, whether store-bought or homemade, is a great head start on a variety of meals the whole family will love.

Italian Meatballs
A tasty alternative to buying frozen meatballs.

- **9 slices white bread, crusts removed**
- **2 cups water**
- **3 pounds ground beef**
- **2 medium onions, chopped very fine**
- **2 tablespoons chopped parsley**
- **½ cup grated Parmesan cheese**
- **3 eggs, lightly beaten**
- **1 tablespoon salt**
- **1½ teaspoons pepper**

Soak bread in 2 cups water and mash with fork. Squeeze out excess water. Crumble ground beef into large bowl. Add bread, onion, parsley, Parmesan cheese, eggs, salt and pepper to beef. Mix well and shape into 1-inch-diameter balls.

Brown in batches in skillet, turning frequently, until cooked through. Remove with a slotted spoon to paper towels. Makes about 120 meatballs.

Barbecue Meatball Hoagies
Perfect for game day or an outdoor party.

- **30 (1-inch) cooked meatballs (thawed if frozen)**
- **½ cup ketchup**
- **½ cup chili sauce**
- **½ cup chopped onion**
- **2 tablespoons white vinegar**
- **1 tablespoon Worcestershire sauce**
- **¼ cup brown sugar**
- **½ teaspoon garlic powder**
- **½ teaspoon dry mustard**
- **4 hoagie rolls, toasted**

Preheat oven to 350 degrees. Place meatballs in ungreased 1-quart baking dish. Combine ketchup, chili sauce, onion, white vinegar, Worcestershire sauce, brown sugar, garlic powder and dry mustard; pour over meatballs.

Cover and bake for about 1 hour. Serve on toasted hoagie rolls. Serves 4. ▶

> **Quick Tip** For speedier cooking, meatballs may be baked on baking sheets at 400 degrees for 12 to 15 minutes.

Shown on this page: Italian Meatballs (page 78) and Barbecue Meatball Hoagies (page 78).

Penne Pasta Bake With Meatballs
Simple and hearty.

12 ounces penne pasta
2½ cups spaghetti sauce
1 (14½-ounce) can diced toma-
toes with Italian seasoning
30 (1-inch) cooked meatballs
(thawed if frozen)
1 cup shredded mozzarella
cheese

Preheat oven to 350 degrees. Grease 2½-quart casserole dish.

Cook penne pasta according to package directions, drain. Meanwhile, in bowl, combine spaghetti sauce and diced tomatoes.

Layer half the pasta and half the sauce in greased casserole. Top with meatballs. Repeat layer of pasta and layer of sauce. Top with mozzarella cheese. Cover and bake for 30 minutes; uncover and bake 20 to 30 minutes more or until bubbling and hot. Serves 6.

Sweet & Sour Meatballs
In this speedy stove-top dish, chunks of pineapple and green pepper complement the tangy sauce.

1 (20-ounce) can pineapple
chunks
⅓ cup water divided
¼ cup apple cider vinegar
2 tablespoons soy sauce
½ cup brown sugar
3 tablespoons cornstarch
1 clove garlic, minced
1 tablespoon ketchup
30 (1-inch) cooked meatballs
(thawed if frozen)
½ green bell pepper, diced
½ red bell pepper, diced
Hot cooked rice

Drain pineapple, reserving juice. Set pineapple aside. Add water to juice to measure 1 cup; pour into large skillet.

Add ⅓ cup water, vinegar, soy sauce, brown sugar, cornstarch, garlic and ketchup. Stir until smooth.

Cook over medium heat until thick, stirring constantly. Add pineapple, meatballs and green and red peppers. Simmer uncovered for 15 to 20 minutes or until heated through. Serve over rice. Serves 6.

Swedish Meatballs
Bring an international feel to your table with this dish of meatballs in sour cream sauce.

1 teaspoon vegetable oil
1 small onion, chopped
½ cup beef broth
2 teaspoons Worcestershire sauce
30 (1-inch) cooked meatballs
(thawed if frozen)
1½ cups sour cream
¼ teaspoon dill weed
Hot cooked noodles or mashed
potatoes
Lingonberry jam (optional)

Heat oil in large skillet over medium heat. Add onion and cook until tender. Add beef broth and Worcestershire sauce; simmer 3 to 4 minutes. Add meatballs; cover and heat until meatballs are hot, about 5 minutes.

Remove meatballs with slotted spoon to serving dish; keep warm.

Add sour cream and dill to skillet; whisk until smooth and heated through. Do not boil.

Pour over meatballs and serve immediately over noodles or mashed potatoes. If desired, serve with lingonberry jam as an accompaniment. Serves 6.

Italian Wedding Soup
Delicious for a light lunch or appetizer.

2 small onions, chopped
1 cup sliced baby carrots
1 teaspoon olive oil
2 quarts (8 cups) chicken broth
½ cup orzo (rice-shaped pasta)

1 cup thinly sliced fresh spinach
Zest of one lemon
30 (1-inch) cooked meatballs
   (thawed if frozen)

In a 2-quart saucepan, sauté onion and carrots in olive oil until just tender.

Add broth; bring to a boil. Add orzo and cook until al dente, about 7 to 8 minutes. Add spinach, lemon zest and meatballs; heat through. Serves 6.

Spaghetti & Meatballs

An underrated classic! Try different pastas for variety.

1 small onion, chopped
3 cloves garlic, peeled and left
   whole

2 tablespoons olive oil
1 (32-ounce) can tomato sauce
1 (12-ounce) can tomato paste
2 cups water
2 tablespoons sugar
2 tablespoons dried oregano
1 teaspoon salt
Dash of pepper
30 (1-inch) cooked meatballs
   (thawed if frozen)
Hot cooked spaghetti

Sauté onion and garlic in oil until soft. Add tomato sauce, tomato paste, water, sugar, oregano, salt and pepper; stir well. Cover and simmer over low heat 1 hour, stirring occasionally. Add meatballs and simmer, covered, 30 minutes more.

Discard garlic before serving over spaghetti. Serves 6. ■

SAVINGS YOU'LL SAVOR

Budget-friendly favorites that are sure to please your family.

Oven Baked Chicken

A crisp, tasty substitute for fried chicken.

1 envelope dry onion soup mix
¾ cup bread crumbs
½ cup mayonnaise
1 frying chicken, cut up

Preheat oven to 400 degrees. Place soup mix and bread crumbs in plastic bag. Shake to blend.

Brush mayonnaise on both sides of chicken pieces. Shake 1 or 2 pieces at a time in plastic bag until coated.

Place chicken on rack in baking dish. Bake 45 minutes.

Serves 4 to 5. ■

Helen Harlos, Ethel, Miss.

Quick Tip If you are watching fat and calories, this recipe works great with skinless pieces.

Easy & Good For You

Island Chicken
Quick, colorful and satisfying

1 pound boned, skinned chicken breasts, cut into ¾-inch cubes
2 tablespoons olive oil
2 potatoes, cut into ½-inch cubes and microwaved 8 to 10 minutes
1 small can (8.25 ounces) whole-kernel corn, drained
¼ cup sliced green pepper
¼ cup sliced red pepper
1 cup salsa
Cooked rice (optional)

Brown chicken in olive oil in a large skillet for 5 minutes. Add potatoes and continue to brown.

Add corn, green and red peppers, and salsa; heat and serve alone or over rice. Serves 4.

Per serving: 302 calories, 27 g protein, 27 g carbohydrate, 10 g fat (2 g saturated), 3 g fiber, 63 mg cholesterol, 347 mg sodium.

Dottie Luttrell, Enid, Miss.

Chewy Fruit 'n' Flax Cookies

2 tablespoons peanut butter
½ cup unsweetened applesauce
6 tablespoons flaxseed
½ cup brown sugar
1 egg
1 teaspoon vanilla extract
½ teaspoon salt
½ cup flour
¾ cup oats
½ cup dark seedless raisins

Preheat oven to 400 degrees. In a large bowl, combine peanut butter, applesauce, flaxseed, brown sugar, egg, vanilla extract and salt. Beat on low until well blended.

Add flour and oats; beat until blended. Stir in raisins.

Drop by teaspoonfuls onto an ungreased baking sheet. Bake 10 minutes or until done. Makes 2 dozen.

Per serving: 124 calories, 3 g protein, 22 g carbohydrate, 3 g fat (1 g saturated), 2 g fiber, 15 mg cholesterol, 104 mg sodium.

Arlene Ranney, Eureka, Calif.

Easy Floret Salad

1 small head cauliflower, cut into
florets
1 bunch broccoli, cut into florets
1 cup thinly sliced celery
1 cup mayonnaise
1 cup sour cream
1 (1-ounce) package ranch-
flavored salad dressing mix
Crushed bits of bacon

Combine cauliflower, broccoli and celery in a large bowl. Set aside

In a small bowl, combine mayonnaise, sour cream and ranch-flavored salad dressing mix. Stir until mixed well. Pour onto vegetables and toss.

Refrigerate until time to serve. Add bits of bacon and toss. Serves 4 to 6.

Per serving: 164 calories, 5 g protein, 20 g carbohydrate, 8 g fat (3 g saturated), 3 g fiber, 17mg cholesterol, 962 mg sodium.

Nancy O'Mary, Rock Island, Ill.

Turkey Sausage Patties

¾ pound ground turkey
1 egg white
¼ teaspoon basil
¼ teaspoon oregano

¼ teaspoon pepper
¼ teaspoon sage
⅛ teaspoon allspice
⅛ teaspoon nutmeg
⅛ teaspoon dill weed
⅛ teaspoon garlic powder
⅛ teaspoon chili powder
(optional)
⅛ teaspoon hot pepper sauce
(optional)
2 tablespoons water

Preheat broiler. In a medium bowl, combine turkey, egg white, basil, oregano, pepper, sage, allspice, nutmeg, dill weed, garlic powder, chili powder, hot pepper sauce and water; mix thoroughly.

Shape into 4 patties and place on rack in shallow pan. Broil 2 to 4 inches from heat 10 to 15 minutes until done. Serves 4.

Editor's note: *Add ¼ teaspoon salt if you are not on a salt-restricted diet.*

Per serving: 101 calories, 12 g protein, 0 g carbohydrate, 5 g fat (2 g saturated), 0 g fiber, 50 mg cholesterol, 74 mg sodium. ■

Arlene Ranney, Eureka, Calif.

Make mealtime easier by planning ahead.

Headstart on Entertaining

Shrimp & Tomato Aspic
A nice addition to any buffet.

- 2 cups tomato juice
- 2 packages unflavored gelatin, dissolved in 3 tablespoons hot water
- Dash salt
- 1 teaspoon hot pepper sauce
- 1 or 2 stalks of celery, diced
- 1 (3-ounce) can shrimp (optional)
- 1 small bottle sliced stuffed olives
- 1 (15-ounce) can stewed tomatoes with liquid
- Mayonnaise

Heat tomato juice. Add gelatin, salt and hot pepper sauce. Pour into a gelatin mold. Let cool in refrigerator until it begins to gel.

Remove mixture from refrigerator and add celery, shrimp, sliced olives and tomatoes. Chill until set.

Serve with a dollop of mayonnaise on each. Serves 8.

Timothy Fennell, Birmingham, Ala.

Breakfast Potato Casserole
Perfect for a hungry family and easily scaled for a crowd.

- 6 cups hash brown potatoes
- 6 eggs, scrambled
- 6 (1-ounce) slices processed cheese
- 6 slices bacon, crumbled

Layer ingredients in a greased 13 x 9-inch baking pan in the following order: potatoes, eggs, cheese and bacon. Cover and refrigerate overnight.

Preheat oven to 325 degrees and bake, uncovered, for 30 to 45 minutes. Serves 6.

Jerry Shaw, Bluffton, Ind.

Lemon Icebox Cake
Delightful, tangy, refreshing

- 1 (18¼-ounce) package lemon cake mix
- 2 (14-ounce) cans sweetened condensed milk
- ½ cup fresh lemon juice
- 1 (12-ounce) container frozen whipped topping, thawed

Bake cake as directed for 8-inch, two-layer cake. When cool, cut each layer in half to make 4 total layers.

Mix condensed milk and lemon juice together. Spread half of the mixture between cake layers.

Fold remaining half of mixture into whipped topping. Frost cake.

Refrigerate overnight. Serves 10 to 12. ■

Sue Wadsworth, Lufkin, Texas

A Taste of Italy

Romano Chicken

- 2 (4-ounce) boneless, skinless chicken breasts
- Salt
- Pepper
- 3 tablespoons flour
- 1 egg, beaten
- ¼ cup shredded Romano cheese
- Oil

Trim chicken breast of all fat. Place in a large plastic bag and pound until ¼ inch thick.

Lightly season chicken with salt and pepper. Dredge in flour, dip in egg and roll in Romano cheese.

Preheat nonstick skillet on medium-high heat. Cook chicken in oil until golden, turning once, about 2 minutes per side.

Editor's Note: *Chicken may be breaded and refrigerated for several hours until ready to cook.*

Fettuccine With Tomato Cream Sauce

- 4 ounces fettuccine noodles, uncooked
- ½ cup heavy cream
- 1 fresh thyme sprig
- ¼ cup chicken stock
- 4 sun-dried tomatoes packed in oil, divided
- Salt
- Freshly ground pepper

Cook fettuccine according to package directions. Drain.

In heavy saucepan, bring cream and thyme sprig to a boil. Lower heat and simmer until cream is reduced by ⅓, about 5 minutes. Remove from heat and let sit 10 minutes.

Remove and discard thyme sprig. Return cream to the heat, add chicken stock and simmer for 5 minutes. Puree 3 sun-dried tomatoes and add to sauce. Salt and pepper to taste.

Cut remaining sun-dried tomato into strips. Toss fettuccine with sauce and garnish with sun-dried tomato strips.

Sweet Cherries Over Ice Cream

- 1 (15-ounce) can dark sweet or Bing cherries
- 2½ teaspoons cornstarch
- 1½ teaspoons sugar
- ½ teaspoon vanilla extract
- ¼ teaspoon almond extract
- 2 tablespoons butter
- 1 cup vanilla ice cream, divided into 2 servings

Drain syrup from cherries into a medium saucepan. Set cherries aside. Add cornstarch, sugar, vanilla and almond extracts and butter; bring to a boil. Boil for 2 minutes until thickened.

Remove from heat and cool slightly. Stir in cherries and serve over ice cream. ■

Sensational Citrus

Used more than any other citrus fruit, lemons not only make meals more inviting, they add zest and zip to everyday foods.

By Emily-Jane Orford

Lemon, Herbs, Fish & Shrimp recipe follows on page 88.

When cold season hits, the first thing I think about is stocking up on fresh lemons and honey. I like to have these two ingredients handy for making Mom's age-old cold remedy, the one that always seems to work better than the over-the-counter drugs. But I don't really need to wait until I'm sick to enjoy a hot (or cold) lemon drink. Lemonade and lemon tea (hot or

Shown on page 86 from the top: Lemon Cookies (page 88), Mom's Hot Lemon Drink (page 88) and Lemon Loaf (page 88).

cold) are popular beverages in our household at any time of the year. Baking with lemons adds variety, too, for the sweet tooth. Lemon loaf and lemon cookies add the much-needed extra vitamin C to our daily diets.

The tart, saucy lemon has been given a bad name over the years. As an adjective, the word lemon describes anything from cars to computers. But the real lemon does work. After all, it is packed full of vitamin C and, in our ever-busy lives, vitamins are often lacking in our diets.

I suppose, like many others, I have always taken the sour, juicy lemon for granted. Its tart juice makes my fish and chicken dishes moist and, as my son aptly puts it, spiky. Sliced, it adds a bit of panache to the dinner plate. I can always buy lemons at my local grocer. But I hadn't realized that this saucy citrus fruit had to be picked green in autumn and winter, then stored until spring when it is in greater demand in grocery stores. I guess I always believed that lemons were more popular during the winter cold season.

Lemons, Herbs, Fish & Shrimp

6 fillets of sole (or any other white fish)
½ pound shelled, uncooked shrimp
2 tablespoons margarine
1 teaspoon grated lemon zest
2 lemons
1 clove garlic, minced
1 teaspoon thyme
½ teaspoon parsley
Hot cooked rice

Preheat oven to 325 degrees. Wash and dry white fish and lay across a 9 x 12-inch casserole dish. Wash the shrimp and layer over top of fish.

Melt margarine and add lemon zest. Squeeze the juice from the lemons and add to margarine mixture along with garlic, thyme and parsley. Pour over fish and shrimp.

Bake for 35 to 45 minutes. (Baking time will vary depending on the thickness of the fish fillets. Fish is cooked when it is all white and flakes apart easily when pricked with a fork. Shrimp is cooked when it turns pink.) Serve hot with cooked rice. Serves 6.

Mom's Hot Lemon Drink

Juice of ½ lemon
1 tablespoon liquid honey
Boiling water

Squeeze lemon into a coffee mug. Add liquid honey and fill with boiling water. Stir. Drink hot. Serves 1.

Lemon Loaf
Loaf
2 tablespoons shortening
1 cup sugar
2 eggs
1½ cups flour
1½ teaspoons baking powder
⅛ teaspoon salt
1 teaspoon grated lemon zest
½ cup hot milk

Glaze
⅓ cup sugar
1 lemon, freshly squeezed
1 teaspoon grated lemon zest

Preheat oven to 325 degrees. Grease 9 x 5 x 3-inch loaf pan.

For loaf, blend shortening and 1 cup sugar. Add eggs one at a time, blending well after each addition.

Sift together flour, baking powder, salt and 1 teaspoon grated lemon zest. Add to egg mixture alternately with milk.

Pour into loaf pan. Bake for 1 hour or until toothpick inserted in center comes out clean. Remove to a plate and cool for 5 minutes.

Meanwhile, mix together sugar, lemon and lemon zest for glaze and pour over hot loaf. Finish cooling and serve at room temperature. Slice and serve with butter, if desired. Makes 1 loaf.

Lemon Cookies
Cookies
½ cup margarine, softened
¾ cup sugar
1 egg
½ cup sour cream
2 teaspoons freshly squeezed lemon juice
½ teaspoon grated lemon zest
1½ cups flour
½ teaspoon baking powder
½ teaspoon baking soda
½ teaspoon salt

Topping
¼ cup sugar
½ teaspoon cinnamon
½ teaspoon grated lemon zest

Mix together margarine, ¾ cup sugar, egg, sour cream, lemon juice and ½ teaspoon grated lemon zest. Add flour, baking powder, baking soda and salt. Blend well. Refrigerate for 1 hour.

Meanwhile, mix together sugar, cinnamon and lemon zest for topping.

Preheat oven to 375 degrees. Lightly grease baking sheet.

Drop batter by teaspoonfuls onto baking sheet. Sprinkle topping over unbaked cookies. Bake for 10 to 12 minutes. Makes 2 dozen. ■

Chocolate Nut Delights

Chocolate Nut Revels

This delicious shortbread is sure to become a tea-time favorite.

1 (6-ounce) package chocolate chips
1 cup chopped pecans
1 cup butter
⅔ cup sugar
¼ teaspoon salt
1 teaspoon vanilla
2 cups sifted flour
Sugar

Preheat oven to 350 degrees.

Melt chocolate chips. Add chopped pecans and cool.

Cream butter, sugar, salt and vanilla; add flour gradually to mixture. Add cooled chocolate mixture. Stir slightly to gently swirl dark and white mixtures together.

Drop by teaspoonfuls onto ungreased cookie sheet. Flatten with a glass dipped in sugar. Bake for 10 to 12 minutes. Makes 4 dozen.

Cecelia Rooney, Point Pleasant, N.J.

Peanut Blossoms

This is my godmother, Sharon Breault's, recipe. I always love it when she makes these for Weimann/Breault gatherings!

1¾ cups flour
1 teaspoon baking soda
½ teaspoon salt
½ cup sugar
½ cup brown sugar
½ cup shortening
½ cup peanut butter
1 large egg
2 tablespoons milk
1 teaspoon vanilla
36 milk chocolate candies
Sugar

Preheat oven to 350 degrees. Combine flour, baking soda, salt, sugar, brown sugar, shortening, peanut butter, egg, milk and vanilla in a large mixing bowl.

Roll dough into balls. Roll each ball in sugar. Place balls on an ungreased cookie sheet.

Bake for 10 minutes or until done. Remove cookies from oven and top each with a chocolate candy. Makes 3 dozen. ∎

Jane Weimann, Woodstock, Conn.

May/June 2005

Traditional Comfort Entrees

My Mother-in-Law's Chicken Curry

- **1 cup finely chopped onion**
- **2 cloves finely chopped garlic**
- **4 tablespoons butter**
- **1 tablespoon plus 2 teaspoons curry powder, divided**
- **½ teaspoon salt**
- **¼ teaspoon cayenne pepper**
- **1 medium fryer, cut up**
- **2 teaspoons ground coriander**
- **Pinch of cinnamon**
- **Pinch of ground cloves**
- **1 cup chicken stock**
- **1 tablespoon tomato paste**
- **Hot cooked rice**

Saute onion and garlic in butter until light brown. Add 1 tablespoon curry powder, salt and cayenne pepper to pan. Stir well and cook for 3 to 4 minutes.

Rub chicken with additional curry powder (to taste) and add it to the pan with the coriander, cinnamon and cloves. Stir in the chicken stock and tomato paste.

Cover and simmer until chicken is tender, 30 to 45 minutes. Serve hot with rice.

Option: A little lemon juice may be squeezed over chicken before serving. Serves 4 to 6

Janice McKee, Berne, Ind.

Beef Stroganoff

This is the very first dish I cooked for my husband when we were dating. It actually came out of one of his mother's cookbooks. We've been married 18 years, and it remains one of our favorites.

- **2 pounds beef sirloin, cut in ¼-inch strips**
- **½ teaspoon salt**
- **1 teaspoon garlic powder**
- **½ teaspoon pepper**
- **1 cup onion, diced**
- **6 to 8 ounces fresh mushrooms**
- **½ cup butter**
- **5 tablespoons flour**
- **1 can condensed beef broth**
- **⅓ cup sour cream**
- **Cooked egg noodles or rice**

Coat beef with mixture of salt, garlic powder and pepper. Sauté beef with onion and mushrooms in butter. Add flour, stirring to coat beef evenly. Pour in beef broth. Simmer 15 minutes and then add sour cream. Simmer an additional 5 minutes. Serve on egg noodles or rice. Serves 6 to 8. ■

Larrinda Bass, Acworth, Ga.

Midwest Farm Cooking

When it comes to great family meals, there's nothing better than fresh-picked fruits and vegetables to add an appetizing touch to those tasty homemade dishes.

By Pat A. Eby

Long before cooking locally grown, high-quality produce became commonplace, my grandmother cooked by the calendar. She packed my grandfather off to Findlay Market in Cincinnati with lists of what to buy from which farmer. In May and June, she asked for plump pea pods, tender lettuces, scallions and new spinach with arrowlike leaves. She steamed the asparagus my grandfather craved: slim spears of saturated green with lush, fat hats. Glistening new Harvard beets pleased my Aunt Lanna's picky palate. I favored Ohio strawberries, red to bursting, with a whiff of sweet ripeness no perfume can match.

For a spring Sunday dinner at the grandparents', circa 1958, my girl cousins and I would set the dining room table with real china and cloth napkins. We cheerfully integrated two patterns of flowered china long before mix-and-match became fashionable. Aunt Lanna picked small bouquets of fragrant lilies of the valley or sweet peas just right for juice-glass vases she placed on the table.

Grandmother Rose would pan-fry chicken in the spring. In a holdover belief from her youth, she swore tender chickens could only be purchased in the spring. She dis-

trusted the pallid supermarket fryers available year-round. Grandmother whipped potatoes with plenty of butter and milk, steamed asparagus a little longer than necessary and tossed a green salad with a homemade vinaigrette dressing.

Dessert would be rhubarb or buttermilk pie, red devil cake, or my favorite, strawberry shortcakes. I can still taste my grandmother's shortcakes. From her, I learned to mash berries with brown sugar to "pull the juice" from the fruits. She whipped real cream to soft peaks with sugar and vanilla. Foolishly, I asked for new-fangled whipped cream in a can. My indulgent grandparents bought it for me, too. Whether you serve your shortcake with real whipped cream or the kind from a can, eat and enjoy.

Spinach, Strawberry & Pecan Salad With Orange Vinaigrette Dressing
Dressing:
- 4 tablespoons orange juice
- 1 tablespoon cider vinegar
- ¼ cup olive oil
- Salt and pepper

Salad:
- 5 cups baby spinach, stems

removed, washed and dried
- ½ small red onion, sliced in thin rings and separated
- ¾ cup pecans
- 6 strawberries, cored and sliced
- 6 whole strawberries for garnish

Mix orange juice with vinegar. Whisk olive oil into juice mixture. Add salt and pepper to taste.

Layer onion rings, pecans and strawberries over spinach. Add dressing. Garnish with whole berry cut in half. Serves 6.

Pan-Roasted New Potatoes
- 1½ pounds small new red potatoes (about 15 to 18 potatoes under 2 inches in diameter)
- 1½ cups low-sodium chicken broth
- 1 tablespoon olive oil
- 2 tablespoons butter
- 3 tablespoons fresh parsley, finely chopped
- Salt and pepper

Wash potatoes and cut out eyes. Slice a small circle of peel from each end. Place potatoes in a single layer in a large 10-inch nonstick skillet.

Mix chicken broth, olive oil, butter and parsley. Pour mixture over ▶

Shown on this page, clockwise from the top: Berry Buttermilk Pie (page 95), Oven-Broiled Asparagus (page 94), Skillet Pork Chops (page 94), Pan-Roasted New Potatoes (page 92) and Spinach, Strawberry & Pecan Salad With Orange Vinaigrette Dressing (page 92).

potatoes. Bring the broth mixture to a boil. Reduce heat to medium-high; cover the pan, venting the cover. Cook about 20 minutes until potatoes are tender.

Flatten potatoes slightly with spatula and cook uncovered until broth evaporates and the potatoes are browned. Turn to brown the other side. Remove from heat; add butter and fresh parsley sprigs if desired.

Note: *When the low-sodium broth and the parsley cook down, the flavors become more intense. Salt and pepper as needed after cooking. Serves 6.*

Skillet Pork Chops
- **24 small saltine crackers**
- **2 tablespoons cornmeal**
- **2 tablespoons flour**
- **½ teaspoon salt**
- **½ teaspoon pepper**
- **1 egg**
- **2 tablespoons cold water**
- **4½-inch thick pork chops**
- **6 tablespoons olive oil**
- **½ cup water**

Crush crackers to a fine consistency in a plastic bag, top open, with a rolling pin or the side of a drinking glass. Mix in cornmeal, flour, salt and pepper. Transfer crumb mixture to a shallow dish.

In a shallow dish, beat egg and cold water together.

Dip each chop in egg mixture, coating all sides, and then dip in crumb mixture.

Heat oil in 10-inch non-stick skillet over medium-high heat. Cook chops 10 minutes on each side. Add water; cover and steam for 25 minutes. Uncover and reduce liquid. Serves 4.

Oven-Broiled Asparagus
- **2 pounds fresh asparagus**
- **3 tablespoons olive oil**
- **Salt and pepper**

Warm a 9 x 13-inch cookie sheet with sides in the oven.

Snap off white bottom of asparagus stalks. Peel stalks if needed. Wash. Toss with olive oil. Layer on baking sheet.

Turn oven to broil. Broil asparagus 5 minutes until slightly browned. Turn asparagus and broil additional 3 minutes.

Sprinkle with salt and pepper to taste. Serves 6.

Sweet & Sour Orange Beets
- **2 (15-ounce) cans sliced baby beets or 2 pounds fresh beets**
- **¼ cup sugar**
- **1 tablespoon cornstarch**
- **½ cup vinegar**
- **Freshly grated zest of 1 orange**
- **2 tablespoons freshly squeezed orange juice**
- **2 tablespoons butter**

For fresh beets, preheat oven to 350 degrees (325 degrees for glass pans). Don't peel or trim the beetroot; remove all but 3 inches of beet greens. Wash and arrange beets in 9 x 13-inch baking pan; add water to ¼ inch deep in pan. Cover tightly with aluminum foil and bake for 1 hour or until tender. Cool and slice ¼ inch thick.

Combine sugar, cornstarch, vinegar, orange zest and orange juice in a double boiler and cook until clear. Stir frequently. Add drained canned or baked sliced beets and simmer 10 minutes. Remove from heat; add butter. Serves 8.

Strawberry Shortcake With Chocolate Sauce & Vanilla Whipped Cream
Strawberries
- **1½ quarts strawberries**
- **¼ cup dark brown sugar**

Biscuits
- **2 tablespoons butter, melted**
- **2 cups baking mix**
- **¼ cup sugar**
- **½ cup buttermilk**
- **Extra sugar to sprinkle on top of biscuits**
- **Chocolate Sauce**
- **Vanilla Whipped Cream**

Wash strawberries quickly in cold water. Hull, slice vertically, and place in large mixing bowl. Mash berries lightly with a fork. Add brown sugar, mix, and set aside for 1 to 2 hours.

Preheat oven to 400 degrees. For biscuits, mix butter, baking mix, sugar and buttermilk in a large bowl until baking mix is moistened. Drop by tablespoon onto ungreased cooking sheet to form 6 biscuits. Dust tops of biscuits with extra sugar.

Bake 14 to 16 minutes until golden brown. Cool on wire racks.

To assemble shortcakes, split biscuits, arrange berries on bottom, spoon on Vanilla Whipped Cream, drizzle Chocolate

Sauce over whipped cream and close with biscuit top. Top with Vanilla Whipped Cream and a strawberry. Serves 8.

Chocolate Sauce
1 cup semisweet chocolate chips
¼ cup butter-flavored shortening
¼ cup light corn syrup
¼ cup cold water

Combine chocolate chips, shortening, corn syrup and water in the top of a double boiler. While chocolate and shortening are melting, stir frequently. When sauce is smooth, remove from heat. Store in the refrigerator. May be reheated in the microwave.

Vanilla Whipped Cream
1 pint heavy whipping cream
2 tablespoons granulated sugar
1 teaspoon vanilla

Chill bowl and beaters in freezer 15 minutes. Whip cream until it starts to thicken. Gradually add sugar. Add vanilla and whip to soft peaks. Don't overbeat the mixture.

Berry Buttermilk Pie
½ cup butter, softened
1¾ cups sugar
3 eggs
1 cup buttermilk
1 teaspoon vanilla
Zest of 1 medium lemon
1 unbaked 9-inch pastry shell
2 cups strawberries
1 tablespoon confectioners' sugar
Whole strawberries for garnish

Preheat oven to 400 degrees.
Cream butter and sugar until light and fluffy. Add eggs one at a time and beat until well blended. Add buttermilk, vanilla and lemon zest. Mix well. Pour into pastry shell. Bake for 5 minutes. Reduce heat to 350 degrees and bake an additional 40 minutes or until the custard sets. Cool on wire rack. Chill before serving.
In blender or food processor, puree berries with confectioners' sugar. Top pie slice with berry sauce. Garnish each piece with a whole strawberry. Serves 8. ■

Use convenient pantry items for a head start.

Sweets Made from the Freezer

Praline-Apple Pie

**1 (3-pound, 1-ounce) frozen
    deep-dish apple pie**
¼ cup butter
1 cup brown sugar, firmly packed
⅓ cup whipping cream
1 teaspoon vanilla extract
1 cup confectioners' sugar
¾ cup chopped pecans, toasted

Preheat oven to 375 degrees. Line baking sheet with aluminum foil.

Open center hole in pie. Cut 4 to 6 slits in top crust. Shield edges with foil to prevent burning. Place pie on baking sheet and bake for 80 minutes. Cool 1 hour.

Bring butter, brown sugar and whipping cream to a boil in a 2-quart saucepan over medium heat, stirring often.

Boil 1 minute and remove from heat. Whisk in vanilla and confectioners' sugar until smooth.

Pour slowly over pie, spreading to cover. Top with pecans. Serves 8.

Carolyn Hayes, Johnston City, Ill.

Cinnamon Rolls

1 loaf frozen bread dough, thawed
**½ cup melted butter or
    margarine plus enough
    additional melted butter
    to brush on dough before
    baking**
**¼ to ½ cup sugar mixed
    with cinnamon to taste**
½ cup chopped pecans
1 cup confectioners' sugar
Milk

Preheat oven to 375 degrees. Spray bottom and side of 9-inch round cake pan.

Roll dough onto floured surface to make 12 x 6-inch rectangle. Brush ½ cup butter over entire surface. Sprinkle with cinnamon and sugar mixture, reserving enough to sprinkle over dough before baking. Add pecans. Roll lengthwise; slice into 8 equal-size pieces. Arrange slices in cake pan. Cover with towel and place in warm place. Let rise to double, about 35 to 40 minutes. Brush with butter and sprinkle with reserved cinnamon and sugar. Bake for 20 to 25 minutes.

To make frosting, combine confectioners' sugar with enough milk to make a stiff frosting. Frost rolls while still warm. Makes 8 rolls. ■

Sybil Brown, Highland, Calif.

Some Like It Picante

These tasty southwestern dishes are sure to fill those cravings for something spicy and, with just a touch of salsa, you can give them an extra kick.

Can man live by beans and corn tortillas alone? Yes—which is good news for poor college students, starving artists and those who just like the way they taste. The proteins found in corn and beans complement one another, and together they provide all the amino acids the human body needs. Beans, corn tortillas and rice often work together to form the base of many Tex-Mex meals.

When we think of Mexican flavors, we associate certain spices, like the chili pepper. The chili pepper is a common Mexican spice and ranges in variety from the mild bell pepper to the very hot Habanero. But what is a chili pepper? If you check the dictionary, you'll find that a chili is a pungent, fresh or dried fruit of any one of several varieties used as a flavoring. The same definition fits the word chili pepper, so the words are interchangeable.

Perhaps you already love Mexican food. If that's the case, then these recipes will be more like comfort food to you. If you're not sure about Tex-Mex, why not give them a try anyway. Not all Tex-Mex has to be hot and spicy. Most sauces and seasoning mixes are available in mild versions, which you can use instead of medium or hot. Then, if you like an extra kick, you can just add a touch of salsa.

Easy Guacamole
- **2 large Hass avocados**
- **2 tablespoons medium salsa**
- **1 tablespoon sour cream**
- **1 tablespoon jalapeno juice**
- **½ teaspoon onion salt**

Peel avocados and remove pits. Place in a bowl and mash. Add the salsa, sour cream, jalapeno juice and onion salt. Combine well. To prevent browning while it waits, carefully cover the top of the guacamole (not the bowl) with plastic wrap. Makes about 2 cups.

Tasty Crispy Tacos
- **1 pound ground beef**
- **1 (1.25-ounce) package taco seasoning**
- **1 medium tomato, diced**
- **1 cup shredded lettuce**
- **Sliced ripe olives**
- **Shredded cheese**
- **Chopped avocado (optional)**
- **Sour cream**
- **Salsa**
- **1 (8-count) package crispy corn taco shells or soft taco tortillas**

Fry the ground beef in a skillet. Drain fat and add taco seasoning according to the package directions. Heat through and set aside.

Prepare the tomato, lettuce, olives, cheese, avocado, sour cream ▶

and salsa in individual bowls for passing around.

Warm the taco shells according to the package directions and fill each one with about 2 tablespoons of taco meat. Place them on a platter for each person to take a shell and continue filling with their choice of the lettuce, olives, tomato, cheese, avocado, sour cream and salsa. Serves 4.

Variation: Tantalizing Taco Salad

Line a crispy flour tortilla salad shell with warmed refried beans and add the shredded lettuce, diced tomato, sliced ripe olives, taco meat, salsa and sour cream according to your taco salad style.

Effortless Chicken Enchiladas

4 small or 3 large boneless, skinless chicken breasts (enough to make 4 cups of shredded or chopped cooked chicken)
1 medium onion, quartered
2 cups water
2 chicken bouillon cubes
1 small can chopped green chilies
1 (10¾-ounce) can cream of chicken soup
1 (10¾-ounce) can cream of mushroom soup
2 (8-ounce) cans mild red enchilada sauce
1½ cups grated cheddar cheese
8 to 10 corn tortillas, torn into 6 pieces each
Salt and pepper

Preheat oven to 350 degrees.

Salt and pepper chicken and place in a 10-inch skillet. Add onion. Cover with water and add bouillon cubes. Bring to a gentle simmer over medium heat. Cover skillet. Reduce heat and continue simmering for about 30 minutes or until the chicken is done. When cool enough to handle, chop or shred chicken.

Combine green chilies, soups and enchilada sauce. Stir in chopped or shredded chicken, half of the cheese, and the tortilla pieces. Spread in a 9 x 13-inch baking pan and sprinkle with remaining cheese. It can be refrigerated for later cooking at this point.

Bake for 35 minutes or until thoroughly heated. Serves 6 to 8.

Spanish Rice

½ medium onion, chopped
½ green pepper, chopped
1 tablespoon oil
1 cup uncooked long-grain rice
1 (8-ounce) can mild tomatoes and green chilies
1 cup water
½ teaspoon salt
¼ cup frozen peas

Cook onion and green pepper in oil until translucent. Mix in the uncooked rice and cook for 2 or 3 minutes, stirring constantly; add the tomatoes and green chilies, water and salt. Simmer for 20 minutes or until rice is tender. Stir in frozen peas. Serves 6 to 8.

Sweet Corn Cakes

1 cup self-rising cornmeal
3 tablespoons sugar
½ cup creamed corn
¼ cup milk
1 tablespoon vegetable oil
Salsa verde
Sour cream
Chopped avocado

Combine the cornmeal and sugar. Stir in the creamed corn, milk and oil. Mixture will be thick. Drop by spoonfuls onto a lightly greased griddle. Turn when bubbles begin to appear on the top.

Quick Tip Are tomatillos little green tomatoes? No, but they are members of the same family as potatoes, tomatoes, eggplant and peppers. They are used frequently in Mexican cooking and are the base for salsa verde or green sauce.

Serve on a base of salsa verde and garnish with a small dollop of sour cream and chopped avocado. Makes 8 to 10.

Quick Tomato Salsa

2 (16-ounce) cans stewed tomatoes
1 teaspoon salt
1 teaspoon sugar
6 whole green onions, chopped
3 cloves garlic, minced
¼ cup chopped, pickled jalapeno
3 tablespoons olive oil
1 lime, juiced
Cilantro (optional)
Tortilla chips

Combine tomatoes, salt, sugar, onions, garlic, jalapeno, olive oil and

lime juice. Add cilantro to taste. Toss together and chill.

Serve with tortilla chips.
Makes about 4 cups.

Mexican Flan

⅓ cup sugar
4 eggs
1 (14-ounce) can sweetened condensed milk
1 (12-ounce) can evaporated milk
1 tablespoon vanilla

Preheat the oven to 325 degrees.
Place the sugar in a small heavy saucepan and heat over medium heat, stirring frequently until melted. Quickly divide the liquid sugar between 8 (6-ounce) glass custard cups, coating the bottom of each one. Don't worry if it doesn't cover evenly. Set aside.

Beat the eggs in a medium-sized mixing bowl and add sweetened-condensed milk, evaporated milk and vanilla. Strain the mixture and pour into the prepared custard cups.

Place the custard cups in a large roasting pan. Set the pan on the oven rack and pour about 1 inch of very hot water in the pan around the custard cups. Bake 40 minutes or until set. Serves 8. ■

Great Dishes Assembled Ahead

Greek Roasted-Pepper Salad

- **3 green bell peppers or 2 green bell peppers plus 1 yellow bell pepper**
- **2 red bell peppers**
- **1 (6-ounce) jar marinated artichoke hearts, drained, patted dry and coarsely chopped (reserve marinade)**
- **Olive oil**
- **½ pound feta cheese, rinsed, patted dry, and crumbled**
- **2 (6-ounce) cans black olives, drained**
- **¾ cup sliced fresh mushrooms**
- **½ cup sliced green onions**
- **6 tablespoons minced fresh parsley**
- **2 tablespoons minced garlic**
- **1½ tablespoons dried oregano, crushed**
- **Juice of 1½ lemons**
- **Salt and freshly ground pepper**
- **Toasted sesame seeds or additional feta cheese (optional)**

Preheat oven to 450 degrees.

Place bell peppers on baking sheet. Roast for 30 minutes, or until skins are blackened and bell peppers have softened slightly. Cool slightly. Peel off skin; discard stems, seeds and membranes. Thinly slice bell peppers. Transfer to large serving bowl.

Pour reserved marinade from artichoke hearts into measuring cup. Add enough olive oil to measure 1⅓ cups. Pour over bell peppers.

Add artichoke hearts, feta cheese, black olives, mushrooms, green onions, parsley, garlic, oregano, lemon juice, and salt and pepper to taste. Toss well to blend thoroughly. Chill for at least 24 hours or for up to 1 week before serving.

To serve, bring salad to room temperature. Garnish with toasted sesame seeds to taste. Serves 10.

Eleanor Craycraft, Sequim, Wash.

Overnight Chicken Casserole

- **2 cups cooked chicken, cubed**
- **2 cups uncooked macaroni**
- **2 cups milk**
- **1 (10¾-ounce) can cream of mushroom soup**
- **1 (10¾-ounce) can cream of chicken soup**
- **1 cup shredded cheese, your choice**
- **½ cup chopped onion**
- **Seasoning, your choice**

Preheat oven to 350 degrees.

Mix together chicken, macaroni, milk, soups, cheese, onion, and preferred seasoning to taste. Put in 9 x 13-inch casserole. Refrigerate 4 hours or overnight. Bake for 1 hour. Serves 6. ■

Karen Farr, Warsaw, Mo.

Savoring the South

As you enjoy these delicious Southern dishes, be sure to include the fellowship of family and friends in your mealtime menu.

By Denis' Ann Thomas

In the South, eating is an event. It's also about socializing, savoring and swapping great stories.

Southern hospitality revolves around food and drink, and the smallest gathering of friends requires an offering of refreshment. Part of the slow speed for which the South is famous for is a desire to savor the good parts, which are usually edible. Perhaps the strong cultural influence to stop and enjoy every moment is the reason so many Southern women are named after flowers.

Southerners like their fellowship to be sweet, so the food and beverages are, too. When Daisy serves a cold glass of Fruit Tea over ice to her neighbor, she's offering a taste of the sweet life, a reminder of how good life is. Corn Flower Pudding isn't a dessert; it's served right alongside the main course like a close brother. It's how things are done around here.

Southern meals often begin with a blessing, and one taste of Petunia's Coleslaw Salad makes her grandpa glad to live another day. Violet is famous at potlucks for her Baked Chicken Tenders, where eatin' and gratitude go hand in hand. Iris's Green Bean & Olive Casserole gets passed around as freely as the praise.

Living in the South isn't just location, it's a state of mind. Something about a good meal and good company encourages contentment.

When we say that Southerners love to eat and talk, it's true. We love both because they nourish our connection with others. Maybe that's why we combine them so often.

Daisy's Fruit Tea
The sweet, fruity flavor is perfect for an afternoon in the shade.

> 1 (12-ounce) can frozen orange-pineapple juice concentrate
> 1 (6-ounce) can frozen lemonade concentrate
> 4 cups water
> 2 family-size tea bags
> 1¼ cups sugar
> Orange for garnish

Thaw juice and lemonade. Boil water and remove from heat. Add tea bags and steep for 15 minutes. Remove tea bags and stir in sugar until dissolved. Add juice and lemonade and mix well. Pour into gallon-size pitcher and add enough water to fill. Stir. Chill and serve over ice with a thin slice of orange to garnish. Makes 1 gallon.

Petunia's Coleslaw Salad

Cabbage, carrots and a sweet Southern sauce make up this Southern standby.

4 cups green cabbage, shredded
2 carrots, peeled and grated
1 cup mayonnaise
2 tablespoons apple cider vinegar
2 tablespoons sugar

Combine cabbage and carrots in a large mixing bowl. In another bowl, whisk mayonnaise, vinegar and sugar together. Pour dressing over cabbage mixture and stir to coat. Cover and chill until serving time. Makes 4 cups.

Blossom's Seasoned Potatoes

Potatoes are part of nearly every meal in the South.

6 medium potatoes, peeled
2 tablespoons olive oil
1 teaspoon seasoned salt
½ teaspoon chili powder
½ teaspoon Cajun seasoning

Preheat oven to 375 degrees. Line a baking sheet with foil and coat with cooking spray.

Slice potatoes into thick fries and place in a large bowl.

In a different bowl, combine olive oil, seasoned salt, chili powder and Cajun seasoning. Drizzle over fries and toss to coat evenly.

Arrange fries on baking sheet and bake for 45 minutes or until done, turning once. Serves 8.

Corn Flower Pudding

This sweet corn casserole side dish pairs well with chicken.

½ cup butter
1 (8½-ounce) box sweet corn bread mix
1 cup sour cream
1 (14-ounce) can whole-kernel corn
1 (14-ounce) can creamed corn
Dried parsley

Preheat oven to 350 degrees.

Melt butter. Combine with corn bread mix, sour cream and 2 kinds of corn; pour into a greased 9 x 13-inch casserole dish. Sprinkle with parsley. Bake for 1 hour. Serves 12.

Iris' Green Bean & Olive Casserole

This is the scrumptious classic with a sophisticated twist.

1 (10¾-ounce) can cream of mushroom soup
½ cup milk
2 teaspoons soy sauce
1 teaspoon pepper
2 (14-ounce) cans French-cut green beans, drained
1 (4-ounce) can black olives, sliced
1 (6-ounce) can French-fried onions, divided

Preheat oven to 350 degrees.

Combine soup, milk, soy sauce and pepper in a large mixing bowl. Add green beans, olives and 1 cup of the French-fried onions; mix. Pour into a 9 x 13-inch casserole dish. Bake for 25 minutes. Sprinkle remaining onions on top and bake for 5 more minutes. Serve immediately. Serves 12.

Violet's Baked Chicken Tenders

A less messy and less fattening version of traditional fried chicken, but it's still acceptable to lick your fingers after eating.

- **1 sleeve round butter-flavored crackers**
- **½ cup Parmesan cheese**
- **½ cup butter, melted**
- **1 tablespoon Dijon mustard**
- **1 teaspoon parsley flakes**
- **¼ teaspoon garlic powder**
- **¼ teaspoon salt**
- **¼ teaspoon pepper**
- **12 to 16 chicken tenders, thawed**

What is a Chicken Tender?

The chicken tender is a thin, tender piece of chicken located between the chicken breast and the rib cage. If you do not have any of these strips on hand, you can easily substitute boneless, skinless chicken breasts by cutting them lengthwise into strips. The average chicken breast will yield three strips.

Preheat oven to 400 degrees. Line a baking sheet with foil and coat with cooking spray.

Crush crackers in sleeve into fine crumbs with a rolling pin. Combine cracker crumbs and Parmesan cheese in a wide bowl.

In a different bowl, mix together melted butter, Dijon mustard, parsley, garlic powder, salt and pepper.

Dip chicken in butter mixture, then dredge in cracker mixture and place on baking sheet, spacing the chicken pieces apart.

Bake for 30 minutes or until browned. Serves 6 to 8.

Rose's Coconut Cream Pie

There's nothing better than a pie made from scratch, but this one can be whipped together in minutes and tastes just as good. This pie disappears so quickly that you might want to make two.

Pie
- **1 piecrust, baked and cooled**
- **1 (3-ounce) package coconut cream instant pudding**
- **1½ cups milk**
- **½ to ¾ cup flaked coconut, divided**

Vanilla Whipped Cream Topping
- **1 pint heavy whipping cream**
- **2 tablespoons sugar**
- **1 teaspoon vanilla**

Combine pudding, milk and ¼ cup of coconut. Pour into cooled piecrust; cover and chill for at least 30 minutes. Toast remaining coconut under a broiler or in a toaster oven and allow to cool, watch closely to prevent burning!

For topping, chill bowl and beaters in freezer 15 minutes. Whip cream until it starts to thicken. Gradually add sugar and then vanilla; whip to soft peaks. Don't overbeat mixture.

Swirl Vanilla Whipped Cream Topping over the pie in a thick layer. Top with toasted coconut. Serve immediately or chill. Serves 8. ■

Unfried & Full of Flavor

Unfried Potatoes

Cajun seasoning adds flavor without the fat.

2 large potatoes, cut into sticks
1 egg white, beaten
1 tablespoon Cajun seasoning

Preheat oven to 400 degrees. Coat baking sheet with nonstick spray.

Toss together potato sticks, beaten egg white and Cajun seasoning.

Arrange potatoes on baking sheet. Bake until crisp, around 40 minutes. Serves 2 to 3.

Per serving: 301 calories, 10g protein, 66g carbohydrates, 1g fat, 0g saturated fat, 0mg cholesterol, 7g fiber, 192mg sodium.

Judy Ervin, Glasgow, Ky.

French Onion Chicken Bake

A tasty, low-fat dinner option.

2 cups thinly sliced onion
⅓ cup fat-free French dressing
4 boneless, skinless uncooked
**   chicken breast halves**

Preheat oven to 350 degrees. Arrange onion evenly in bottom of 9 x 9-inch baking dish. Place French dressing in a small bowl. Coat chicken pieces in dressing. Arrange chicken evenly over onion. Drizzle any remaining dressing over chicken. Cover and bake 30 minutes. Uncover and bake another 10 to 15 minutes. For each serving, place a chicken piece on a plate and evenly spoon onion and sauce over top. Serves 4.

Note: *Can be done with any fat-free dressing.*

Per serving: 173 calories, 24g protein, 12g carbohydrates, 3g fat, 1g saturated fat, 63mg cholesterol, 2g fiber, 254mg sodium. ■

Karen Farr, Kansas City, Mo.

Planning Great Meals

Here's our all-new collection of recipes! Plus we're offering these menu suggestions to help you plan great meals.

Kid-Pleasing Lunch

Chili Dog Wraps, 111
Sherilyn's Vegetable Dip, 108
Carrot & Celery Sticks
Orange Pops, 114

Lunch With the Ladies

Apricot Chicken Salad, 112
Apple Gelatin Mold, 109
Fresh Blueberry Tea Cake, 115

Speedy Weeknight Supper

Oven-Baked Halibut in Foil, 111
Breaded Tomatoes, 112
Green Pea Salad, 108
Chocolate Snack, 114

Vegetarian Luncheon

Vegetable Swiss Quiche, 113
Mesclun & Goat Cheese Salad, 121
Macadamia Macaroons, 114

Hearty Dinner

Maxyne's So-Easy, So-Good
Baked Pork Chops, 111
Copper Penny Salad, 109
Swiss Asparagus Au Gratin, 113
Pink Angel Summer Cake, 115

Recipe Contest Winners

Cherry Ice Cream, Butterfinger Ice Cream, Citrus Blast Sherbet and Old-Fashioned Custard Ice Cream were the big winners of our May/June 2005 contest.

Cherry Ice Cream

Sally Sue Campbell, Greeneville, Tenn.

> 2 (14-ounce) cans sweetened condensed milk
> 1 cup light brown sugar
> 2 (8-ounce) jars maraschino cherries, chopped, juice reserved
> 7 cups milk

With mixer, mix sweetened condensed milk and brown sugar.

Add maraschino cherries and reserved juice. Mix well. Pour into freezer can. Fill to the freezer fill line with milk—about 7 cups. Stir well and freeze according to manufacturer's directions. Makes about 1 gallon.

Butterfinger Ice Cream

Nancy Monroe, Statesville, N.C

> 2 cups sweetened condensed milk
> ¾ cup smooth peanut butter
> 6 (2.1-ounce) Butterfinger candy bars
> 6 cups whole milk
> 1 pint heavy whipping cream

Stir sweetened condensed milk and peanut butter together until smooth. Chop candy bars and stir in. Add milk and whipping cream. Pour into ice cream freezer. If not full to fill-line, add more milk. Freeze according to manufacturer's directions. Makes about 6 quarts.

Citrus Blast Sherbet

Dorothy Morris, Shelley, Idaho

> 2 cups water
> 1 envelope unflavored gelatin
> 1 cup sugar
> ½ cup light corn syrup
> 1 cup milk
> ⅔ cup freshly squeezed orange juice
> ⅓ cup freshly squeezed lemon juice
> ¼ cup freshly squeezed lime juice
> 4 drops red food coloring
> 4 drops yellow food coloring

Place water in a small saucepan; sprinkle gelatin over water and let set for 1 minute. Add sugar and corn syrup.

Stir over low heat until dissolved. Let cool.

In a medium bowl, combine milk, citrus juices and red and yellow food coloring. Stir in cooled mixture.

Pour mixture into an ice cream maker and freeze according to manufacturer's directions. Makes about 5 cups.

Old-Fashioned Custard Ice Cream

Cecelia Rooney, Pt. Pleasant, N.J.

- **2 cups milk, divided**
- **1 tablespoon flour**
- **¾ cup sugar**
- **2 egg yolks, slightly beaten**
- **2 cups heavy cream**
- **1 tablespoon vanilla**
- **¼ teaspoon salt.**

In 2-quart saucepan, heat 1½ cups milk until very hot. Mix the flour, sugar and remaining ½ cup milk in a bowl; slowly add the hot milk and stir until smooth. Return to the pan and cook over moderate heat, stirring constantly, for about 8 minutes.

Temper the egg yolks with a little of the milk mixture, then stir yolk mixture into pan. Cook 1 additional minute, then strain and cool.

Add the cream, vanilla and salt. Chill. Freeze in a hand-cranked or electric freezer following the manufacturer's directions. Makes 1½ quarts. ■

Recipes From Our Readers

Home cooks share their favorite recipes, quick-to-prepare comfort foods, good for family, friends and special occasions.

Spicy Plum Relish

Kit Rollins, Cedarburg, Wis.

- **1½ pounds ripe plums, pitted, finely chopped in food processor**
- **2 oranges, cut into segments, chopped (2 cups)**
- **3 tablespoons minced lemon balm, mint or cilantro**
- **¼ to ½ teaspoon minced jalapeno pepper**
- **¼ to ⅓ cup sugar or equivalent sugar substitute**

Combine plums, oranges, lemon balm, jalapeno pepper and sugar substitute. Refrigerate several hours for flavors to blend. Serve with grilled or smoked meats, game or poultry. Makes about 2½ cups.

Spinach Squares

Dorothy Witkowski, Burbank, Ill.

2 eggs, beaten
1 cup milk
½ cup margarine or butter
1 package frozen chopped
   spinach
1 cup flour
1 (16 oz) package grated cheddar
   cheese
½ cup chopped onion
1 teaspoon baking powder
1 teaspoon salt (optional)

Preheat oven to 350 degrees.
Combine eggs, milk and margarine.
Add spinach, flour, cheese, onion, baking powder and salt; mix well. Pour into a 10 x 15-inch pan and bake for about 35 minutes. Cut into 1-inch squares. They may be eaten hot or cold. Serves 15 to 20.

Orange Ginger Wings

Helen Harlos, Ethel, Miss.
Oh, so good!

2 cups flour
3 teaspoons seasoned salt
2 teaspoons garlic salt
25 chicken wings cut in 3 sections
   each, tips discarded
⅓ cup oil
2 cups orange marmalade
1 cup ketchup
½ cup soy sauce
¾ teaspoon ground ginger

In large resealable plastic bag, combine flour, seasoned salt and garlic salt; shake. Add chicken, several pieces at a time. Shake to coat.

In skillet, heat oil. Brown wings; drain.

Mix together marmalade, ketchup, soy sauce and ginger. Pour over wings and stir to coat.

Over medium-low heat, cover skillet and continue cooking for 10 to 15 minutes. Serves 8 to 12.

Sherilyn's Vegetable Dip

Helen Harlos, Ethel, Miss.

½ cup mayonnaise
2 cups sour cream
2 teaspoons seasoned salt
2 teaspoons parsley flakes
2 teaspoons dill seed
2 teaspoons instant onion flakes
1 teaspoon flavor enhancer

Mix together mayonnaise, sour cream, salt, parsley flakes, dill seed, onion flakes and flavor enhancer. Serve with fresh veggies. Keep refrigerated. Makes 2½ cups.

Green Pea Salad

Helen Harlos, Ethel Miss.
I start with the basic recipe and add the ingredients to my family's taste.

1 (16-ounce) bag frozen peas
2 tablespoons chopped green
   pepper
2 tablespoons chopped celery
2 tablespoons shredded
   cheese
1 small jar pimentos
1 tablespoon chopped onion
1 tablespoon relish
2 hard-boiled eggs
2 tablespoons mayonnaise

In large bowl, combine peas, green pepper, celery, cheese, pimentos, onion, relish and eggs. Gently stir in mayonnaise. Chill. Serves 4 to 6.

Copper Penny Salad

Judy Ervin, Glasgow, Ky.

2 pounds carrots
⅓ cup water
1 cup sugar
½ cup oil
1 teaspoon salt
½ teaspoon black pepper
½ teaspoon dry mustard
¼ cup chopped green peppers
½ cup chopped onion
1 (10¾-ounce) can tomato soup

Wash, peel, and slice carrots into ¼-inch slices. Place carrots and water in a covered casserole dish. Cook in microwave oven on HIGH (stirring twice) until the carrots are almost tender, about 12 to 20 minutes. Drain and set aside.

In small covered casserole, combine sugar, oil, salt, pepper, dry mustard, green peppers, onion and soup. Heat and stir until sugar is thoroughly dissolved. Pour over the carrots. Stir again. Let marinate in the refrigerator at least 8 hours or overnight. Serve at room temperature. Serves 6 to 8.

Apple Gelatin Mold

Jo Ann Ervin, Glasgow, Ky.

1 (3-ounce) package
   cherry gelatin
1 cup boiling water
½ cup apple juice
½ cup water
1 apple, peeled and chopped
½ cup chopped celery

Dissolve gelatin in boiling water. Combine juice and ½ cup water; stir in gelatin. Refrigerate until slightly thickened. Add apple and celery. Mix well. Refrigerate until set. Serves 4 to 6.

Southwest Bean Salad

Eleanor Craycraft, Sequim, Wash.

Salad:
1 (15½-ounce) can kidney beans,
   rinsed and drained
1 (15½-ounce) can black beans,
   rinsed and drained
1 (15½-ounce) can garbanzo
   beans, rinsed and drained
3 celery ribs, thinly sliced
1 red onion, thinly sliced in
   quarter rounds
1 large tomato, peeled, seeded
   and diced

Dressing:
¾ cup thick and chunky salsa
¼ cup oil
¼ cup lime juice
1½ teaspoons chili powder
1 teaspoon salt (optional)
½ teaspoon ground cumin
1 cup corn kernels
1 cup thinly sliced olives

In a large bowl, combine kidney beans, black beans, garbanzo beans, celery, onion, tomato, corn and olives. Lift gently with hands several times to combine evenly.

In a small bowl, mix together salsa, oil, lime juice, chili powder, salt and cumin; blend well. Pour over salad mixture and toss to coat.

Cover and place in refrigerator at least 2 hours to chill thoroughly. Toss again before serving in a lettuce-lined bowl. Serves 10. ▶

Trim outer leaves from fennel; remove and discard stalks. Cut bulb in half vertically, discarding core. Cut each half crosswise into ¼-inch slices.

Heat oil in nonstick skillet over medium-high heat. Add fennel and onion, stirring constantly, 7 to 10 minutes, or until browned. Reduce heat and add shrimp, parsley, lemon peel, lemon juice, salt and pepper; stir well until heated. Serves 4.

Pork & Cauliflower Stir-Fry

Edith Ruth Muldoon, Baldwin, N.Y.

> 1 pound lean pork, cut in 1-inch
>   pieces
> 2 cloves garlic, minced
> ½ teaspoon chili powder
> ½ teaspoon ground cumin
> ½ teaspoon salt
> 1 tablespoon canola oil
> 1 head cauliflower (about 2
>   pounds), cut in small florets
> ½ cup water
> ½ cup ketchup

Toss pork with garlic, chili powder, cumin and salt.

In nonstick skillet, heat the oil and brown the pork, stirring occasionally for 3 to 4 minutes. Transfer to plate.

Add cauliflower to skillet and cook for 2 minutes. Pour in water; cover and cook 7 minutes, or until cauliflower is crisp-tender.

Add pork and ketchup to the skillet; cook and stir 2 minutes, until the pork is heated through. Serves 4.

Norwegian Meat Pie

Hazel Hullinger, Decatur, Ill.

> 4 eggs, divided
> 2½ cups milk,divided
> 1½ cups bread cubes
> ¾ pound ground beef
> ½ teaspoon Worcestershire sauce
> ½ teaspoon lemon juice
> 1 tablespoon chopped onion
> 1 teaspoon salt
> 5 strips bacon
> ¼ pound sharp processed cheese,
>   shredded
> ½ cup chopped celery
> ½ teaspoon salt
> ½ teaspoon garlic salt

Meat Crust

Preheat oven to 400 degrees.

Beat 1 egg with ½ cup milk; add bread cubes; let stand 5 minutes. Add beef, Worcestershire sauce, lemon juice, onion and salt; mix well.

Line bottom and sides of 10-inch pie pan with meat mixture.

Filling

Fry bacon until crisp; crumble and sprinkle over meat in pan. Then sprinkle with cheese and celery.

Slightly beat remaining 3 eggs; add 2 cups milk, salt and garlic salt. Pour

gently into meat shell. Bake for 15 minutes. Reduce heat to 350 degrees and bake for 30 minutes or until custard tests done. Serves 6.

Shrimp With Fennel & Red Onion

Kit Rollins, Cedarburg, Wis.

> 1 large fennel bulb
> 2 tablespoons virgin olive oil
> 2 cups red onion, sliced ¼ inch
>   thick
> 1 pound medium shrimp, cooked,
>   peeled, de-veined
> 3 tablespoons chopped parsley
> 1 teaspoon grated lemon peel
> 2 teaspoons fresh lemon juice
> ½ teaspoon salt
> ¼ teaspoon pepper

Chili Dog Wraps

Karen Farr, Kansas City, Mo.

10 (5- or 6-inch) corn tortillas
10 beef hot dogs
1 (15-ounce) can chili
1 (16-ounce) jar thick and chunky salsa
1 cup shredded cheddar cheese

Preheat oven to 350 degrees. Grease 9 x 13-inch dish.

Soften tortillas as per package directions. Place 1 hot dog and 2 tablespoons chili on each tortilla. Roll up and place seam side down in baking dish.

Spoon salsa over tortillas. Spray a sheet of foil with cooking spray. Cover dish with foil, sprayed side down, and bake for 25 minutes. Sprinkle with cheese and bake uncovered, for another 5 minutes. Serves 5.

Oven-Baked Halibut in Foil

Gwen Campbell, Sterling, Va.

4 (12 x 12-inch) pieces
aluminum foil
Oil
4 (6-ounce) halibut fillets, or fish
of choice
1 large rib celery, strings
removed, chopped
1 onion, chopped
¼ cup butter or margarine,
melted
2 tablespoons fresh lemon juice
¼ teaspoon salt
½ teaspoon paprika
¼ teaspoon pepper

Preheat oven to 375 degrees. Lightly oil foil pieces.

Place fish on oiled foil. Top each fillet with chopped celery and onion. Combine butter, lemon juice, salt, paprika and pepper; pour over fillets.

Close foil tightly on all edges with double folds. Bake for 10 to 15 minutes until fish easily flakes with fork. Serves 4.

Maxyne's So-Easy, So-Good Baked Pork Chops

Eleanor Craycraft, Sequim, Wash.

4 boneless pork chops,
1 to 1¼ inches thick
1 egg, beaten
Salt and pepper, to taste (use
very little salt, as soup is salty)
Fine, dry bread crumbs
1 tablespoon shortening
2 (10¾-ounce) cans cream of
mushroom soup
2 tablespoons sherry (optional)
Mashed potatoes

Preheat oven to 350 degrees.

Dip pork chops in egg; sprinkle lightly with salt and pepper, then dip in bread crumbs to coat thoroughly.

Melt shortening in a skillet and brown chops over medium heat until golden brown.

Arrange browned chops in a single layer in a 10 x 10-inch baking dish.

Combine mushroom soup with sherry and spoon over chops. Bake, covered, for 1½ hours. Serve with mashed potatoes. Serves 4. ▶

Sausage Casserole

2 pounds bulk seasoned sausage
2 cups shredded cheddar cheese
1 (10¾-ounce) can cream of
    chicken soup
1 cup sour cream
1 (8-ounce) container French
    onion dip
1 cup chopped onion
¼ cup each of green and red bell
    peppers, chopped
2 teaspoons garlic, minced
Salt and pepper
1 (30-ounce) package frozen hash
    browns, thawed

In skillet, brown sausage and drain. Preheat oven to 350 degrees.

In a large mixing bowl combine cheese, soup, sour cream and onion dip; set aside.

Sauté onion, peppers and garlic until tender and add to soup mixture. Fold in hash browns and mix well; add salt and pepper to taste. Spread half of hash brown mixture over bottom of 9 x 13-inch greased baking dish. Spread half of sausage over hash browns. Repeat. Top with remaining sausage. Bake for about 1 hour. Serves 8.

Apricot Chicken Salad

Jo Ann Ervin, Glasgow, Ky.

½ cup plain yogurt
¼ cup mayonnaise
3 tablespoons apricot preserves
2 teaspoons grated fresh ginger
½ teaspoon salt
½ teaspoon pepper
1 cup sliced almonds, toasted
1 (6-ounce) package dried apri-
    cots, chopped
3 cups cooked chicken, chopped
¾ cup sliced celery
Bibb lettuce leaves

Whisk together yogurt, mayonnaise, apricot preserves, ginger, salt and pepper in large bowl. Add almonds, apricots, chicken and celery, tossing gently. Serve on lettuce leaves. Serves 4 to 6.

Breaded Tomatoes

Cecelia Rooney, Pt. Pleasant, N.J.

8 to 10 medium-firm fresh
    tomatoes
½ cup butter, melted
1 cup crushed saltine crackers
1 tablespoon grated Parmesan
    cheese

Cheese Sauce

2 tablespoons butter
2 tablespoons flour
Dash white pepper
1½ cups milk
3 tablespoons Parmesan cheese

Preheat oven to 475 degrees. Grease a shallow baking dish.

Peel and core tomatoes, but leave them whole. Dip each tomato in melted butter.

In a small bowl, combine crushed crackers and Parmesan cheese. Roll tomatoes in crumb mixture, gently press crumbs onto tomatoes and place in a single layer in baking dish. If there are any crumbs or butter left, combine them and sprinkle over tomatoes.

Bake for 15 minutes or until tomatoes are heated through and begin to brown, (watch, as they burn easily).

For cheese sauce, melt butter in a medium saucepan. Stir in flour; add milk all at once. Cook and stir over medium heat until thickened and bubbly. Remove from heat and stir in Parmesan cheese. Serve over tomatoes. Serves 8 to 10.

Peel and cut potatoes into ¼ x ½-inch strips.

In bowl, combine egg white, chili powder, garlic powder and onion powder; beat well. Add potatoes and toss to coat. Place in a single layer on baking sheets. Bake, uncovered, for 20 to 25 minutes until golden brown. Serves 2 to 4

Swiss Asparagus Au Gratin

Timothy Fennel, Birmingham, Ala.

½ cup water
1½ pounds fresh asparagus spears, trimmed
2 tablespoons Dijon mustard
2 ounces finely shredded Swiss cheese
½ cup seasoned bread crumbs
2 tablespoons margarine, melted
Salt and pepper

Preheat oven to 400 degrees.

Bring water to boil; add asparagus. Cook 3 to 4 minutes and drain, (asparagus will still be crisp). Toss in Dijon mustard. Place in 10 x 6-inch baking dish.

Mix together cheese, bread crumbs, margarine, add salt and pepper to taste. Reserve ¼ cup mixture for topping.

Toss with asparagus. Top with remaining ¼ cup bread crumb mixture. Bake 15 to 20 minutes or until cheese mixture is lightly browned. Serves 4 to 6.

Sweet Potato Fries

Arlene Ranney, Eureka, Calif.

1 pound sweet potatoes
1 egg white
2 teaspoons chili powder
¼ teaspoon garlic powder
⅛ teaspoon onion powder
Nonstick cooking spray

Preheat oven to 400 degrees. Coat 2 baking sheets with nonstick cooking spray.

Vegetable Swiss Quiche

Cecelia Rooney, Pt. Pleasart, N.J.

½ cup chopped zucchini
½ cup chopped broccoli
⅓ cup chopped tomato
¼ cup chopped onion
1½ cups grated Swiss cheese
1 (9-inch) unbaked pie shell
¾ cup milk
½ cup sour cream
½ cup cottage cheese
2 tablespoons flour
2 eggs
⅛ teaspoon seasoned salt

Preheat oven to 375 degrees.

Distribute zucchini, broccoli, tomato and onion with cheese evenly in pie shell.

Combine milk, sour cream, cottage cheese, flour, eggs and seasoned salt and pour over vegetable mixture. Bake for 40 minutes. Let stand 5 minutes before serving. Serves 8. ▶

Orange Pops
Mrs. Barbara Spittle, Wingate, N.C.

> 1 (3-ounce) package orange
>   gelatin
> 1 (.15-ounce) package unsweet-
>   ened orange soft drink mix
> 1 cup sugar
> 2 cups boiling water
> 2 cups cold water
> 12 (3-ounce) paper cups
> 12 popsicle sticks

Dissolve gelatin, soft drink mix and sugar in boiling water. Stir in cold water and pour into paper cups. Freeze until almost firm; add popsicle sticks and freeze until firm. Makes 12.

Macadamia Macaroons
Cecelia Rooney, Pt. Pleasant, N.J.

> 2½ cups shredded sweetened
>   coconut
> 1 cup unsalted macadamia nuts
> 1 (14-ounce) can sweetened
>   condensed milk
> 1 teaspoon vanilla
> 20 saltine crackers, finely crushed
> 2 egg whites
> 6 ounces semisweet chocolate,
>   chopped and melted

Preheat oven to 350 degrees.

Place coconut and nuts on a baking pan. Bake until lightly toasted, about 10 minutes, stirring frequently. Let cool.

In a large bowl, combine sweetened condensed milk and vanilla. Stir in coconut and nuts and crushed crackers; blend well.

Beat egg whites until stiff, then gently fold into coconut mixture. Drop by rounded tablespoonfuls onto a lightly greased baking sheet.

Bake for 12 to 14 minutes or until golden around the edges. Let cool completely. When cool, dip the cookie bottom in the melted chocolate and place on waxed paper. Refrigerate until set. Makes 30.

Chocolate Snack
Galelah Dowell, Fairland, Okla.
For the love of chocolate!

> 1 sheet ready-made frozen
>   puff pastry
> 1 (8-ounce) package semisweet
>   chocolate
> ½ cup chopped walnuts or pecans
> 2 tablespoons butter or
>   margarine
> Confectioners' sugar
> Shaved chocolate

Thaw pastry 20 minutes. Preheat oven to 425 degrees.

On a floured board, roll pastry sheet to 14-inch square. In center of square,

place chocolate, nuts and butter. Pull pastry edges together, twist and turn. Place on ungreased baking sheet and bake 20 minutes. Let stand at least 10 minutes. Sprinkle with confectioners' sugar and shaved chocolate. Serves 6.

Key Lime Dessert
Julia Malnar, Gilbert, Minn.

> 2 cups crushed graham crackers
> ½ cup margarine, melted
> 1½ (14-ounce) cans sweetened
>   condensed milk
> 4 egg yolks
> 1 cup lime juice
> 1 (8-ounce) container frozen
>   whipped topping, thawed

Preheat oven to 350 degrees.

Combine graham cracker crumbs and margarine; mix well. Press into 9 x 9 x 2-inch pan. Combine sweetened condensed milk, yolks and lime juice. Pour over crust. Bake 20 minutes or till set. Cool for ½ hour. Top with whipped topping. Serves 9.

French Apple Pie

Cecelia Rooney, Pt. Pleasant, N.J.

Pie

        6 cups sliced tart apples
        1 teaspoon cinnamon
        ¼ teaspoon nutmeg
        ¾ cup milk
        2 eggs
        2 tablespoons butter, softened
        1 cup sugar
        ½ cup baking mix

Streusel

        1 cup baking mix
        ½ cup chopped nuts
        ⅓ cup brown sugar
        3 tablespoons firm
          butter

Preheat oven to 325 degrees. Grease 10 x 1½-inch pie plate.

For pie, combine apples, cinnamon and nutmeg. Turn into prepared pie plate.

Beat together milk, eggs, butter, sugar and baking mix on high speed for 1 minute, or until smooth. Pour over apple mixture.

For streusel, combine baking mix, nuts, brown sugar and butter until crumbly. Sprinkle over pie. Bake 55 to 65 minutes or until knife inserted in center comes out clean. Cool. Serves 8.

Rhubarb Custard Bars

Julia Malnar, Gilbert, Minn.

Crust

        1½ cups flour
        ½ cup sugar
        ⅓ teaspoon salt
        ½ cup butter

Filling

        ⅓ cup flour
        ½ cup sugar
        ½ cup milk
        3 eggs
        5 cups chopped rhubarb

Topping

        ½ cup sugar
        1 (8-ounce) package cream
          cheese
        1 teaspoon vanilla
        1 cup whipped cream

Preheat oven to 350 degrees. Spray a 13 x 9-inch baking pan.

For crust, combine flour, sugar and salt. Cut in butter until it resembles cornmeal. Press in pan. Bake until browned.

For filling, combine flour and sugar. Add milk and eggs. Stir until blended; add rhubarb. Pour over crust. Bake for 40 minutes.

For topping, beat together sugar, cream cheese and vanilla until smooth. Fold in whipped cream; spread over crust. Makes 24 bars.

Pink Angel Summer Cake

Mrs. Chris Biggin, Lyons, Ill.

        1 pint strawberries, washed and
          hulled
        ½ pint fresh raspberries
        2 tablespoons sugar
        2 tablespoons orange juice, divided
        ¼ cup strawberry jam
        6 ounces purchased angel food cake,
          half of a 12-ounce cake
        8 ounces vanilla yogurt

Slice strawberries and set half of them aside with the raspberries. Place remaining strawberries in a mixing bowl with the sugar and 1 tablespoon orange juice. Mash with fork and let stand until they are juicy.

Combine jam and remaining 1 tablespoon orange juice.

Slice cake horizontally into 3 layers using a serrated knife. Spread jam onto bottom and middle layers and reassemble cake. When ready to serve, overlap 2 slices on each of 4 dessert plates.

Stir reserved strawberries and raspberries into mashed berries. Top each cake slice with a spoonful of berries and a dollop of yogurt. Serve immediately. Serves 4.

Fresh Blueberry Tea Cake

Rita Kitsteiner, Tucson, Ariz.

        2 cups flour
        2 teaspoons baking powder
        1 cup sugar
        ¼ teaspoon salt
        ⅓ cup shortening
        ¾ cup milk
        1 egg
        1 teaspoon grated lemon peel
        1 cup blueberries
        Confectioners' sugar (optional)
        Whipped cream (optional)

Preheat oven to 350 degrees. Grease an 8 x 8-inch pan.

Sift together flour, baking powder, sugar and salt. Cream shortening and alternately add to flour mixture with milk. Beat for 2 minutes. Add egg and beat for 1 minute. Combine lemon peel with berries and fold into batter. Pour into pan. Bake for about 50 minutes.

Serve plain or with a dusting of confectioners' sugar and a dollop of whipped cream. Serves 8. ■

Speedy Vegetarian Italian

Spaghetti With Zucchini, Tomatoes & Mozzarella
1 (8-ounce) package spaghetti
2 medium zucchini, chunked
2 tablespoons butter
1 (15-ounce) can Italian-style stewed tomatoes
1 (8-ounce) package shredded mozzarella cheese
½ cup half-and-half or milk
½ teaspoon salt
⅛ teaspoon basil

Prepare spaghetti according to package directions. Meanwhile, in 10-inch skillet over medium heat, cook zucchini in hot butter for 5 minutes or until tender.

When spaghetti is done, drain and return to pot. Add zucchini, tomatoes, mozzarella, half-and-half, salt and basil. Over low heat, toss spaghetti mixture until cheese is melted. Serve immediately. Serves 4.

Butter Dips
⅓ cup butter
2¼ cups flour
1 tablespoon sugar
3½ teaspoons baking powder
1½ teaspoons salt
1 cup milk

Preheat oven to 375 degrees.
Melt butter in a 13 x 9-inch pan.
Mix flour, sugar, baking powder and salt in medium bowl. Stir in milk. Knead

dough on a lightly floured surface. Pat into a rectangle ½ inch thick and cut into strips about ½ inch wide.

Roll strips in butter and arrange in pan.

Bake for 15 to 20 minutes. Serves 4 to 6.

Bananas Foster
6 tablespoons butter
½ cup brown sugar
**2 large bananas, peeled and cut
into 1-inch chunks**
1 teaspoon rum flavoring
Vanilla ice cream

Melt butter in large skillet. Add brown sugar and cook over low heat, stirring constantly, until sugar is melted. Boil 1 minute and add bananas and rum flavoring. Spoon sauce over bananas and cook until slightly softened.

Serve immediately over ice cream.

Serves 4. ■

SAVINGS YOU'LL SAVOR

Budget-friendly favorites that are sure to please your family.

Sam's Salmon Loaf

**1 (15-ounce) can salmon,
undrained**
1 cup fresh bread crumbs
2 beaten eggs
½ cup diced celery
**½ cup evaporated milk or
regular milk**
2 tablespoons melted butter
1 tablespoon minced parsley
2 teaspoons diced onion
½ teaspoon salt
½ teaspoon crumbled sage
½ teaspoon lemon juice
Dash of freshly ground pepper

Preheat oven to 350 degrees. Butter a loaf pan.

Flake undrained salmon into a medium bowl. Add bread crumbs, eggs, celery, milk, butter, parsley, onion, salt, sage, lemon juice and pepper. Stir until well combined. Pack firmly into loaf pan. Bake for 40 minutes. Serves 4. ■

Kit Rollins, Cedarburg, Wis.

Mother's Day Brunch

Mother's Day is a great time to show you care. Honor your mother with a special treat—a yummy brunch she can sit back and enjoy in the company of those she treasures most.

By Judy Shaw

Fixing food for others is often the way I show them how much they mean to me.

One of the best presents I can give my mother for Mother's Day is a brunch, usually on Saturday, where all four of her daughters gather around the table to eat, talk and laugh. We rarely get to spend time together without worrying about husbands or children.

The Overnight Cardamom Waffles recipe is one my mother made as a special treat for us when we were children. They are delicious served with maple syrup or the Warm Apple-Walnut Compote. My youngest sister, Carol, contributed the coffee recipe. She perfected it by serving it to us at any special occasion.

No matter who you are cooking for, you'll find these dishes simple, satisfying and a great way to show you care.

Warm Apple-Walnut Compote
    2 tablespoons butter
    4 cups Granny Smith apples,
        peeled, cored and cut into
        small cubes
    1 tablespoon grated fresh ginger
    ½ cup brown sugar
    ½ cup chopped walnuts
    Waffles

Shown on the facing page, clockwise from the top: Overnight Cardamom Waffles (page 119), Carol's Caramel Coffee (page 119), Warm Apple-Walnut Compote (page 119) and Spicy Turkey Sausage (page 119).

Combine butter, apples, ginger, brown sugar and walnuts in 2-quart saucepan. Bring to a boil; reduce heat and simmer until apples are very soft, about 20 minutes.

Serve warm over waffles. Makes 4 cups.

Spicy Turkey Sausage
    1 pound ground turkey meat
    1 teaspoon chili powder
    1 tablespoon paprika
    1 teaspoon salt
    1 teaspoon onion powder
    1 teaspoon garlic powder
    ½ teaspoon cayenne pepper
    ½ teaspoon ground cumin
    ½ teaspoon dried oregano
    ½ teaspoon dried thyme
    ½ teaspoon freshly ground
        black pepper

In a large mixing bowl, add the turkey.

In a small mixing bowl, combine the chili powder, paprika, salt, onion powder, garlic powder, cayenne pepper, cumin, oregano, thyme and black pepper together. Mix well. Toss the turkey with the seasoning blend and mix well. Cover and refrigerate for 24 hours. Form the turkey into 4 patties and broil or grill until juices run clear. Serves 4.

Carol's Caramel Coffee
    ½ cup plus 2 tablespoons
        ground coffee
    1 cup caramel topping
    Water
    Aerosol whipped topping

Place coffee in filter in brew basket of 12-cup coffeemaker.

Pour cold water for 12 cups of coffee in coffee maker. Place caramel topping in empty coffee pot. Brew coffee. Stir coffee and topping until well mixed. Pour into coffee cups and top with aerosol whipped topping. Yummy!

Carol Clemons, Macy, Ind.

Overnight Cardamom Waffles
    2 cups flour
    2 tablespoons sugar
    2 tablespoons grated orange peel
    1 package dry yeast
    1 teaspoon cardamom
    1 teaspoon salt
    ½ teaspoon baking soda
    1½ cups milk
    ½ cup butter
    3 eggs

Combine flour, sugar, orange peel, yeast, cardamom, salt and baking soda in mixer bowl.

Heat milk and butter over low heat until very warm, 120 to 125 degrees.

With mixer on low speed, gradually add liquid to flour mixture. Beat just until combined. Add eggs and increase speed to medium; beat 3 minutes.

Cover and refrigerate overnight. Bake according to waffle iron instructions. Serves 6 to 8. ∎

Jerry Shaw, Bluffton, Ind.

West Coast Flavors

When it comes to healthy eating, the West Coast does it naturally. From fresh fish to avocados and figs, these healthful dinner ideas are a treat no matter where you live.

What is California cuisine? What are the West Coast flavors? It's all about natural goodness, freshness and lots of fruits and vegetables. California, in particular, with its mild climate, provides the rest of the country with fresh fruits and vegetable year round. Salads made with baby greens, herbs, dates, walnuts and goat cheese, fresh breads from local bakeries, broiled figs drizzled with sweet balsamic vinegar syrup and mascarpone cheese, turkey sandwiches with sliced avocado and juicy tomatoes, grilled fish and the liberal use of vinaigrette dressings are just a part of the eclectic blend of the tastes and cultures found on the West Coast.

Add in crunchy apples from Washington, salmon from Alaska and bright and juicy cherries or berries from Oregon, and you have bushels of fresh and exciting flavors.

Figs for Thought

Figs can be part of almost any special diet. They satisfy a sweet tooth without adding any fat. Three or four figs is a delicious and easy way to add a serving of fruit to reach the daily recommendation of five fruits and vegetables.

Mesclun & Goat Cheese Salad

Vinaigrette

> 2 tablespoons red wine vinegar
> 1 tablespoon soy sauce
> Freshly ground black pepper
> Salt
> ½ cup extra-virgin olive oil

Salad

> 8 cups mesclun (mixed baby
>   greens, about ¾ pound), rinsed
>   and spun dry
> 12 dried dates, pitted and cut
>   lengthwise into thin strips
>   (about 1 cup)
> 6 ounces soft goat cheese, cut into
>   pieces, at room temperature
> 1 cup walnut halves, lightly toasted

To make vinaigrette: In a small bowl, whisk together vinegar, soy sauce, and pepper and salt to taste. Add oil in a stream, whisking until emulsified. Vinaigrette may be made 1 day ahead and chilled, covered. Bring vinaigrette to room temperature and whisk before proceeding.

In a bowl, toss mesclun with vinaigrette and divide among 8 salad plates. Top salads with dates, goat cheese and walnuts. Serves 8.

Quick Tip What is mesclun? It is a mixture of young leafy greens, often including young lettuces, used as salad. In the packaged lettuces at the grocer, it is often called "spring mix."

The California Sandwich

> 2 ounces sliced Provolone cheese
> 1 small avocado
> 8 ounces peppered turkey,
>   thinly sliced
> Mixed sprouts
> 4 slices multigrain bread
> Ranch dressing

Thinly slice cheese and avocado. Divide cheese, avocado, turkey and sprouts equally and layer on 2 slices of bread. Spread with ranch dressing to taste; top with remaining slices of bread. Serves 2.

Classic Grilled Alaska Salmon

> 3 pounds Alaska salmon
>   fillets (thawed)
> ⅓ cup fresh lemon juice
> ⅔ cup brown sugar
> ½ cup soy sauce
> 2 tablespoons Dijon-style mustard
>   or 2 tablespoons minced shallots
>   or onions or 2 teaspoons chili
>   powder or 1 teaspoon pepper
>   blend (optional)

Arrange salmon in single layer on baking pans; brush with lemon juice.

In small bowl, blend brown sugar and soy sauce. Brush sauce evenly over fillets. Add optional seasoning, if desired.

Broil salmon on grill for 10 minutes per inch of thickness, about 5 to 6 inches from heat. Brush with any remaining sauce. Serves 8.

Glazed Figs With Soft Cheese Sauce

The figs served with the Blue Cheese Cream sauce make a delicious appetizer. Served with the sweetened cream sauce, they become a unique dessert.

> ½ cup orange juice
> ¼ cup balsamic vinegar
> ¼ cup sugar
> 1 teaspoon orange zest
> ½ teaspoon vanilla
> 16 fresh figs or 20 dried figs
> Blue Cheese Cream
> Sweet Cheese Cream

Combine the orange juice, balsamic vinegar, sugar and zest in a small saucepan. Boil over high heat, stirring to dissolve the sugar. Reduce heat to medium and simmer for 5 minutes. Take off heat and stir in vanilla.

If using dried figs, stir into warm glaze and heat through.

If using fresh figs, cut them in half and cover with glaze; broil cut side up until lightly caramelized. Serve with sauce of choice.

▶

Blue Cheese Cream

2 cups soft cheese, such as
mascarpone or cream or goat
½ cup heavy cream
¼ cup Gorgonzola cheese

Sweet Cheese Cream

2 cups soft cheese, such as
mascarpone or cream or goat
½ cup heavy cream
2 tablespoons confectioners' sugar
¼ teaspoon vanilla

For either cheese cream, whip soft cheese with an electric mixer until smooth. Continue whipping and slowly add the cream in a steady stream. Add sugar and vanilla or the Gorgonzola respectively and continue whipping until fairly smooth. Serves 4.

Apple Crisp

4 medium tart cooking apples,
sliced (4 cups)
⅔ cup brown sugar
½ cup flour
½ cup quick-cooking or
old-fashioned oats
⅓ cup butter or margarine,
softened
¾ teaspoon cinnamon
¾ teaspoon nutmeg
Cream or ice cream, if desired

Preheat oven to 375 degrees. Grease bottom and sides of 8 x 8 x 2-inch pan.

Arrange apples in pan. Mix together brown sugar, flour, oats, butter, cinnamon and nutmeg; sprinkle over apples.

Bake about 30 minutes or until topping is golden brown and apples are tender. Serve with cream or ice cream. Serves 4.

Cherry-Berry Pie

12 ounces frozen mixed
berries, drained
¼ cup plus 1 tablespoon sugar,
divided
1 tablespoon flour
1 (21-ounce) can cherry pie filling
½ teaspoon almond extract
2 refrigerated unbaked piecrusts
1 egg, lightly beaten

Preheat oven to 375 degrees.

In a large bowl, combine mixed berries, ¼ cup sugar and flour. Add pie filling and almond extract. Set aside.

Gently unfold bottom crust onto pie plate. Pour berry filling into unbaked crust. Cover with top crust and cut slits for venting. Seal edges by fluting.

Brush top crust with beaten egg and sprinkle lightly with sugar. Bake for 45 minutes or until bubbling appears in the middle of pie. Cover pie with aluminum foil halfway through baking. Let set for 20 minutes before serving. Serves 6. ■

Beautiful Sweet-Tooth Temptations

Raspberry Linzer Cookies
 1 cup butter, softened
 1¼ cups sugar, divided
 2 eggs, divided
 2½ cups flour
 ¼ teaspoon salt
 Confectioners' sugar
 ½ cup ground almonds
 ¾ cup raspberry preserves

Preheat oven to 350 degrees. Grease baking sheets.

In a mixing bowl, cream butter and ¾ cup sugar, beating until light and fluffy. Add egg yolks, one at a time, beating well after each addition.

Combine flour and salt and gradually add to the creamed mixture, mixing well.

Shape dough into a ball and chill 30 to 45 minutes or until firm.

On a surface dusted with confectioners' sugar, roll half of the dough to ⅛-inch thickness. Cut with a 2½-inch round cookie cutter. Repeat with remaining dough. Take half the cookies and cut a ½-inch circle in the center with a round cutter.

Combine almonds with remaining ½ cup sugar.

Beat egg whites until frothy. Brush cookies with holes in the center with egg white and sprinkle with almond mixture. Place on baking sheets and bake for 6 to 8 minutes or until lightly browned. Cool completely.

Spread 2 teaspoons raspberry preserves over the solid cookies. Place cookies with center cutout, almond side up, on top of preserves, creating a pretty sandwich. Makes 2 dozen.

Cecelia Rooney, Pt. Pleasant, N. J.

Gooey Brownies
Brownies
 1 (18¼-ounce) box German
   chocolate cake mix
 ½ cup butter, melted and cooled
 1 egg
 1 cup chopped nuts

Topping
 8 ounces soft cream cheese
 2 eggs
 1 teaspoon vanilla
 4½ cups confectioners' sugar

Preheat oven to 350 degrees.

Mix together cake mix, butter, egg and nuts. Spread in an ungreased 13 x 9 x 2-inch metal pan.

For topping, beat together cream cheese, eggs, vanilla and confectioners' sugar. Pour over the brownie batter and bake 40 minutes or until cheese topping turns lightly golden. Do not overbake.

Remove from oven and cool before cutting into bars. The topping will remain somewhat gooey. Makes 24 bars. ■

Anneliese Deising, Plymouth, Mich.

Flavors of New England

New England specialties remind us of a simpler time and bring a flavorful blend of easy-to-prepare favorite foods to tables everywhere.

Lynn M. Michaud

Traditional New England dinners, chowders and stews were one-pot meals originating in Colonial times when they were cooked in a fireplace over an open fire. Biscuits were cooked in a frying pan or Dutch oven and served as the side dish. Many of these early dishes are still popular today.

New England is also known for maple syrup and blueberries. Some of the local ingredients introduced to colonists by the natives were corn, beans, pumpkins, fish, game birds, and berries. The Indians taught the colonists to tap maple trees, boil down the sap and make maple syrup.

Later arrivals contributed to the developing New England flavors: the French brought different cooking styles and the Irish introduced potatoes to the New World. The Italians showed the tomato wasn't poisonous by using it to make the now frequently served sauce.

During the Great Depression, cooks managed with what they had and shared with others. Neighbors and strangers alike shared the taste and spirit of New England.

When you sample these New England specialties, picture where they were created. A cold winter night warmed by chowder or baked beans.

Fortified for a crisp autumn morning of apple picking by blueberry pancakes soaked in maple syrup.

Following true Yankee ingenuity, these recipes are equally delicious with substitutions based on ingredients readily available in the cook's area. Unlike Colonial times, well-stocked grocery stores allow you to enjoy food the way it is eaten in New England, or you can make the dish all your own with local ingredients.

Catch of the Day Chowder
- 2 tablespoons butter
- ¼ cup celery, diced
- 1 cup onion, diced
- ¾ teaspoon sea salt
- 2 cups chunks of fish (cod, salmon, clams, etc.)
- 1½ tablespoons flour
- 1 cup chicken broth or fish stock
- 2 cups 1 percent milk
- 2 cups precooked potatoes cut in uneven chunks
- 1 teaspoon hot pepper sauce
- 1 tablespoon light soy sauce
- ¼ teaspoon black pepper
- ⅛ teaspoon nutmeg
- 1 teaspoon cognac

Melt the butter in a 3-quart saucepan and sauté the celery and onion until soft. Add the salt and fish and continue to sauté until the fish begins to flake. Stir in flour, then blend in broth and milk.

Add the potatoes, hot pepper sauce, soy sauce, black pepper, nutmeg and cognac. Continue to cook over low heat (do not boil) until the mixture thickens. Serves 4 (meal servings) or 6 (appetizer servings).

Shown on this page, clockwise from the top: Fried Cabbage (page 126), Boiled Dinner (page126) and Corn Bread Pudding Cake (page 127).

Maple Syrup Pancakes

- ½ cup 1 percent milk
- 1 egg
- ½ cup maple syrup
- 1 teaspoon baking powder
- 1 cup flour
- 1 tablespoon butter
- Oil or cooking spray

Place milk, egg, maple syrup, baking powder, flour and butter in a blender and blend until a batter is formed. Heat a griddle or frying pan and lightly grease with oil or cooking spray.

Pour out batter to form 3-inch pancakes. Allow them to cook on 1 side until bubbles begin to form. Flip over and fry the other side until golden. Serves 4 with 3 pancakes each.

New England Baked Beans

- 2 cups white beans or
    black-eyed peas
- 6 cups water plus additional
    as needed
- Ham bone or 1 cup of diced ham
- ½ tablespoon butter
- 1 cup onion
- ½ cup molasses
- ½ cup ketchup
- 1 tablespoon mustard
- 1 tablespoon light soy sauce
- 1 teaspoon hot pepper sauce
- ½ teaspoon garlic salt

Soak beans in 6 cups water overnight; drain. Place beans in a slow cooker; add additional water just to cover the beans and add the ham bone or ham.

Cook on high for 5 to 6 hours until the beans are soft. Save the cooking liquid.

In a 2-quart saucepan, melt the butter and sauté the onion until soft; add molasses, ketchup, mustard, soy sauce, hot pepper sauce and garlic salt for the sauce. Stir in beans and ham and 1½ cups of the reserved cooking liquid (more can be added if you like your beans with more sauce).

Heat thoroughly and allow to sit for at least 30 minutes. Warm them again and serve. Serves 8.

Fried Cabbage

- 1 tablespoon olive oil
- ½ cup diced onions
- 5 cups shredded cabbage
- ½ cup apple, diced
- ½ teaspoon Cajun seasoning
- ⅛ teaspoon salt
- Dash of pepper

Heat the oil in a frying pan; add onions, cabbage, apple, Cajun seasoning, salt and pepper; cover to allow steam to cook vegetables. Stirring frequently to prevent burning, cook until the cabbage has softened. Serves 6.

Boiled Dinner

- 5 medium whole potatoes, peeled
- 1 to 2 carrots per person, peeled
    and cut in 3-inch sticks
- 1 pound turnips peeled and cut
    into large chunks
- 2 cups water
- 2½ pounds corned beef or
    smoked shoulder ham
- Spice packet from corned beef or
    3 bay leaves and 1 clove garlic

Layer potatoes, carrots, turnips, water, corned beef or shoulder ham, and spice packet in a slow cooker; cook on high for 5 to 6 hours.

Serve meat on platter; surround with vegetables; reserve cooking liquid for Gravy. Serves 4 to 6.

Gravy

- 1 tablespoon butter
- 1½ tablespoons flour
- 2 cups reserved cooking liquid
    (strain out the spices)

Melt butter in saucepan and add flour to make a roux. Add the reserved cooking liquid and stir until it thickens. Makes 2 cups.

Corn Bread

　1½ cups flour
　1 cup cornmeal
　¼ cup maple syrup
　¼ teaspoon salt
　2 teaspoons baking powder
　1 egg
　1 cup 1 percent milk
　1 tablespoon vegetable oil
　⅛ teaspoon cinnamon

Preheat oven to 350 degrees. Grease an 8 x 8- or 9 x 9-inch baking pan.

Combine flour, cornmeal, maple syrup, salt, baking powder, egg, milk, oil and cinnamon. Stir just until mixed into a batter.

Pour the batter into the greased pan and bake for 18 minutes or until golden brown patches form on the top.

Corn Bread Pudding Cake

　4 cups cubed Corn Bread (recipe on this page)
　¼ cup dried cranberries, blueberries, cherries or raisins
　1 cup 1 percent milk
　1 egg
　1 (6-ounce) container lemon yogurt
　⅓ cup maple syrup
　1 teaspoon spiced rum
　⅛ teaspoon cinnamon

Preheat oven to 325 degrees. Grease a 1½-quart baking pan.

Place half the corn bread in greased baking pan and spread with dried fruit. Cover with remaining corn bread.

In a blender, puree the milk, egg, yogurt, maple syrup, rum and cinnamon and pour over the corn bread. Bake for 50 minutes or until a strand of dry spaghetti inserted into the center comes out clean. Serves 8. ■

What is corned beef?

Corning is a form of curing; it has nothing to do with corn. Back in the days before refrigeration, meat had to be preserved. In those days, the meat was dry-cured in coarse "corns" of salt. Pellets of salt, some the size of kernels of corn, were rubbed into the beef to keep it from spoiling.

Today, brining—the use of salt water—has replaced the dry salt cure, but the name "corned beef" is still used, rather than "brined" or "pickled" beef. Commonly used spices that give corned beef its distinctive flavor are peppercorns and bay leaf. Of course, these spices may vary regionally.

While brining is not necessary to preserve meat in the current age of refrigeration, the flavor of corned beef is one that is still popular today. In addition to being a traditional part of a boiled dinner, corned beef is also the base for a classic Reuben sandwich.

Classic Steak Dinner

Beef Tenderloin Steaks With Mushroom Sauce

- **2 (4- to 6-ounce) well-trimmed beef tenderloin steaks (filet mignon)**
- **½ teaspoon garlic salt**
- **½ teaspoon pepper, divided**
- **½ teaspoon olive oil**
- **½ tablespoon butter**

Mushroom Sauce

- **½ tablespoon butter**
- **½ teaspoon olive oil**
- **½ small minced onion**
- **1 (10-ounce) package sliced fresh mushrooms, either white or a mix of white mushrooms and wild mushrooms**
- **½ teaspoon salt**
- **¼ cup chicken stock**

Generously sprinkle steaks on both sides with garlic salt and ¼ teaspoon pepper. Place 10-inch skillet over medium heat until very hot. Add olive oil and butter. Add steaks and cook 8 to 10 minutes for medium-rare or until desired doneness, turning steaks over once. Transfer steaks to platter; keep warm.

To drippings in skillet, add oil, butter and minced onion. Cook until translucent, stirring often. Add mushrooms, salt and remaining ¼ teaspoon pepper; cook until liquid evaporates and mushroom mixture is golden, 8 to 10 minutes, stirring frequently. Add stock and heat through, stirring constantly. Spoon mushroom sauce over steaks. Serves 2.

Quick Slaw for Two

1 cup packaged precut cabbage mix
¼ cup diced celery
1 small diced apple
3 tablespoons mayonnaise
1 to 2 teaspoons sugar
1 tablespoon vinegar
¼ teaspoon salt
Chopped walnuts (optional)

Combine cabbage mix, celery and apple. Mix together mayonnaise, sugar, vinegar and salt. Toss with cabbage mixture until well combined. Add chopped walnuts. Serves 2.

Twiced-Baked Potato

1 large russet baking potato
Aluminum foil
¼ teaspoon salt
Dash of pepper
2 teaspoons butter
2 tablespoons sour cream
Small amount of milk
    for thinning
2 tablespoons grated cheese

Preheat oven to 350 degrees.
Microwave potato for 3 to 4 minutes. Wrap in foil and continue baking in oven until tender, about 20 minutes. When cool to the touch, open foil and cut potato in half. Carefully scoop out pulp, leaving thin shell.
Mash pulp with salt, pepper, butter and sour cream. Thin with milk, if necessary. Carefully stuff shell; sprinkle with grated cheese.

Bake for 15 minutes or until heated through. Serves 2.

Frozen Berries With Hot White Chocolate Sauce

4 ounces white chocolate
    buttons or grated white
    chocolate
5 ounces heavy cream
¼ teaspoon almond extract
8 ounces frozen berries

Place chocolate buttons, heavy cream and almond extract in a heatproof bowl over a pan of simmering water for 20 to 30 minutes, stirring every so often. When the sauce is hot, proceed.
Divide berries between 2 dessert plates and leave at room temperature for 10 to 15 minutes, to lose a little of their chill. Drizzle chocolate sauce over berries and serve. Serves 2. ■

July/August 2005

Cool & Creamy Classic Desserts

Margaret's English Trifle

There are many recipes for trifle, and this is a good one. My mother-in-law is expected to bring this to every family reunion.

**1 pound cake
Strawberry jam
½ cup sherry, divided
1 (29-ounce) large can of pears
1 (6-ounce) package vanilla pudding mix, prepared according to package directions
Whipped cream**

Slice the entire pound cake into ½-inch slices. Spread the slices with strawberry jam. Layer half the slices in the bottom of a pretty bowl. Sprinkle with ½ of the sherry.

Cut the pears into 1-inch pieces. Spread over the first layer of pound cake.

Add another layer of pound cake slices. Sprinkle with remaining sherry. Pour the vanilla pudding over the top. Chill until set.

Serve with whipped cream. Serves 10 to 12.

Alice Robinson, Berne, Ind.

Grandma's Cheese Cake

I like old recipes that remind me of my childhood and taste so good. This is my grandmother's "Cheese Cake" made with cottage cheese, which is actually baked in a pie plate. The recipe is over 100 years old, but I still love it and bake it often. I hope you enjoy it as much as I.

**1 cup cottage cheese
2 rounded tablespoons flour
1 cup sugar
¼ teaspoon salt
2 eggs, beaten
1 teaspoon vanilla
2 cups milk
1 (9-inch) unbaked pie shell
Cinnamon for sprinkling on top.**

Preheat oven to 450 degrees.

Place cottage cheese in blender and whip till smooth. Pour into mixing bowl and add flour, sugar, salt, eggs and vanilla. Mix until smooth. Add milk and mix until blended.

Pour into unbaked pie shell. Sprinkle with cinnamon. Bake in oven for 10 minutes, then reduce heat to 300 degrees and bake for 60 to 70 minutes. The center should be slightly wobbly, but will thicken as it cools. Serves 8. ■

Dolly Schell, e-mail

Fourth of July Cookout

Picnics, parades and fireworks. It's time for America's birthday party and everyone is invited to the celebration.

By Connie Moore

Happy 229th birthday, America! The celebration of our nation's birth has moved far beyond the drum-and-fife parade and primitive fireworks of 200 years ago. Today's gala bashes feature musically choreographed displays of exploding color. Whether you were born in the United States, have emigrated here, or are just visiting for a while, everyone can find a reason to celebrate the freedom won when our country was founded.

Although there is no set menu, traditions are hard at work on the Fourth, the same as other holidays. Hamburgers, chicken, and hotdogs for the kids load up the grill, while garden-fresh salads, beans and chips fill out the table. Cool refrigerator desserts, hand-cranked ice cream or an ice-cold watermelon are good ending choices.

Your Fourth of July feast can be easy and enjoyable when you make use of the slow cooker and make-ahead recipes. Light your grill for the burgers and chicken skewers and you're ready for a stress-free celebration.

So pour yourself a tall glass of iced tea and head outside to enjoy the day, the food and fireworks with family and friends.

Note: Lots of Fourth of July games and activities can be found on the Internet by using the key words "Fourth of July facts" on your search engine.

Garden Delight Salad
Colorful and fresh, this is a county-fair winning recipe.

3 cups fresh green beans, snapped
2 cups fresh corn kernels
½ cup shredded carrots
½ green pepper, seeded, chopped
¼ cup chopped sweet or green onions
3 small radishes, sliced
1 medium tomato, seeded, chopped
¾ to 1 cup Italian salad dressing

In boiling water, cook beans for about 10 minutes until tender-crisp. During last 3 minutes of cooking time, add corn. Drain vegetables well.

In large bowl, combine beans, corn, carrots, green pepper, onions, radishes and tomato. Toss lightly.

Pour salad dressing over vegetables. Toss lightly. Cover and refrigerate at least 4 hours or overnight to chill thoroughly.

Toss lightly again to serve. Serves 10.

Quick Tip This recipe lends itself to different kinds of vegetables. Raw zucchini or yellow squash, fresh peas, Roma flat beans and different tomato varieties are all possibilities.

Bean & Sweet Onion Salad
The lightly sweet and sour combination of flavors makes this a satisfying side dish.

3 (15-ounce) cans light and/or dark kidney beans, rinsed, drained
1 cup diced sweet onions
¾ cup sweet pickles, diced
4 hard-boiled eggs, diced
2 to 3 tablespoons vinegar
2 to 3 tablespoons sugar

In large bowl, combine beans, onions and pickles. Add diced eggs. Dissolve vinegar and sugar together. Sprinkle over salad and toss.

Refrigerate until serving time. Serves 8.

Shown on this page, clockwise from the top: Fourth of July Trifle (page 136), Grilled Chicken-Bacon Skewers (page 134), Pepper Jack Burgers (page 134), Slow Cooker Baked Beans (page 135) and Garden Delight Salad (page 132).

Grilled Chicken-Bacon Skewers

*Chicken strips are always
a favorite of the kids.*

**8 boneless, skinless chicken
breast halves
1 pound bacon**

Quick Tip If using wooden
skewers, soak for about ½ hour in
water to reduce chance of burning.

Shown on this page, clockwise from
the top: Fourth of July Trifle (page 136),
Grilled Chicken-Bacon Skewers (page 134),
Garden Delight Salad (page 132) and Bean
& Sweet Onion Salad (page 132).

**1 cup lemon juice
1 cup honey
4 teaspoons lemon-pepper
    seasoning
¾ teaspoon seasoning salt**

Heat grill to medium-hot.

Cut chicken in long, thick strips.
Lay strips of bacon on chicken. Thread
meat onto skewers ribbon style. (Line a
cookie sheet with waxed paper for an
easy-to-clean-up work surface.)

Blend together lemon juice, honey,
lemon-pepper seasoning and seasoning salt. Reserve about ¼ cup of mixture for basting during grilling. Pour the
rest into a shallow glass dish and place
prepared skewers on top. Turn so all
meat is coated with liquid. Cover and

refrigerate at least 1 hour.

Place skewers on grill. (Discard rest
of liquid in dish.) Grill until chicken is no
longer pink and bacon is crisp. Baste at
least once during grilling time with the
reserved liquid. Serves 8.

Pepper Jack Burgers

*Zesty pepper-jack cheese adds
a surprise to every bite.*

**2 pounds lean ground beef
⅓ cup dry bread crumbs
2 tablespoons ketchup
2 teaspoons onion powder
½ cup shredded Pepper Jack cheese
8 hamburger buns
Condiments of choice**

In a mixing bowl, combine beef, bread crumbs, ketchup and onion powder. Mix well and divide into 16 portions.

On waxed paper, shape patties to about ¼-inch thickness. Top 8 of the patties with shredded cheese. Place other 8 patties on top of cheese. Press meat together firmly and seal edges well. Cover and refrigerate until grilling time.

Grill over medium-hot coals. Cook first side until no longer pink. Turn burgers carefully and continue to grill over medium coals until meat is cooked thoroughly (170 degrees and no longer pink, juices running clear). Serve on toasted buns with favorite condiments. Serves 8.

Slow Cooker Baked Beans
Everyone loves baked beans and they are even easier when baked in the slow cooker.

- **2 (15-ounce) cans pork and beans with liquid**
- **1 (15-ounce) can kidney beans with liquid**
- **1 (15-ounce) can baby lima beans, drained**
- **1 (15-ounce) can whole-kernel corn, drained**
- **½ cup brown sugar**
- **1 teaspoon salt**
- **½ cup ketchup**
- **1 teaspoon mustard**
- **2 tablespoons vinegar**
- **¾ cup chopped onions**

Place pork and beans, kidney beans and lima beans in slow cooker with corn, brown sugar, salt, ketchup, mustard, vinegar and onions. Cook on low for 3 to 5 hours (or according to appliance instructions). Serves 8 to 10.

Fried Green Tomatoes
An old-fashioned side dish.

- **½ cup cornmeal**
- **½ cup flour**
- **1 teaspoon salt**
- **½ teaspoon pepper**
- **5 large green tomatoes, just starting to ripen, sliced ½-inch thick**
- **Oil for frying**

In shallow dish, combine cornmeal, flour, salt and pepper. Dip tomato slices into mixture and fry in about ½-inch oil until brown and crisp. Drain on paper towels and serve hot. Serves 8.

Fourth of July Trifle

Wave the flag with this red, white and blue dessert.

- **1 (8-ounce) package cream cheese, softened**
- **2 cups cold milk, divided**
- **1 (4-serving-size) box instant vanilla pudding mix**
- **2½ cups pound-cake cubes**
- **1 cup strawberry preserves**
- **2 cups sliced fresh strawberries**
- **2 cups fresh blueberries**
- **Fresh whole strawberries and blueberries, or mint leaves, for garnish**

In mixing bowl, blend cream cheese and 1 cup of the milk on medium speed with electric mixer. Add pudding mix and remaining 1 cup of milk. Beat on low for 3 minutes.

In a tall, clear 1½-quart serving bowl (to show off layers), place half of the cake cubes. Spread half of the preserves over cake. Layer strawberries over top. Spoon half of pudding mixture over top of berries. Make sure layers are spread to sides of bowl. Repeat layers using rest of cake, preserves, blueberries and pudding. Garnish top of trifle with whole berries, and mint leaves, if desired. Cover with plastic wrap and chill. Serves 8.

Icebox Turtle Cake

Make this easy and luscious cake to chill until ready to serve.

- **1 (18.25-ounce) package devil's food cake mix**
- **1 (12.25-ounce) jar fat-free caramel ice cream topping, divided**
- **1 (8-ounce) container reduced-fat frozen whipped topping, thawed**
- **½ cup toasted pecans**

Preheat oven according to cake mix package directions. Grease and flour a 13 x 9-inch pan. Prepare cake mix and bake cake according to package directions. Bake cake until done.

Remove cake from oven and immediately poke holes over entire surface. Pour half of the caramel topping over cake and allow to soak in. Cool cake completely.

Frost top of cake with whipped topping. Drizzle remainder of caramel topping over cake and sprinkle with pecans. Refrigerate until ready to serve. Serves 9 to 12. ■

Quick Tip To toast pecans, spread nuts in microwave-safe shallow dish and cook on HIGH for 30 to 45 seconds. Stir and cook for 30-second intervals until nuts are hot and lightly toasted. Cool completely before using.

Quick & Easy Baking

Easy Cheese Coffee Cake

2 (8-ounce) tubes refrigerated crescent roll dough
2 (8-ounce) packages cream cheese, softened
¾ cup sugar
1 egg, separated
1 teaspoon lemon juice
½ teaspoon vanilla
1 cup raisins
½ cup chopped pecans
Confectioners' sugar

Preheat oven to 350 degrees. Grease a 9 x 13 x 2-inch pan.

Spread 1 can crescent roll dough in bottom of prepared pan. Press edges to seal; set aside.

Beat cream cheese and sugar; add egg yolk, lemon juice and vanilla. Stir in raisins. Spread over dough in pan. Top with second package of crescent roll dough. Press all the edges together to seal. Whisk egg white and brush over top of cake. Sprinkle with chopped pecans.

Bake for 35 to 40 minutes; cool. Top with a sprinkling of confectioners' sugar before serving.

Serves 12.

Helen Harlos, Ethel, Miss.

Louisiana Stranger's Cake

1 (18-ounce) yellow cake mix
1 cup water
½ cup chopped pecans
4 eggs
½ cup oil
1 (16-ounce) container coconut pecan frosting

Preheat oven to 350 degrees. Grease and flour a bundt pan.

Mix together cake mix, water, pecans, eggs, oil and frosting. Pour into prepared pan and bake 35 to 45 minutes. Serves 12. ■

Helen Harlos, Ethel, Miss.

Shown on this page: Grilled Vegetable Kabobs (page 141) and Marinated Flank Steak (page 139).

Simple Summer Grilling

Whether you call it grilling, barbecuing or a good old-fashioned cookout, why not join the grilling fun this summer?

Outdoor kitchens are a popular trend for taking full advantage of long, warm summer evenings. Even if you can't afford an outdoor kitchen, having a grill outside your kitchen door expands your summer cooking options greatly. It keeps your kitchen cool and can be your friend when you want to stay outside instead of going inside to fix something to eat. Once you work out a system to make it quick and easy, you'll find yourself cooking on the grill more often. Some people grill all year round—even in the snowy North.

Grilling is cooking meat, vegetables or fruits over hot to moderately hot, direct heat. It is best suited for cuts of meat that are tender, but you can expand your choices by marinating less tender cuts of meat for a period of time by placing them in a zip-top bag and refrigerating them until ready to grill.

It is also great for the quick cooking of vegetables and fruit. You can even warm your hamburger buns, or toast bread on the grill.

Marinated Flank Steak
Spicy and versatile, this flank steak is great on salads or in fajitas.

1 teaspoon garlic powder
1 teaspoon oregano
½ teaspoon ground chipotle
½ teaspoon ground cumin
½ teaspoon freshly ground
   black pepper
½ cup red wine
½ cup soy sauce
1 (2- to 3-pound) flank steak

Mix garlic powder, oregano, chipotle, cumin and black pepper. Add red wine and soy sauce.

Place flank steak in gallon-sized zip-top plastic bag. Pour marinade over steak and refrigerate 4 to 16 hours.

Grill over medium-high heat for 6 minutes per side for rare, 7 minutes per side for medium, or 8 minutes per side for well done.

Remove from grill and let rest 10 minutes. Slice thinly across the grain. Serves 8.

Quick Tip Steak and marinade may be frozen together until ready to use. Place in the refrigerator in the morning to thaw to have it ready to grill in the evening.

Quick & Easy Grilled Chicken
Grilled chicken doesn't get any easier!

4 boneless, skinless chicken
   breast halves
¼ cup soy sauce

Pound the chicken breasts to flatten them slightly. Place in a large zip-top plastic bag with soy sauce. Marinate for 15 to 30 minutes while the grill is heating. Marinate for no more than 30 minutes.

Grill chicken breasts for 10 to 15 minutes on each side. Discard the soy sauce. The chicken will release from the grill when it is ready to turn. Serves 4. ▶

Great Grilled New York Strip Steak

Use this method for any tender cut of steak.

4 (6-ounce) strip steaks
Oil for brushing
Garlic salt
Freshly ground pepper

Brush the strip steaks with oil. Sprinkle generously with garlic salt and freshly ground pepper. Set aside while heating the grill.

Place steaks on hot grill and cook for 5 to 6 minutes on each side, turning only once. Cook for longer if you prefer a more well done steak. Serves 4.

Rosemary Balsamic Chicken

Pairing honey with the tang of mustard and balsamic vinegar gives this tender chicken a lot of flavor.

1½ tablespoons Dijon mustard
1 tablespoon honey
1½ teaspoons rosemary
1 clove minced garlic
1 tablespoon red wine vinegar
½ cup chicken broth
¼ cup balsamic vinegar
2 tablespoons olive oil
4 boneless, skinless chicken breast halves

Combine Dijon mustard, honey, rosemary, garlic, red wine vinegar, chicken broth and balsamic vinegar. Whisk in olive oil. Set aside.

Lightly pound chicken breasts to a uniform thickness and place in a zip-top plastic bag. Pour marinade over chicken and refrigerate 2 to 4 hours.

Grill chicken breasts over medium-high heat. Marinade can be simmered for 10 minutes and served as a sauce over cooked chicken. Serves 4.

Quick Tip A grill is an open fire, and anything you cook on it needs to be monitored carefully. We highly recommend setting a timer, so you won't forget to keep your eye on the food.

Grilled Vegetable Kabobs

A fun way to get your kids to eat their veggies.

8 fresh mushrooms
2 zucchini
1 large onion
12 whole cherry tomatoes
Teriyaki sauce for brushing the kabobs

Clean mushrooms and cut zucchini and onion into chunks, keeping sizes fairly uniform. Thread vegetables onto skewers, alternating at least two of each vegetable, adding extra onions between some of the vegetables, to taste.

Right before grilling, brush with teriyaki sauce. Grill 20 minutes or until tender. Do not overcook. Makes 4 skewers.

Grilled Nectarines & Pound Cake

Grilled nectarines and balsamic glaze served with a purchased pound cake make a simple ending to your picnic.

½ cup orange juice
¼ cup balsamic vinegar
¼ cup sugar
1 teaspoon orange zest
4 nectarines
4 (1-inch) slices pound cake
Sweetened whipped cream

Combine the orange juice, balsamic vinegar, sugar and zest in a small saucepan. Boil over high heat, stirring to dissolve the sugar. Reduce heat to medium and simmer for 5 minutes.

Set aside to cool while grilling the nectarines and pound cake.

Halve the nectarines and grill cut side down until browned and slightly soft. It takes 5 or 10 minutes. During the last few minutes, place the slices of pound cake on the grill to warm them.

Serve grilled nectarines with pound cake; drizzle with balsamic sauce and top with whipped cream. Serves 4. ■

Grilling Fruits & Vegetables

Grilled Vegetables

Grilling vegetables used to be considered a novelty, but grilling intensifies the flavors by evaporating some of the liquid and allows them to remain bright and delicious. Because of the nature of grilling a variety of vegetables on the grill, consider serving them at room temperature.

- Vegetables should be cut to expose the maximum surface area to the grill, which helps them cook quickly and thoroughly.
- Skewer smaller vegetables, such as cherry tomatoes and button mushrooms, to keep them from falling through the grill. Skewering works well for slices of some larger vegetables like onions.

- Just before grilling, brush the vegetables with olive oil, and then sprinkle with salt and pepper.

Good candidates for grilling:
- Zucchini and summer squash
- Eggplant
- Onions
- Mushrooms (especially portabellas)
- Tomatoes
- Corn on the cob
- Endive, radicchio or fennel

Grilled Fruit

It doesn't take long for the fruit to become slightly warm and soft and to take on the sweet flavor of the caramelizing.

- Nectarines
- Peaches
- Plums
- Pineapple
- Bananas

Halve the fruits and place them directly on the grill, cut side down. It will only take 5 or 10 minutes. Watch carefully.

Vegetables & Salads

Lime-Pear Gelatin Salad
Cool and refreshing any time.

1 (8-serving-size) box lime gelatin
2 cups boiling water
1 (8-ounce) package cream
    cheese, cubed
1 (29-ounce) can pears with juice

Dissolve gelatin in boiling water; add cream cheese. In blender, puree pears with juice. Add gelatin mixture and blend until smooth. Pour into 8-cup bowl or mold and refrigerate overnight. Serves 12 to 15.

Jerry Shaw, Bluffton, Ind.

Kung Fu Salad
This salad keeps well in the refrigerator for several days.

1 (14½-ounce) can French-style
    green beans, drained
1 (6-ounce) can sliced water
    chestnuts

1 (15-ounce) can chow mein
    vegetables, drained
1 large onion, sliced
Salt to taste
Pepper to taste
2 to 3 cups sliced celery
¾ cup sugar
¾ cup cider vinegar

Mix together green beans, water chestnuts, chow mein vegetables, onion, salt, pepper, celery, sugar and vinegar. Refrigerate overnight before serving. Keeps for weeks. Serves 6 to 8.

Dottie Luttrell, Enid, Miss.

Orange Blossom Carrots
Excellent with roast game hens and rice.

2 pounds baby carrots
¼ cup melted butter
¼ cup brown sugar
¼ cup frozen orange juice
    concentrate, thawed
½ cup mandarin orange pieces

Plan Ahead

When you know there are busy days ahead, having dishes that hold well, prepared and waiting in the refrigerator, can really save you time. Many salads can be made several days in advance and most gelatin will hold one to two days before serving.

½ teaspoon salt
Pinch of cinnamon

Preheat oven to 350 degrees. Butter a 1½-quart baking dish.

Cook carrots until tender; drain. Place in prepared baking dish.

Combine butter, brown sugar, orange juice concentrate, mandarin orange pieces, salt and cinnamon; pour over carrots. Cover and refrigerate overnight. Remove from refrigerator at least 30 minutes before baking. Turn to recoat carrots with sauce. Bake, uncovered, for 20 to 25 minutes, or until thoroughly heated. Serves 4 to 6. ■

Eleanor Craycraft, Sequim, Wash.

Fun at Camp Grandma

Summer days at Grandma's are a time for children to learn the joys of cooking and to create lasting memories.

By Vicki Steensma

We are blessed with eight wonderful grandchildren, and we relish the idea of having them come for visits. However, eight at a time is rather overwhelming at this stage in life, so I created a more two-on-two approach for Grandpa and myself by having "Camp Grandma" during the summer months. Camp Grandma is usually four days long and includes two grandchildren at a time. We play age-appropriate games, craft something special to take home to Mom and Dad, walk in the field nearby, go canoeing in the river that borders our property, and dig for dinosaur bones at "Bone Mountain." (A pile of dirt where I deliberately buried old cow jawbones to thrill the little ones.)

One of the most fun elements of the camp is that the children, no matter how old they are, always want to help fix the food we eat. Gracie is just 2, so she helps stir the food, and Nate and Trey, who are older, can help make the sandwiches and help Grandpa start a campfire. Anna, who will make her debut at Camp Grandma this year at the age of 1, will no doubt just enjoy eating! Sometimes the older grandkids have ideas on how to keep Grandma and Grandpa busy when they arrive. It is never boring. I hope you are able to have fun this summer with your children and grandchildren, and be sure to include them in the preparation of some edible memories!

Tropical Island Chicken

Serve over cooked white rice for a complete meal.

- **4 pounds bone-in chicken thighs or legs**
- **1 teaspoon ginger**
- **1 teaspoon paprika**
- **1 tablespoon onion powder**
- **2 tablespoons garlic salt**
- **2 tablespoons Worcestershire sauce**
- **1 cup ketchup**
- **¼ cup soy sauce**
- **1 (20-ounce) can crushed pineapple with juice**
- **¼ cup brown sugar**

Preheat oven to 400 degrees. Spray a 9 x 13-inch baking dish with cooking spray.

Let the kids arrange chicken pieces on prepared baking dish.

In a small bowl, mix together ginger, paprika, onion powder and garlic salt. Add the Worcestershire sauce and mix well. Divide this mixture and brush half over the chicken pieces. Bake for 15 minutes. Turn chicken pieces and baste with remaining half of Worcestershire sauce mixture; bake for an additional 15 minutes.

In a medium bowl, combine ketchup, soy sauce, pineapple and brown sugar. Carefully spoon the pineapple/soy sauce mixture over baked chicken. Bake an additional 30 minutes. Serve hot. Serves 6 to 8.

Wiggly Piggly Spaghetti

Serve with a tossed salad and baked bread for a filling meal.

- **1 pound bacon**
- **1 pound spaghetti**
- **3 cloves garlic, minced**
- **5 tablespoons olive oil**
- **Salt to taste**
- **Pepper to taste**
- **Grated Parmesan cheese to taste**

Cook bacon until crisp. Drain well; crumble.

Prepare spaghetti according to package directions.

Process garlic cloves through a garlic press. (Kids can do this and have fun pressing it through the "holes.") Combine with olive oil.

Toss together spaghetti, bacon, garlic and olive oil. Season with salt and pepper. Sprinkle with Parmesan cheese. Serves 4 to 6.

Soft Pretzels

Kids of all ages will have fun making these and eating them! Playing with dough is never boring!

- **2 (16-ounce) loaves frozen bread dough (or package of frozen dinner-roll dough balls, thawed)**
- **1 egg white, slightly beaten**
- **1 teaspoon water**
- **Coarse salt**

Preheat oven to 350 degrees. Spray a cookie sheet with nonstick cooking spray.

Separate and roll bread into 24 (1½-inch) balls. Roll each ball into a rope 14½ inches long. Have the children plan and design pretzel shapes (letters or numerals).

Place pretzels 1 inch apart on a prepared cookie sheet. Combine egg white and water; brush on pretzels. Sprinkle with coarse salt.

Place a shallow pan filled with 1 inch of boiling water on bottom rack of oven; place cookie sheet with pretzels on the rack above the pan of water and bake for 20 minutes or until golden brown. Makes 24 pretzels.

Fruit Juice Cream Pops

A child can help measure ingredients, insert wooden sticks and arrange paper cups.

- **1 (6-ounce) can frozen 100-percent juice concentrate**
- **2 cups plain yogurt**
- **2 teaspoons vanilla**
- **6 (5-ounce) paper cups**
- **6 wooden sticks**

Mix together juice concentrate, yogurt and vanilla. Pour about ⅓ cup of mixture into each paper cup. Insert a wooden stick for a handle. Cover and freeze until firm. Serves 6.

Note: *To remove a pop easily, hold the paper cup under running tap water for a few seconds.*

Bugs on a Bench

Kids think this is great fun to make and fun to eat as well! Makes a great midday snack!

5 stalks celery, cut in half
½ cup peanut butter
¼ cup raisins

Spread each celery half with peanut butter. Place raisins in a row across the top of the peanut butter. Serves 5.

Variations: *You can use nuts or sunflower seeds or other nugget-type food instead of the raisins.*

Peanut Butter Bread Pudding

This tasty, kid-friendly dessert is good for you, but don't tell the kids.

2 cups milk
½ cup sugar
2 eggs
3 tablespoons peanut butter
3 slices whole-wheat bread
Whipped cream or jelly (optional)

Preheat oven to 350 degrees. Spray 1-quart baking dish with cooking spray.

Scald milk and slowly stir in sugar.

Beat eggs; gradually combine with milk mixture.

Spread peanut butter on bread and cut into small cubes. Place bread cubes in prepared baking dish; pour in milk/egg mixture.

Set the baking dish in a pan of hot water. Place in oven on center rack and bake for 1¼ hours or until set. Top with whipped cream or a dollop of jelly before serving, if desired. Serves 4 to 6.

Orange Frosty

A perfect after-dinner treat before those roasted marshmallows over a fire.

½ cup frozen orange juice
concentrate
1 cup milk or plain yogurt
1 teaspoon sugar, optional
4 to 5 ice cubes

Place orange juice concentrate, milk or yogurt, sugar and ice cubes in blender or food processor; blend.

For variation: add a ripe banana, a ripe peach or a cup of fresh strawberries. You may want to adjust the sugar amount as desired. Makes 4 (½-cup) servings.

Blue Lagoon

To create your own edible terrarium, layer "dirt" and "sand" cookie crumbs, then plant with candy "leaves" and "trees."

2 (4-serving-size) packages
blue-colored gelatin
Milk
Chocolate sandwich cookies,
finely crushed
Vanilla wafers, finely crushed
Peanut butter–flavord sandwich
cookies, coarsely crushed
Whipped topping
Candy "trees" and "leaves"
Blue food coloring

Prepare gelatin as directed on package. Pour into large glass bowl. Refrigerate until set; about 1½ hours.

Top gelatin with a layer of chocolate sandwich cookie crumbs and vanilla wafer cookie crumbs. Add crushed peanut cookies to resemble a terrarium. Tint whipped topping with blue food coloring to create waves and use candy to resemble trees and leaves. Serves 10 to 12.

Dirt Pudding

Kids like to crush the cookies in a plastic zip-top bag with a rolling pin.

1 (4-serving-size) package instant
vanilla pudding mix
1 (4-serving-size) package instant
chocolate pudding mix
4 cups milk, divided
1 cup whipped topping, divided
20 chocolate sandwich cookies,
finely crushed
Gummy worms

Prepare vanilla and chocolate pudding mixes in separate bowls according to package directions. Let stand 5 minutes.

Gently stir ½ cup whipped topping into each bowl of pudding.

Sprinkle 1 tablespoon of cookie crumbs on bottom of 8 (6-ounce) dessert cups. Layer each with ¼ cup vanilla pudding, 1 tablespoon cookie crumbs and ¼ cup chocolate pudding. Sprinkle cups evenly with remaining cookie crumbs.

Refrigerate at least 1 hour or until ready to serve. Before serving, insert 3 gummy worms into each dessert cup. Serves 8. ■

Butterscotch & Chocolate

Butterscotch Bars

1 (18-ounce) package white cake mix
1 (4-serving-size) package instant butterscotch pudding mix
1 cup milk
1 egg
1 cup chopped pecans
¾ cup butterscotch baking chips

Preheat oven to 350 degrees. Grease and flour a 9 x 13 x 2-inch pan.

In large bowl, combine cake mix, pudding mix, milk and egg. Beat on low speed until blended, about 1 minute. Stir in pecans. Spread batter in prepared pan and sprinkle butterscotch chips evenly over top.

Bake for 30 to 35 minutes or until tester comes out clean. Serves 12 to 16.

Karen Farr, Warsaw, Mo.

Chocolate Wows

After you bite one of these decadent cookies, you will know why I call them Wows.

⅓ cup flour
¼ cup cocoa powder
1 teaspoon baking powder
1 teaspoon salt
6 (1-ounce) squares semisweet chocolate, chopped
½ cup unsalted butter
2 large eggs
¾ cup sugar
1½ teaspoons vanilla
2 cups chopped pecans
1 (6-ounce) package semisweet chocolate chips

Preheat oven to 325 degrees. Grease 2 large cookie sheets.

In a bowl, combine flour, cocoa powder, baking powder and salt.

In a heavy 2-quart saucepan, melt chocolate squares and butter over low heat, stirring frequently until smooth. Remove and cool.

In a large bowl, beat eggs and sugar at medium speed until light and fluffy and lemon-colored, about 2 minutes. Reduce speed to low. Add cooled chocolate mixture, flour mixture and vanilla. Beat just until blended.

Helpful Tips

- To keep cookies a uniform size, use a spring-handled ice cream scoop.
- Use popcorn to pack fragile cookies. It fills the empty spaces between cookies and is lightweight.
- Do not store crispy cookies with soft ones. The soft cookies will make the crispy ones turn soft.
- Store cookies in an airtight container. They will stay fresh for several days.

Increase speed to medium; beat an additional 2 minutes. Stir in pecans and chocolate chips.

Drop by rounded teaspoonfuls 2 inches apart on prepared cookie sheets. With a spatula, spread batter into 2-inch rounds.

Bake until tops are shiny and cracked, about 15 minutes. Cool 10 minutes on cookie sheet. Transfer to wire racks to cool completely. Makes 48 cookies. ■

Cecelia Rooney, Pt. Pleasant, N.J.

Planning Great Meals

Here's our all-new collection of recipes! Plus we're offering these menu suggestions to help you plan great meals.

Kid-Friendly
Cream of Tomato Soup, 150
Chili-Cheese Fingers, 150
No-Bake Chocolate
Peanut Butter Balls, 156

Ladies' Luncheon
Fresh Tomatoes &
Mozzarella, 150
Poached Cold
Cucumber Chicken, 153
Buttermilk Fruit Salad, 157

Game Night
Warm Layered Sandwich, 153
Bacon-Ranch Potato Salad, 152
Salted Peanut Bars, 156

Easy Weeknights
Lemon Broccoli Chicken, 153
Broccoli
French bread
Earthquake Cake, 157

Welcome Friends
Honey-Orange Game Hens, 154
Fruit & Cabbage Salad, 152
Your favorite warm rolls
Banana Pie Delight, 157

Recipe Contest Winners

We knew when we chose the generic term "barbecuing" for our summer contest, that we would get different versions of what barbecuing means. We were looking forward to seeing what you'd send us.

We weren't disappointed! We made sauce, roasted brisket, slow-cooked stew meat, marinated ribs and chicken. … We tasted a lot of different meats. We finally chose our four first place winners, each for a different category. All of these prizewinners will receive a gift from Gourmet Standard cookware.

Jim Bratton of Atascadero, Calif., is our winner for his zippy barbecue sauce.

Jonni Gonzales of Lyndon, Wash., took top honors for Billy Bob's Barbecue beef brisket.

Mollie Ballou of Florissant, Mo., sent us a winning recipe for yogurt-dipped grilled chicken.

Cecelia Rooney, Pt. Pleasant, N.J., who is a regular contributor to *Home Cooking*, won in the pork category for her Mustard-Glazed Spareribs.

Billy Bob's Barbecue

Jonni Gonzales, Lyndon, Wash.

- **1 (3 to 4 pound) boneless brisket**
- **1 medium onion, sliced**
- **1 clove garlic, minced**
- **1 (18-ounce) bottle barbecue sauce**

Preheat oven to 350 degrees.

Place meat, fat side up, on rack in baking pan. Place onion and garlic on top of brisket. Bake 1 hour. Pour barbecue sauce over meat; cover, bake about 2 hours or until meat almost falls apart. Skim off fat. Cut meat against the grain. Serves 12 to 16.

Grilled Chicken

Mollie Ballou, Florissant, Mo.

- **½ cup dried bread crumbs**
- **¼ teaspoon onion powder**
- **¼ teaspoon garlic powder**
- **⅓ teaspoon salt**
- **¼ teaspoon cayenne pepper**
- **⅛ teaspoon ground ginger**
- **⅓ cup plain yogurt**
- **4 skinless chicken breast halves**

Combine bread crumbs, onion powder, garlic powder, salt, cayenne pepper and ground ginger in a shallow dish or pan. Place yogurt in a shallow dish. Dip chicken in yogurt, then into crumb mixture. Place on prepared grill, flesh side up, over medium heat. Bake 20 minutes, turn, and bake 15 minutes more or until fork-tender. Serves 4.

Barbecue Sauce

Jim Bratton, Atascadero, Calif.

> **1 cup ketchup**
> **1 cup dark brown sugar**
> **1 cup dark molasses**
> **2 tablespoons liquid smoke**
> **2 tablespoons garlic powder**
> **2 tablespoons onion powder**
> **2½ tablespoons ground pepper**
> **¼ cup beer (optional) to help dissolve the brown sugar**

Mix ketchup, brown sugar, molasses, liquid smoke, garlic powder, onion powder, pepper and beer in a saucepan. Heat to a quick boil, then simmer, stirring occasionally, until sauce thickens slightly (5 to 10 minutes). While still warm, pour into a canning jar or airtight container. Makes 3 cups.

Mustard-Glazed Spareribs

Cecelia Rooney, Pt. Pleasant, N.J.

> **1 to 2 racks (about 4 pounds) pork spareribs**
> **2 teaspoons fresh rosemary**

> **2 medium garlic cloves, minced**
> **Salt and freshly ground pepper**
> **⅓ cup dark brown sugar**
> **¼ cup coarse-grained Dijon mustard**
> **2 tablespoons plus 1½ teaspoons cider vinegar**
> **1 tablespoon molasses**
> **1½ teaspoons dry mustard**

Preheat oven to 350 degrees.

Mix rosemary, garlic, salt and pepper, and rub on spareribs. Bake spareribs for 1 hour, turning once. Cool completely, cover and chill.

Place brown sugar, Dijon mustard, vinegar, molasses and dry mustard in saucepan. Bring to a simmer. Cook 5 minutes, then cool.

Prepare barbecue grill on medium heat. Place ribs on grill rack, meaty side up. Spread with half of sauce. Cook until bottom side is crisp (about 5 minutes). Turn, spread bottom with sauce, and cook until top side is glazed (about 5 minutes). Transfer to serving platter. Cut into individual ribs and serve immediately. Serves 4. ■

Recipes From Our Readers

Home cooks share their favorite recipes—quick-to-prepare comfort foods, good for family, friends and special occasions.

Tomato Pie

Karen Farr, Warsaw, Mo.

A wonderful way to use the overabundance of tomatoes when they're in season.

> **2 to 3 large tomatoes, thickly sliced**
> **2 to 3 green onions, chopped**
> **1 (9-inch) deep-dish baked pie shell, cooled**
> **Salt to taste**
> **Pepper to taste**
> **Basil to taste**
> **1 cup mayonnaise**
> **1 cup shredded sharp cheddar cheese, or preferred cheese**

> **3 slices bacon, crisp-cooked, crumbled**
> **¼ cup Parmesan cheese**

Preheat oven to 350 degrees.

Alternate layers of tomatoes and onions in pie shell. Sprinkle with salt, pepper and basil.

Combine mayonnaise and cheddar cheese; spread over tomatoes. Sprinkle with bacon and Parmesan cheese. Bake for 30 minutes.

Serves 6 to 8.

Shrimp-Filled Tomatoes

Dottie Luttrell, Enid, Miss.

- 4 cups shrimp, cleaned and cooked
- 1 cup Italian dressing
- 8 medium tomatoes
- 1½ cups diced celery
- ½ cup diced cucumber
- 4 tablespoons chopped green onion
- 2 tablespoons lemon juice
- 4 tablespoons mayonnaise
- Salt to taste
- Pepper to taste

Combine shrimp with Italian dressing and refrigerate overnight.

Place tomato stem side down and slice (not quite through) into 5 sections. Scoop out some of the center to make room for filling. Chill tomatoes upside down to drain.

Drain shrimp; reserve 20 for "wings." Chop remaining shrimp and combine with celery, cucumber, onion, lemon juice, mayonnaise, salt and pepper.

Sprinkle inside of tomatoes with salt. Tuck whole shrimp into sections of tomato. Fill with salad mixture. Serves 8.

Fresh Tomatoes & Mozzarella

- 1½ pounds tomatoes, cored
- 1 pound fresh mozzarella cheese
- ¾ to 1 teaspoon fine sea salt or fleur de sel
- Freshly ground black pepper
- ⅓ cup packed basil leaves, torn or cut into thin strips
- ¼ cup extra-virgin olive oil

Slice tomatoes and cheese into ¼-inch-thick slices. Arrange on a serving platter or individual plates in an alternating pattern, with 2 to 3 slices of tomato for every piece of cheese.

Season with salt and pepper to taste. Sprinkle basil leaves over top of salad and drizzle with olive oil. Serve at room temperature. Serves 6 to 8.

Cream of Tomato Soup

Arlene Ranney, Eureka, Calif.

- 4 cups peeled, seeded and chopped tomatoes
- ¼ cup chopped onion
- 6 tablespoons butter or margarine
- ¼ cup flour
- 1½ teaspoons salt
- ⅛ teaspoon pepper
- ½ teaspoon baking soda
- 2 cups half-and-half
- 2 cups milk
- Crackers or croutons

Simmer tomatoes and onion in butter over low heat; place in blender and puree. Return to pot and heat thoroughly.

Combine flour, salt and pepper; add to tomato mixture. Stir in baking soda, half-and-half and milk; mix well. Heat thoroughly and serve with crackers or croutons. Makes 2 quarts.

Tip: *To freeze soup, simmer tomatoes and onion in butter over low heat. Place in blender and puree; cool and freeze. When ready to make soup, thaw tomatoes and heat. Make rest of soup using instructions above.*

Chili-Cheese Fingers

Gwen Campbell, Sterling, Va.
Serve with your favorite TV program and drinks of your choice!

- 1 cup grated extra-sharp cheddar cheese

¼ cup butter or margarine
1 teaspoon chili powder
¼ teaspoon ground cumin
8 slices white bread, crusts removed

Blend cheddar cheese with butter, chili powder and cumin.

Toast 1 side of bread. Spread with cheese mixture. Cut each slice into 4 "fingers." Arrange on cookie sheet. Broil just until golden, watching carefully to avoid burning. Makes 32 snacks.

Pimento-Cheese Spread

Helen Harlos, Ethel, Miss.
This is great in sandwiches.

1 pound processed cheese, shredded
1 cup mayonnaise
½ cup finely chopped pimentos

In a large bowl, combine cheese with mayonnaise and pimentos until well blended. Keep refrigerated. Makes 6 cups spread.

Brie in Puff Pastry

Galelah Dowell, Fairland, Okla.

1 sheet frozen puff pastry, thawed
¼ cup sliced almonds, toasted (optional)
¼ cup chopped fresh parsley
1 pound round Brie cheese
1 egg
1 tablespoon water
Crackers

Preheat oven to 400 degrees.
Unfold pastry sheet on lightly floured surface. Roll into a 14-inch square; cut off corners to make a circle.

Sprinkle center of pastry with almonds and parsley; top with cheese round. Fold 2 opposite sides of pastry over cheese. Trim remaining 2 sides to 2 inches from edge of dough. Fold in these 2 remaining sides and press edges to seal. Place seam side down on baking sheet. Decorate top with pastry scraps, if desired. Whisk together egg and water; brush on top of pastry.

Bake for 20 minutes or until golden. Let stand 1 hour before serving with crackers. Serves 12.

Cheese Ball

Mary Stowell, Pahrump, Nev.

1 (5-ounce) jar Old English cheddar cheese, at room temperature
1 (5-ounce) jar Roka blue cheese, at room temperature
1 (8-ounce) package cream cheese, at room temperature
1½ tablespoons wine vinegar
Garlic salt to taste
1 cup chopped pecans

Blend Old English cheese, blue cheese and cream cheese with wine vinegar and garlic salt in medium-sized bowl. Shape into a ball. Wrap in waxed paper, foil or transparent wrap and chill until firm, about 30 minutes. Unwrap ball; roll in chopped pecans and refrigerate until ready to serve. Serves 8 to 10. ▶

Fruit & Cabbage Salad

Eleanor Craycraft, Sequim, Wash.

This is delightful on a hot day with plain broiled chicken, hot rolls and a lot of iced tea.

2 oranges, peeled and sectioned
2 apples, diced
2 cups shredded cabbage
1 cup seedless grapes
Pineapple, diced (optional)
½ cup heavy whipping cream
1 tablespoon sugar
1 tablespoon lemon juice
¼ teaspoon salt
½ cup mayonnaise

Place oranges, apples, cabbage, grapes and pineapple in bowl; set aside.

Beat cream until stiff; stir in sugar, lemon juice, salt and mayonnaise.

Gently fold whipped cream mixture into fruit. Serves 6.

Wild Rice Salad

Dottie Luttrell, Enid, Miss.

1 cup cooked wild rice, cooled
2 cups cooked chicken, chopped, cooled
1 cup finely chopped celery
1 cup chopped green pepper
½ cup crumbled crisply cooked bacon
½ cup finely chopped nuts
1 tablespoon lemon juice
½ cup or more mayonnaise

Lettuce
3 hard-boiled eggs, sliced

Combine rice and chicken with celery, green pepper, bacon, nuts, lemon juice and mayonnaise.

Serve salad on a bed of lettuce topped with sliced eggs. Serves 4 to 6.

Salmon Salad

Dottie Luttrell, Enid, Miss.

1 (16-ounce) can red salmon
Juice of 1 lemon
2 tablespoons chopped chives
1 small onion, sliced and separated into rings
¼ teaspoon rosemary
6 whole ground black peppercorns
½ teaspoon salt
1 cup sour cream
Lettuce
Tomato

Combine salmon with lemon juice, chives, onion, rosemary, peppercorns, salt and sour cream. Serve on a bed of lettuce with tomato. Serves 4.

Bacon-Ranch Potato Salad

Judy Ervin, Glasgow, Ky.

2 pounds red potatoes, quartered
Oil
Salt to taste
Pepper to taste
1 cup chopped, cooked smoked bacon
1 cup diced red onion

¼ cup freshly chopped parsley
1 cup ranch dressing

Preheat oven to 350 degrees.

In a large bowl, lightly coat potatoes with oil. Season with salt and pepper. Spread evenly on a large sheet pan. Bake for 25 to 35 minutes until tender; cool.

Combine bacon, onion, parsley and ranch dressing; toss with potatoes. Season with additional salt and pepper. Keep refrigerated. Serves 6 to 8.

Lemon Broccoli Chicken

Arlene Ranney, Eureka, Calif.

4 boneless, skinless chicken
   breasts
Salt and pepper to taste
1 tablespoon oil
1 (10¾-ounce) can cream of
   broccoli soup
¼ cup milk
Juice of 1 lemon

Season chicken breasts with salt and pepper. Heat oil in skillet; brown chicken breasts.

Combine soup, milk and lemon juice. Add to chicken and heat to a boil. Cover, reduce heat and cook until chicken is done. Serves 4.

Warm Layered Sandwich

Helen Harlos, Ethel Miss.

1 (1-pound) round loaf Italian
   bread
2 tablespoons honey mustard
¼ pound thinly sliced deli turkey
¼ pound thinly sliced hard salami
¼ pound sliced mozzarella cheese
2 slices red onion,
   separated into rings
¼ pound thinly sliced deli ham
¼ pound sliced Colby-jack cheese
1 medium tomato, sliced
Lettuce leaves

Preheat oven to 450 degrees.

Cut bread in half crosswise; carefully hollow out top and bottom leaving a ¾-inch shell. Spread honey mustard on both halves.

On the bottom half, layer ingredients starting with turkey, then salami, mozzarella cheese, onion, ham and Colby-jack cheese.

Replace top half of sandwich. Wrap

in aluminum foil and place on a baking sheet. Bake for 25 to 30 minutes or until heated through.

To serve, remove top half of sandwich and layer with tomatoes and lettuce. Replace top and cut into wedges. Serves 6.

Poached Cold Cucumber Chicken

Gwen Campbell, Sterling, Va.

¾ cup dry white wine
1½ cups canned chicken broth
½ cup fresh lemon juice
8 boneless, skinless chicken
   breast halves
1 medium cucumber, peeled,
   finely chopped
¼ teaspoon salt
¼ teaspoon pepper
1 cup mayonnaise
⅛ teaspoon poultry seasoning
2 cups cold cooked rice
Cold, crisp lettuce leaves

Combine wine, chicken broth, lemon juice and chicken breasts in a 12-inch skillet; bring to a simmer. Cover and poach over low heat 20 minutes. Remove chicken; cool.

Mix together cucumber, salt, pepper, mayonnaise and poultry seasoning.

Serve by placing a lettuce leaf on each plate, top with cold rice and chicken breast half; top with cucumber sauce. Serves 8. ▶

½ cup light cream
½ teaspoon salt
Pepper to taste

Broiled Salmon

¼ cup melted butter
1½ tablespoons lemon juice
4 (¾-inch-thick) medium salmon
   steaks or choice of fish

Preheat oven to broil.

Combine butter and lemon juice; brush generously on salmon steaks. Place on broiler rack 3 inches from heat; broil 6 minutes. Turn and brush again with butter/lemon mixture. Broil for an additional 6 minutes, or until fish is opaque throughout.

For sauce, combine cucumber, onion, horseradish, cream, salt and pepper; heat to serving temperature. Serve each steak topped with cucumber sauce. Serves 4.

Skillet Creole Fish

Eleanor Craycraft, Sequim, Wash.

¼ cup flour
1 teaspoon paprika
½ teaspoon salt
¼ teaspoon pepper
1 pound orange roughy fillets or
   any mild white fish
2 medium onions, sliced
2 to 3 green peppers, cut into
   small chunks
2 tablespoons butter
¼ cup dry white wine
2 servings hot cooked rice

On a sheet of waxed paper, combine flour, paprika, salt and pepper; blend well. Dip each fillet into the

Honey-Orange Game Hens

Galelah Dowell, Fairland, Okla.

¾ cup orange juice
¾ cup honey
3 tablespoons soy sauce
3 cloves garlic, minced
1 tablespoon cider vinegar
3 (4¾ pounds total) game hens,
   cut in half lengthwise

Preheat oven to 400 degrees.

In large zip-top plastic bag, combine orange juice, honey, soy sauce, garlic and vinegar. Add game hens, reseal and shake to combine. Refrigerate 3 hours or overnight.

Remove game hens from marinade and place skin side up on broiler pan; roast for 20 minutes.

Boil marinade for 10 minutes until slightly syrupy.

Remove game hens from oven and brush with honey-orange syrup. Return to oven and roast an additional 10 minutes or until instant-read thermometer reads 160 degrees. Place hens

under broiler 2 minutes to crisp skin, if desired. Serves 6.

Note: Serve over fruited white-and-wild rice.

Broiled Salmon With Cucumber Sauce

Eleanor Craycraft, Sequim, Wash.

Cucumber Sauce

½ cup peeled, seeded cucumber,
   grated medium-coarse or
   diced small
2 tablespoons grated onion
1½ tablespoons well-drained
   horseradish

seasoned flour to coat; set aside.

Brown onion and green peppers in melted butter in medium skillet; cook until tender, remove from skillet and set aside.

Place fillets in skillet and cook until lightly browned on both sides. Return vegetables to skillet and add wine. Cover and cook over low heat about 3 to 5 minutes, or until fish is opaque and begins to flake when lightly touched with fork.

Serve with rice. Serves 2.

Note: A peeled, seeded, diced tomato may be added when the vegetables are returned to skillet. Good with a sprinkling of garlic powder and marjoram.

Lump Crab Cakes

Cecelia Rooney, Pt. Pleasant, N.J.

- ½ cup + 2 tablespoons unsalted butter
- ¼ cup heavy cream
- 3 tablespoons minced shallots
- 1 pound lump crabmeat, shells removed
- 1 teaspoon dry mustard
- Cayenne pepper to taste
- ½ teaspoon Old Bay seasoning
- ⅓ cup chopped scallions, green part only
- ¾ cup Panko or regular bread crumbs, divided
- 2 large eggs, beaten
- 2 tablespoons water
- ⅓ cup flour
- ¼ cup oil
- Tartar sauce

Melt butter; add cream and shallots. Cook on low heat for 2 minutes; set aside.

Mix together crabmeat, dry mustard, cayenne pepper, Old Bay seasoning, scallions and ¼ cup bread crumbs. Fold into butter mixture; spread evenly in 8 x 10-inch pan. Cover and refrigerate 4 hours. Cut into 6 equal portions.

Beat eggs with water. With floured hands, form each crab portion into a ball; roll in flour, egg wash, then in bread crumbs.

Heat 2 tablespoons butter and oil in a heavy skillet. Sauté crabcakes until golden, turning once. Serve with tartar sauce. Serves 6.

Seaside Prawns & Pineapple Kabobs

Galelah Dowell, Fairland, Okla.

- 4 (12-inch) kabob skewers
- 1 (8-ounce) can pineapple chunks, drained (reserve 2 tablespoons juice)
- ½ cup bottled marinade: toasted sesame, honey and mustard, or gourmet teriyaki
- 16 fresh or frozen jumbo prawns, thawed, or shrimp with tails, deveined
- 1 small red bell pepper, cut into 1-inch squares

Preheat oven to broil. Soak bamboo skewers in water 30 minutes to prevent burning.

Combine reserved pineapple juice and marinade in large bowl; remove ¼ cup mixture; set aside. Add prawns to bowl; toss well to coat; remove.

Place 1 pineapple chunk in curve of each prawn; thread alternately with red pepper onto skewers, leaving space between pieces. Broil 4 inches from heat source for 4 minutes. Turn and brush with reserved pineapple/ marinade mixture. Cook an additional 3 to 4 minutes, or until prawns turn evenly pink. Serves 4. ▶

Chocolate Muffins With Gooey Centers

Carol Forcum, Marion, Ill.

    2 cups flour
    2 tablespoons cocoa powder
    ½ teaspoon baking soda
    ½ teaspoon salt
    ½ cup sugar
    ½ cup grated milk chocolate
    2 eggs
    2 teaspoons vanilla
    6 tablespoons butter, melted and
        cooled
    1 cup sour cream
    ½ cup dark chocolate squares
    2 tablespoons dark chocolate
        chunks or chocolate chips

Preheat oven to 350 degrees. Grease or spray 15 muffin cups.

Combine flour, cocoa powder, baking soda, salt, sugar, milk chocolate, eggs, vanilla, butter and sour cream in a mixing bowl. Beat for 1 minute on low until combined; turn to high and beat for 1 additional minute.

Spoon half the batter into muffin cups. Place a square of dark chocolate in each cup and top with remaining batter. Press several chocolate chunks or chocolate chips on top of muffins. Bake for 15 minutes, until puffy. Centers will still be gooey. Makes 15 muffins.

No-Bake Chocolate Peanut Butter Balls

Arieal Smith, Glasgow, Ky.

    ½ cup light or dark corn syrup
    2 cups honey-nut creamy or
        chunky peanut butter
    2 cups graham cracker crumbs

    1 cup confectioners' sugar
    1 cup semisweet chocolate chips,
        melted

Combine corn syrup, peanut butter, graham cracker crumbs and confectioners' sugar; mix until smooth. Shape into 1-inch balls. Place on waxed-paper–lined cookie sheet. Drizzle with melted chocolate, or dip balls in chocolate. Chill for 30 minutes to set. Makes 2½ dozen.

Salted Peanut Bars

Karen Farr, Warsaw, Mo.

    4 cups dry-roasted or honey-
        roasted peanuts
    1 (10-ounce) package miniature
        marshmallows
    ½ cup butter
    1 (14-ounce) can sweetened
        condensed milk
    1 (10-ounce) package peanut
        butter pieces
    ½ cup creamy peanut butter

Line a 13 x 9-inch pan with foil; spray with cooking spray. Evenly spread half the peanuts in pan.

In a 3-quart saucepan, melt marshmallows and butter over medium-low heat. Stir in sweetened condensed milk, peanut butter pieces and peanut butter; mix until smooth. Quickly pour over peanuts in pan. Sprinkle with remaining peanuts, gently pressing into bars. Chill 1 hour or until firm; cut into 1 x 1½-inch bars. Store, covered, in refrigerator. Makes 60 bars.

Chinese Noodle Candy

Ruth Ann Johnson, Humboldt, Iowa

    1 (6-ounce) package chocolate chips
    1 (6-ounce) package butterscotch
        chips
    1 (3-ounce) can chow mein noodles
    1 cup broken nuts

Melt chocolate and butterscotch chips over hot water, stirring until smooth. Fold in chow mein noodles and nuts. Let mixture cool about ½ hour, and then drop clusters onto waxed paper; let set. Makes 2 dozen.

Banana Pie Delight

Lisa Langston, Conroe, Texas

A yummy and quick pie to serve!

> 2 bananas, sliced
> 1 graham cracker pie crust
> 1 (4-serving-size) package instant vanilla pudding mix
> 1¾ cups milk
> 1 (12-ounce) container non-dairy whipped topping
> Maraschino cherries, chopped
> Pecans, chopped

Layer bananas in graham cracker pie crust.

Combine pudding mix with milk; fold in whipped topping. Pour over bananas in crust. Sprinkle cherries over pie and top with pecans. Refrigerate. Serves 8.

Earthquake Cake

Karen Farr, Warsaw, Mo.

> 1 cup coconut
> 1 cup chopped pecans
> ½ cup white chocolate chips
> 1 (18-ounce) package devil's food cake mix
> 1 (8-ounce) package cream cheese, softened
> ½ cup butter or margarine
> 3½ cups confectioners' sugar
> 1 teaspoon vanilla

Preheat oven to 350 degrees. Grease a 9 x 13 x 2-inch pan.

Sprinkle coconut, pecans and white chocolate chips evenly in bottom of prepared pan.

Mix cake according to package directions; pour over ingredients in pan.

In medium bowl, thoroughly blend cream cheese, butter, confectioners' sugar and vanilla. Drop by spoonfuls on top of cake, covering entire surface. Do not stir. Bake for 40 to 45 minutes. Serves 12.

Super-Moist Chocolate-Mayo Cake

Galelah Dowell, Fairland, Okla.

> 1 (18.25-ounce) package chocolate cake mix
> 1 cup mayonnaise
> 1 cup water
> 3 eggs
> 1 teaspoon cinnamon (optional)

Preheat oven to 350 degrees. Grease and flour a 9 x 13 x 2-inch pan.

Combine cake mix, mayonnaise, water, eggs and cinnamon. Pour into prepared pan. Bake as directed on cake box. Serves 12.

Buttermilk Fruit Salad

Hazel Hullinger, Decatur, Ill.

> 1 (4-serving-size) package instant vanilla pudding mix
> 1½ cups buttermilk
> 1 (8-ounce) container whipped topping
> 1 (16-ounce) can mandarin oranges, drained
> 1 (20-ounce) can pineapple tidbits, drained
> 1 package fudge-striped shortbread cookies, broken into dime-sized pieces
> ¼ cup miniature marshmallows

Combine pudding mix, buttermilk and whipped topping. Fold in mandarin oranges, pineapple, cookie pieces and marshmallows. Chill. Serves 8. ■

Quick Chicken Florentine Meal

On a busy weeknight, this meal can be on the table in around 30 minutes. To make this happen, follow these easy steps:

1. Preheat the oven.

2. Bake the puff pastry shell.

3. While the shell is baking, chop onions and garlic.

4. Start cooking the onions.

5. Slice spinach and set aside.

6. Chop or shred chicken—this is a great way to use leftovers, or buy already-cooked chicken breast.

7. Add garlic to onions, cook 1 minute, then add flour and seasonings. Whisk in broth.

8. Cook until thickened, add chicken and reduce heat to simmer. The soup will hold at this point until you are ready to finish it and serve.

9. Clean fruit.

10. Mix cream cheese and chocolate syrup and set aside.

11. Plate salad greens and oranges segments.

12. Add cream & spinach to soup.

13. Whisk dressing together and dress salads.

14. Fill the tart right before you need to serve.

Field Greens With Orange Vinaigrette

**2 tablespoons orange juice
    concentrate**
3 tablespoons red wine vinegar
¼ teaspoon salt
**¼ teaspoon freshly ground
    black pepper**
¼ teaspoon garlic powder
2 tablespoons olive oil
6 cups mixed field greens
**1 (11-ounce) can mandarin
    orange segments, drained**
Fresh Parmesan shavings

Whisk together orange juice concentrate, vinegar, salt, pepper and garlic powder. While still whisking vigorously, drizzle in olive oil, whisking until mixture is emulsified.

Divide greens between 4 salad plates. Arrange orange segments on each plate. Top with Parmesan shavings and drizzle with vinaigrette. Serves 4.

Chicken Florentine Soup

¼ cup butter
½ cup onions, finely chopped
½ teaspoon minced garlic
⅓ cup flour
Pinch of cayenne pepper
Salt to taste
Freshly ground black pepper to taste
4 cups chicken stock
**1½ cups cooked chicken breast,
    cubed or shredded**
4 cups spinach, thinly sliced
¾ cup heavy cream

In a heavy-bottomed, 3-quart saucepan over medium heat, melt butter. Add onions and cook until onions are tender, 7 to 10 minutes. Add garlic

and cook 1 minute more.

Stir in flour, cayenne pepper, salt and black pepper. Cook 1 to 2 minutes.

Slowly whisk chicken stock into butter/flour mixture. Bring to a boil and cook several minutes until thickened. Add chicken.

Remove from heat and stir in spinach and heavy cream. Serve immediately. Serves 4.

Easy Chocolate Fruit Tart

**1 sheet frozen puff pastry,
    thawed**
½ cup whipped cream cheese
**¼ cup chocolate syrup plus more
    for drizzling**
1½ cups blueberries
½ cup strawberries

Preheat oven to 400 degrees.

Cut ¾ inch from each side of puff pastry. Place square on baking sheet. Trim two longer pieces to match

shorter and place one strip on top of each side of square, overlapping on the corners and making sure outside edges are even.

Bake in preheated oven for 15 to 18 minutes. The center will puff up. Carefully slit center square around edge and press it down. Cool.

Combine cream cheese and chocolate syrup. Spread into center of puff pastry shell. Arrange blueberries and strawberries over filling and drizzle with additional chocolate syrup. Serves 4. ■

Shown on this page: Cool & Fresh
Pasta Salad (page 162) and California
Sunburst Salad (page 162).

Picnic Salads That Can Take the Heat

It's time to welcome those lazy, hazy, crazy days of summer with picnics at the park or ball field, family reunions and block parties, holiday barbecues and more.

By Linda Coss

Good friends, the great outdoors and mouthwatering food are all ingredients for a terrific time. No picnic spread would be complete without a garden-fresh salad—bountiful bowls of potato salads, vegetable salads and pasta salads make the most of summer produce and tempt warm-weather appetites. And so that you can be sure that your salads are at their freshest and best even when the temperature's rising, this collection of savory salads are specially developed to beat the heat.

Fruited Carrot Salad
This salad is a favorite of my son Kevin.

- 3 tablespoons raspberry, white wine or rice vinegar
- 2 tablespoons canola oil
- 2 tablespoons olive oil
- ½ teaspoon ground cinnamon
- Freshly ground black pepper to taste
- 1 (1-pound) bag peeled baby-cut carrots
- ⅔ cup mixed dried fruit bits (buy the variety that contains raisins, apples, apricots and peaches)

In a small bowl or measuring cup, whisk together the raspberry vinegar, canola oil, olive oil, cinnamon and black pepper. Set aside.

Using a food processor that has been fitted with a shredding disc, grate the carrots. Place carrots in a serving bowl and add dried fruit bits and the oil/vinegar mixture; mix well. Refrigerate for at least 4 hours. Serves 8.

Linda's Corn Salad
This quick and attractive corn salad is a great side dish to serve with chicken or beef.

- 1 (11-ounce) can whole-kernel corn, drained, chilled or 2 cups fresh or frozen kernals
- 3 tablespoons sun-dried tomatoes packed in oil, drained and diced (reserve ½ tablespoon oil)
- 2 tablespoons minced green onions, tops only
- 1 tablespoon balsamic vinegar
- 1 teaspoon bottled minced garlic

- 1 teaspoon crumbled dried oregano leaves
- Black pepper to taste

Place corn, sun-dried tomatoes, sun-dried tomato oil, green onion tops, balsamic vinegar, garlic, oregano leaves and black pepper in serving bowl; mix well. Serve immediately or refrigerate. Serves 6.

New Potatoes With Sun-Dried Tomato Dressing
This flavorful potato dish is one of my favorites.

- 2 pounds tiny new red potatoes, washed
- ¼ cup olive oil
- ¼ cup balsamic vinegar
- ½ cup julienne-sliced sun-dried tomatoes packed in oil, cut in half lengthwise
- 1 tablespoon salt-free seasoning blend
- 2 green onions, chopped

Place potatoes in a 3-quart pan and add enough water to just cover potatoes. Cover and bring to a boil over high heat. Reduce heat and simmer, covered, for 10 minutes or until a fork can easily pierce the center of the largest potato; drain.

To prepare dressing, whisk together olive oil, balsamic vinegar, sun-dried tomatoes and seasoning blend in a small bowl. Place drained potatoes and chopped green onions in serving bowl. Pour dressing over potatoes and toss gently to coat. Chill. Serves 6.

California Sunburst Salad

For best results at your picnic, pack the ingredients separately, and then assemble the salad just before serving.

- **2 tablespoons olive oil**
- **3 tablespoons white wine vinegar**
- **2 tablespoons orange juice**
- **2 teaspoons Dijon mustard**
- **½ teaspoon dried dill weed**
- **1 teaspoon sugar**
- **Salt to taste**
- **Freshly ground black pepper to taste**
- **1 (7-ounce) package ready-to-eat butter lettuce with radicchio, torn into bite-sized pieces**
- **1 medium orange, peeled, sectioned, and cut into small pieces**
- **1 medium-sized ripe avocado, peeled and sliced**
- **4 medium or 3 large stalks celery, thinly sliced**
- **½ medium cucumber, peeled, cut in half lengthwise and thinly sliced**
- **3 tablespoons sweetened dried cranberries**

To make dressing, place olive oil, white wine vinegar, orange juice, Dijon mustard, dill weed, sugar, salt and pepper in small bowl; mix well with fork. Set aside.

Combine prepared lettuce, orange, avocado, celery, cucumber and dried cranberries in serving bowl. Toss with dressing and serve immediately. Serves 5.

Cool & Fresh Pasta Salad

Because this fruity pasta salad is so refreshing, it's perfect for a picnic on a hot summer day. Plus, it's very low in fat and loaded with vitamin C!

- **1 (12-ounce) package tri-colored rotini**
- **1 tablespoon oil**
- **½ teaspoon peeled, minced fresh gingerroot**
- **2 tablespoons soy sauce**
- **1 (16-ounce) bag frozen stir-fry vegetables (including sugar snap peas, broccoli, green beans, carrots, celery, water chestnuts, onions and red pepper)**
- **1 (20-ounce) can pineapple chunks (reserve juice)**
- **⅓ cup frozen orange juice concentrate, thawed**

Cook pasta following manufacturer's instructions; drain.

While pasta is cooking, heat oil in 12-inch skillet over medium-high heat. Add gingerroot, soy sauce and frozen vegetables to skillet; sauté for approximately 6 minutes, stirring frequently, until vegetables are thawed and heated through.

Place drained pasta, cooked vegetable mixture, canned pineapple with juice and orange juice concentrate in large serving bowl; mix well. Cover and refrigerate at least 8 hours. Serves 10 to 12.

Angel-Hair Pasta With Sesame-Ginger Dressing

This pasta is equally delicious served hot as a side dish or cold as a salad.

- **1 small zucchini**
- **1 medium carrot, peeled**
- **1 (8-ounce) package angel-hair pasta**
- **1½ teaspoons bottled minced garlic**
- **1 (½ x ½ x ¼-inch) piece of fresh gingerroot, peeled**
- **¼ cup rice vinegar**
- **3 tablespoons canola oil**
- **1 tablespoon sesame oil**
- **Salt to taste**
- **Black pepper to taste**

In a 4-quart pot, bring 2½ quarts of water to a boil over high heat.

While water is boiling, shred zucchini and carrot using a food processor or grater. Place the grated vegetables in a colander.

Cook angel-hair pasta over low heat for 3 to 4 minutes, stirring occasionally; drain over vegetables in colander.

Place garlic, gingerroot, rice vinegar, canola oil, sesame oil, salt and pepper in a food processor or blender process until completely smooth.

Place cooked pasta-vegetable mixture in serving bowl. Add dressing and toss to coat. Serve immediately or refrigerate and use as a cold salad. Serves 6 to 8. ■

About the Author

Linda Coss is an author and freelance writer who lives in Southern California. She can be reached via email at LindaCoss @FoodAllergyBooks.com.

Healthy & Tasty Recipes

Far East Chicken Cantonese

- **1 cup celery, diagonally sliced into 1-inch pieces**
- **1 cup thinly sliced carrots**
- **1 cup green onions, cut into small rings; green part cut into strips**
- **¼ cup slivered almonds**
- **1 tablespoon butter**
- **1 tablespoon cornstarch**
- **¼ teaspoon ginger**
- **⅛ teaspoon nutmeg**
- **1 (20-ounce) can pineapple tidbits, drained (reserve ¾ cup juice)**
- **2 tablespoons soy sauce**
- **1 teaspoon fresh lemon juice**
- **1 cup fat-free, low-sodium chicken broth**
- **2 cups roughly chopped cooked chicken**
- **1 (5-ounce) can thinly sliced water chestnuts, drained**
- **3 cups hot cooked rice**

In a large, nonstick skillet, sauté celery, carrots, onions and almonds in butter until onions are golden brown.

Combine cornstarch, ginger, nutmeg, reserved pineapple juice, soy sauce, lemon juice and chicken broth; mix until well blended. Add to the sautéed vegetables. Cook until mixture thickens, stirring constantly. Add pineapple, chicken and water chestnuts. Cover; simmer for 10 to 15 minutes.

Serve over hot cooked rice. Serves 6.

330 calories, 20 g protein, 45 g carbohydrates, 8 g fat, 2 g saturated fat, 47 mg cholesterol, 4 g fiber, 406mg sodium.

Gwen Campbell, Sterling, Va.

Low-Fat Double-Apple Cake With Yogurt Sauce

Cake

- **3 egg whites**
- **1½ cups sugar**
- **1 cup applesauce**
- **1 teaspoon vanilla**
- **2 cups flour**
- **1½ teaspoons cinnamon**
- **1 teaspoon baking soda**
- **¼ teaspoon salt**
- **4 cups peeled, cored, thinly sliced tart apples**

Yogurt Sauce

- **1½ cups plain or vanilla yogurt**
- **3 tablespoons brown sugar or to taste**
- **1 teaspoon vanilla or lemon juice**

For cake, preheat oven to 350 degrees Lightly grease or spray a 13 x 9 x 2-inch pan.

In a large bowl, beat egg whites until slightly foamy; stir in sugar, applesauce and vanilla.

On a piece of waxed paper, combine flour, cinnamon, baking soda and salt; add to applesauce mixture and blend well.

Arrange apple slices over bottom of prepared pan. Gently pour batter over apples and spread evenly. Bake for 35 to 40 minutes or until a wooden pick inserted in center comes out clean. Cool on wire rack.

For Yogurt Sauce, combine yogurt, brown sugar and vanilla; stir until smooth. Spoon on each cake serving. Serves 12.

248 calories, 5 g protein, 56 g carbohydrates, 1 g fat, 0 g saturated fat, 2 mg cholesterol, 2 g fiber, 190 mg sodium.

Eleanor Craycraft, Sequim, Wash.

Low-Fat Warm Fruit Cocktail Dessert

- **1 (16-ounce) can light fruit cocktail, drained (reserve juice)**
- **1 (9-ounce) package golden yellow cake mix**
- **Whipped topping**

Preheat oven to 350 degrees. Spray a 9 x 9 x 2-inch pan with cooking spray.

Blend reserved fruit cocktail juice and cake mix. Gently fold fruit into batter; pour into prepared pan and bake 40 to 45 minutes or until top is golden.

Top each serving with whipped topping. Refrigerate leftovers. Serves 5 to 6.

249 calories, 3 g protein, 45 g carbohydrates, 7 g fat, 3 g saturated fat, 11 mg cholesterol, 1 g fiber, 329 mg sodium. ■

Karen Farr, Warsaw, Mo.

Thirst Quenchers

This summer, try some refreshing variations of the traditional family favorite—freshly squeezed lemonade.

Beverages shown on this page, left to right: Limeade (page 165), Strawberry Lemonade (page 165) and Lemonade (page 165).

When the summer sun pours on the heat, there is nothing more refreshing than a tall glass of ice-cold lemonade, iced tea or ginger ale.

While instant powders and frozen concentrates are speedy, the taste difference of freshly squeezed fruit or freshly brewed tea can't be beat.

One way to speed the process of making most cold drinks is to make and keep Simple Syrup in your refrigerator. It is easy to make and keeps for weeks.

Easily adjust the sweetness of any beverage by using more or less simple syrup to taste.

Simple Syrup
3 cups sugar
3 cups water

Combine sugar and water in a medium saucepan. Heat over medium heat, stirring occasionally, until all sugar is dissolved. Cool and store in a tightly covered container in the refrigerator. Makes 6 cups.

Lemonade

A refreshing old-fashioned favorite that satisfies your thirst.

1 cup freshly squeezed lemon juice, strained
⅔ to 1 cup Simple Syrup
4 cups water

Combine lemon juice, Simple Syrup and water in a pitcher. Refrigerate until cold; serve over ice. Serves 4.

Strawberry Lemonade

For an easy variation, try adding fresh strawberries.

1 cup sliced strawberries
2 tablespoons sugar
Lemonade

Mash strawberries with sugar and let stand 15 minutes. Spoon strawberries into bottoms of tall glasses. Fill with ice and lemonade. Stir. Serves 4.

Limeade

If you haven't tried limeade, give this zingy drink a chance.

1 cup lime juice
1⅓ to 1½ cups Simple Syrup
4 cups water

Combine lime juice, Simple Syrup and water. Chill before serving. Pour over ice in tall glasses. Serves 4.

Peach Iced Tea

Peach nectar adds a twist to everyday iced tea.

2 quarts water
2 quart-sized tea bags
1 (12-ounce) can peach nectar
½ cup Simple Syrup

Bring water to a boil; remove from heat, add tea bags and steep for 5 minutes.

Discard tea bags and stir in peach nectar and simple syrup. Chill well before serving. Serve in tall glasses over ice. Makes ½ gallon.

Homemade Ginger Ale

Enjoy the spicy taste of ginger ale any time when you keep this syrup handy.

2 cups sugar
2 cups water
1 cup peeled, sliced gingerroot
8 ounces club soda or
**   seltzer water**
Lime wedges

Combine sugar, water and gingerroot in a medium saucepan; bring to a boil. Reduce heat and simmer until mixture has reduced slightly.

Strain gingerroot from syrup.

To make ginger ale, combine 2 tablespoons syrup with club soda. Pour over ice and serve with a squeeze of lime wedge. Store syrup in the refrigerator for several weeks. Makes 16 (8-ounce) servings. ■

Lemons & Limes

Choose lemons/limes that are brightly colored and heavy for their size. The lime most commonly used is the Persian. Key limes are much smaller and, when ripe, have a smooth, greenish-yellow peel.

- **1 medium lemon equals 2 to 3 tablespoons juice and 2 to 3 teaspoons zest .**
- **1 medium Persian lime equals 1½ tablespoons juice and 1½ teaspoons zest.**

Hamburger Casserole

This is inexpensive, easy and very good!

1 pound ground beef
½ cup chopped onion
Salt to taste
Pepper to taste
1 (10¾-ounce) can tomato soup
1 (15-ounce) can cut green beans, drained
1⅓ cups instant potato flakes
1 egg, beaten
Parmesan cheese

Preheat oven to 350 degrees. Grease a 1½-quart casserole dish.

Brown beef with onion; drain. Season with salt and pepper; stir in tomato soup and green beans. Place in prepared dish.

Prepare instant potatoes as package directs, omitting milk and adding egg. Spoon potato mounds over casserole. Sprinkle with Parmesan cheese. Bake for 30 minutes. Serves 4 to 6. ∎

Helen Harlos, Ethel, Miss.

How to Save on Food

Plan your meals ahead of time, or at least keep a list of your family's favorite meals so you can:

1. Plan your grocery list ahead of time.
2. Plan around what's in season.
3. Only buy in bulk if you have a way to store the extra for use later.
4. Stretch your expensive foods by using them in casseroles.

Easy Main Dishes

Creamy Country Chicken & Vegetables

- **1½ pounds peeled potatoes, cut into 1-inch pieces**
- **½ pound baby carrots**
- **1 cup chopped onion**
- **2 to 2½ pounds bone-in, skinless chicken thighs**
- **2 (0.87-ounce) packages chicken gravy mix**
- **1½ cups water**
- **1 teaspoon dried thyme**
- **¼ teaspoon poultry seasoning**
- **1 teaspoon salt**
- **1 cup reduced-fat sour cream**

Place potatoes, carrots and onion in slow cooker. Top with chicken.

In a small bowl, combine gravy mix, water, thyme, poultry seasoning and salt. Pour mixture over chicken and vegetables. Cover; cook on low 8 hours.

Place chicken and vegetables on platter; cover to keep warm. Whisk sour cream into drippings in slow cooker. Pour over chicken and vegetables. Serves 6.

Karen Farr, Warsaw, Mo.

Meal in a Slow Cooker

- **1 (10¾-ounce) can cream of chicken soup**
- **1 soup can milk or water**
- **1 pound round steak**
- **1 medium onion, sliced**
- **1 (8-ounce) package penne rigate, cooked**

Combine soup and milk or water; spoon into slow cooker; place round steak and onions on top. Simmer on low for 8 hours.

Serve over penne rigate. Serves 4. ■

Mary Stowell, Pahrump, Nev.

Slow Cooker Comeback

With the addition of timers and the sleek new styling, slow cookers are more popular than ever. They do require a little advance planning, but the convenience of having a home-cooked meal ready when you arrive home from work, or the ball game, or the chauffeur run for the day is worth the planning ahead it takes to make using your slow cooker a success.

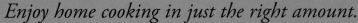

Savory Chicken Dinner

So-Easy Chicken Quarters for Two
Baked chicken goes from ordinary to special with great seasonings.

2 chicken hindquarters
(drumsticks with thighs
attached)
Garlic salt
Pepper to taste
Paprika to taste

1 (10¾-ounce) can cream of
onion soup
¼ cup water or white wine

Preheat oven to 325 degrees.
Sprinkle chicken with garlic salt, pepper and paprika. Place in a baking dish just large enough to accommodate the pieces flat without overlapping (a 1½-quart casserole dish should be just right).

Mix soup with water or wine until smooth; pour over chicken and again sprinkle lightly with paprika. Cover and bake for 1 hour; uncover and continue baking for an additional 15 minutes. Serves 2.

Note: *Particularly good with rice, peas and slivered celery steamed in parsley-butter.*

Eleanor Craycraft, Sequim, Wash.

Herbed Wild Rice Salad for Two

½ cup cooked wild rice
½ cup cooked brown rice
1 ounce scallions, minced
1 ounce shallots, minced
¼ cup minced green pepper
¼ cup minced carrots
¼ cup minced cucumber
1 tablespoon fresh, chopped
    parsley
2 tablespoons oil
1½ teaspoons water
1 teaspoon lemon juice
¼ teaspoon basil
¼ teaspoon tarragon
Dash of salt
Dash of pepper

Combine wild rice, brown rice, scallions, shallots, green pepper, carrots, cucumber and parsley.

In a small jar, combine oil, water, lemon juice, basil, tarragon, salt and pepper; shake vigorously to mix well.

Just before serving, pour well-blended dressing over salad mixture and toss gently. May be served chilled or at room temperature in a lettuce cup. Serves 2.

Note: *Excellent for a special summer meal with chilled, poached salmon steaks, chilled cucumber sauce, chilled asparagus cooked al dente and grape tomatoes.*

Eleanor Craycraft, Sequim, Wash.

Two Popovers

1½ teaspoons melted butter,
    divided
1 medium egg, at room
    temperature
¼ cup whole milk, at room
    temperature
1 teaspoon sugar
⅛ teaspoon salt
¼ cup flour

Preheat oven to 425 degrees. Rub ½ teaspoon butter into 2 muffin cups. Place in oven while preparing batter.

Whisk together remaining 1 teaspoon butter, egg, milk, sugar and salt in medium-sized mixing bowl until blended. Gradually stir in flour until mixture is smooth.

Remove hot muffin pan from oven and pour batter into 2 prepared muffin cups. Fill the unfilled muffin cups with water halfway up. Bake for 10 minutes; reduce heat to 350 degrees and bake an additional 15 minutes. Do not open the oven door until the popovers bake at least 25 minutes. Run a knife around each popover to remove. Makes 2.

Karen Farr, Warsaw, Mo.

Pear Crisp

Really delicious—a perfect blend of fruit and spices.

1 medium Bartlett pear, peeled
    and sliced
1 tablespoon dried cranberries
4 tablespoons brown sugar
3 tablespoons flour
½ teaspoon ground cinnamon
⅛ teaspoon ground ginger
2 teaspoons butter
2 tablespoons oatmeal
1 tablespoon sliced almonds

Preheat oven to 375 degrees. Butter 2 (10-ounce) ramekins.

Divide pear slices and cranberries

between prepared ramekins.

Combine brown sugar, flour, cinnamon and ginger. Cut in butter until crumbly. Stir in oatmeal and almonds. Sprinkle evenly over fruit.

Bake 20 to 25 minutes or until pear mixture is bubbly and topping is golden brown. Serves 2. ■

September/October 2005

Granny's Cookie Jar

Frances' Ginger Cookies

This cookie is a favorite of my seven grandkids—from the eldest in college to the kindergartener. They love to sandwich ice cream (usually peach or vanilla) between two cookies.

- **1½ cups butter**
- **2 cups sugar, plus some for rolling**
- **½ cup molasses**
- **2 eggs**
- **4 cups flour**
- **4 teaspoons baking soda**
- **2 teaspoons cinnamon**
- **1 teaspoon ginger**
- **1 teaspoon cloves**

In a large saucepan, melt butter (or melt in a large glass bowl in the microwave). Remove from heat and beat in sugar, molasses and eggs.

In a bowl, combine flour, baking soda, cinnamon, ginger and cloves; stir into butter mixture until thoroughly mixed. Refrigerate several hours or overnight.

When ready, preheat oven to 350 degrees. Scoop out dough and shape into ½-inch balls. Roll in granulated sugar. Arrange at least 3 inches apart on a baking sheet. Bake for 8 to 10 minutes or until firm and brown. Cool on wire racks. Baking less time will give you a chewy cookie; baking more will make them crisp.

Frances Guthrie, Dublin, Va.

Grandma Worman's Cookies

Grandma made these delicious, soft sugar cookies without measuring any of the ingredients. My mother was the first to try to write the recipe so we could still enjoy them after she was gone.

- **2 cups sugar**
- **1 cup shortening**
- **2 eggs**
- **5 cups flour**
- **1 teaspoon baking soda**
- **1¼ teaspoons nutmeg**
- **1 teaspoon salt**
- **2 teaspoons baking powder**
- **1 cup buttermilk**
- **Sugar**

Preheat oven to 375 degrees.

Cream together sugar, shortening and eggs.

Sift together flour, baking soda, nutmeg, salt and baking powder. Add to creamed mixture alternately with buttermilk.

Chill dough. Drop by teaspoonfuls onto a greased cookie sheet. Dip bottom of a glass into sugar and press to flatten cookies. Bake 10 to 12 minutes. Makes about 5 dozen. ■

Jerry Shaw, Bluffton, Ind.

Apples, Apples, Apples!

From classic Waldorf salad to the perfect deep-dish pie, nothing captures the fresh, crisp taste of fall better than our easy apple recipes.

Having been grown in many parts of the country since the Colonial era, it's not surprising apples are considered our official American fruit. Now more than any other time of year, you'll find a glorious array of these red, green and golden beauties at a farmer's market near you. As this collection of apple treats deliciously demonstrates, apples are prized not only for their just-picked flavor, but their versatility, too. Thanks to these tempting recipes, you'll discover how equally comfortable apples are prepared on the stovetop, in the oven, or just tossed in a salad. Plus, to help you pick the best apples to use, don't miss our helpful Harvest Apple Guide on page 175.

Deep-Dish Apple Pie

Here's a pie perfect for a bumper-crop supply of tart Granny Smith or Winesap apples. If you don't have a deep-dish pie pan, this pie works well in a regular cake pan.

Crust
- 2½ cups flour
- 1½ teaspoons sugar
- 1½ teaspoons salt
- 1 cup shortening
- 1 egg, beaten, with added water to total ½ cup liquid
- 1 teaspoon vinegar

Preheat oven to 350 degrees.

In mixing bowl, combine flour, sugar and salt. Cut in shortening. Stir together egg/water mixture with vinegar; add all at once to flour mixture; stir to make dough. Roll out on floured surface. Place pastry in 9-inch round cake pan or 9-inch deep-dish pie pan.

Filling
- 1½ cups sugar
- ½ cup flour
- 1 teaspoon cinnamon
- 1 teaspoon nutmeg
- ¼ teaspoon salt
- 8 cups peeled, cored and sliced apples
- 2 tablespoons butter, melted

For filling, stir together sugar, flour, cinnamon, nutmeg and salt. Place sliced apples in pastry-lined pan. Sprinkle with sugar mixture. Drizzle with melted butter.

Topping
- 1 cup flour
- ½ cup brown sugar
- ½ cup butter, melted

For topping, stir together flour and brown sugar; add butter and stir until crumbly. Sprinkle over pie.

Bake for 1 to 1½ hours. Serves 8.

Cinnamon Candy–Glazed Baked Apples

No other dessert lets the honest-to-goodness taste of apples shine like baked apples.

- 1 cup sugar
- ¼ cup cinnamon candies
- 1 cup water
- 4 large baking apples
- 2 teaspoons lemon juice
- 1 teaspoon butter

Preheat oven to 375 degrees. Lightly grease small baking dish.

In small saucepan, combine sugar and cinnamon candies with water; boil, stirring until sugar dissolves. Reduce heat; simmer uncovered 2 minutes. Remove from heat. Pare top ⅓ of apples. Core apples, leaving bottom intact.

Brush apples with lemon juice; arrange in baking dish. Dot centers with butter; brush generously with sugar-and-cinnamon glaze. Bake, uncovered, 1 hour, brushing frequently with rest of glaze. Serve warm or cold. Serves 4.

Quick Tip This version of baked apples is particularly kid-friendly, thanks to the cinnamon candy glaze. Red Rome, Fuji or Golden Delicious apples are ideal here, because they retain their shape so well in baking.

Shown on opposite page, Deep-Dish Apple Pie (page 172) and Cinnamon Candy–Glazed Baked Apples (page 172).

Applesauce Oatmeal Muffins

It's a snap to whip up these scrumptious crumb-topped spice muffins. They're not only perfect for breakfast, but also lovely paired with a cup of afternoon tea.

- **1½ cups rolled oats**
- **1¼ cups flour**
- **1 teaspoon baking powder**
- **¾ teaspoon baking soda**
- **¾ teaspoon cinnamon**
- **¾ tablespoon salt**

- **1 cup applesauce**
- **½ cup milk**
- **½ cup brown sugar**
- **3 tablespoons oil**
- **1 egg**

Preheat oven to 350 degrees. Line muffin cups with paper baking cups.

Combine oats, flour, baking powder, baking soda, cinnamon and salt. Add applesauce, milk, brown sugar, oil and egg; mix just until dry ingredients are moistened. Fill muffin cups almost full.

Topping

- **¼ cup rolled oats**
- **2 tablespoons brown sugar**
- **1 tablespoon margarine, melted**
- **¼ teaspoon cinnamon**

For topping, combine oats, brown sugar, margarine and cinnamon; sprinkle evenly over muffins before baking. Bake for 20 to 22 minutes. Serve warm. Makes 12 muffins.

Homemade Apple Butter

Long, gentle simmering creates a fabulously rich spread that's a perfect balance of sweet and tart flavors. Pack in pretty jars as a gift from your kitchen for the coming holiday season.

- **5 to 7 pounds Jonathan, Winesap or Red Delicious apples**
- **2½ cups apple cider**
- **4½ cups sugar**
- **1 tablespoon cinnamon**
- **1 tablespoon grated lemon zest**
- **1½ teaspoons ground cloves**
- **½ teaspoon salt**

Cut unpeeled apples into quarters and remove cores. Place in a large stockpot. Add apple cider. Place over high heat. Bring to a boil; reduce heat to low. Simmer, stirring occasionally, until the apples are tender and puffy, about 2 hours.

Process the apple mixture in a food processor or blender until smooth to yield 6 to 7 cups of pulp.

Combine apple pulp, sugar, cinnamon, lemon zest, cloves and salt in a large saucepan and mix well. Place over medium heat. Bring to a boil, stirring occasionally. Simmer over low heat, stirring occasionally, until thickened, about 1 hour. Makes 3½ cups.

Galelah Dowell, Fairland, Okla.

Waldorf Salad

Dates and raisins replace the traditional grapes in this classic fruit salad with creamy lemon dressing. Choose a red-skinned apple that's good for eating out of hand—like Gala, Cortland, Empire or Macintosh.

4 red apples, cored and cubed
2 tablespoons fresh lemon juice
1 cup sliced celery
1 cup chopped walnuts
¾ cup chopped dates
¾ cup raisins
½ cup mayonnaise
Green lettuce leaves

In large salad bowl, coat apples with lemon juice. Mix in celery, walnuts, dates, raisins and mayonnaise. Serve on bed of lettuce leaves. Serves 6 to 8.

Apple Crisp

Call a crisp, or "spoon pie," the ultimate comfort dessert—a warm and wonderful finale to a casual supper or fruitful wake-up call when served for brunch. A good baking apple is the variety of choice for the filling, like Braeburn, Granny Smith and Jonagold.

4 cups sliced baking apples
⅔ to ¾ cup brown sugar
½ cup flour
½ cup rolled oats
¾ teaspoon cinnamon
¾ teaspoon nutmeg
⅓ cup soft butter

Preheat oven to 375 degrees. Grease an 8 x 8-inch pan.

Put sliced apples in prepared pan. Mix brown sugar, flour, oats, cinnamon, nutmeg and butter until crumbly. Spread over apples.

Bake 30 to 35 minutes or until apples are tender and topping is brown. Serves 4. ∎

Harvest Apple Guide

Take your pick. This time of year it's easy to enjoy an apple a day!

- **Braeburn:** October to July. Color ranges from orange to red over a yellow background. Rich, sweet-tart, spicy flavor. Very firm, juicy and crisp. Great for snacking or baking.

- **Cortland:** September to April. Smooth, shiny red skin. Sweet and juicy with a hint of tartness. Excellent for snacking, salads and baking.

- **Empire:** September to August. Bright red with bright yellow streaks. Creamy and juicy white flesh. Wonderful blend of sweet and tart flavors. Excellent for snacking and salads.

- **Fuji:** October to August. Extra-large with reddish-pink skin and super-sweet flesh. Crisp, firm texture makes it great for baking as well as salads.

- **Gala:** September to June. Pink-orange stripes over a yellow background. Crisp and juicy with a mellow sweet flavor. Excellent for snacking and salads.

- **Golden Delicious:** September to June. Golden yellow skin, tangy, juicy and sweet. Excellent for eating and sauce. Holds its shape well in baking.

- **Granny Smith:** Available year-round. Bright green skin, firm texture. Moderately tart. Excellent pie apple, for snacking and salads.

- **Jonagold:** September to April. Red tinged with orange. A cross between a Golden Delicious and Jonathan apple, this variety has a refreshing tangy-sweet flavor. Excellent for eating, baking and pies.

- **Jonathan:** September to April. Yellow with bright red streaks. Crisp and juicy, tart with a sweet finish. Excellent for eating and sauces.

- **MacIntosh:** September to June. Shiny red skin with streaks of green and yellow. Sweet-tart and very juicy. Excellent for eating and sauce.

- **Red Delicious:** Available year-round. This bright red, heart-shaped fruit is America's favorite snacking apple. Sweet and crunchy, it's also excellent for salads.

- **Red Rome:** October to May. Deep red skin with yellow or green markings. Mildly tart, retains its shape well in baking, but also an excellent sauce apple.

- **Winesap:** October to April. Deep red skin, juicy and firm. Moderately tart, rich flavor. Good for eating, baking and sauce.

Make mealtime easier by planning ahead.

Homestyle Casseroles

Keith's Creamy Cheese-Potato Casserole

- **5 pounds russet potatoes, cooked**
- **1½ cups butter**
- **1 pint sour cream**
- **2 (8-ounce) bags cheddar and Monterey Jack cheese**
- **9 sprigs fresh chives, chopped**
- **1 (7-ounce) jar bacon bits, divided**
- **Salt and pepper to taste**
- **1 (8-ounce) bag sharp cheddar cheese**
- **Cooking spray**

Spray a 9 x 13-inch pan with cooking spray. Set aside.

Mash potatoes with butter and add sour cream; mash until creamy. Add cheddar and Monterey Jack cheese, chives and ½ jar bacon bits. Season with salt and pepper. Sprinkle with remaining bacon bits and sharp cheddar cheese.

Refrigerate up to 48 hours.

To serve, preheat oven to 350 degrees. Bake uncovered 45 minutes or until cheese melts and becomes bubbly. Serves 12 to 15.

Carol Mentze, San Marcos, Calif.

Quesadilla Casserole

- **Vegetable cooking spray**
- **1 (16-ounce) can refried beans**
- **1 (8-ounce) can tomato sauce**
- **1 (4-ounce) can chopped green chilies**
- **1 teaspoon ground cumin**
- **1 teaspoon chili powder**
- **1 teaspoon garlic powder**
- **4 (8-inch) flour tortillas**
- **2 cups shredded cheddar cheese, divided**
- **Cooking spray**

Spray an 8-inch round cake pan with cooking spray.

In a small bowl, combine refried beans, tomato sauce, chilies, cumin, chili powder and garlic powder. Place 1 tortilla in prepared cake pan. Spread ¼ of bean mixture over tortilla. Repeat with second tortilla and bean mixture. Sprinkle 1 cup cheese over bean mixture. Repeat with remaining tortillas and bean mixture. Sprinkle remaining 1 cup cheese over top. Cover and refrigerate.

To serve, preheat oven to 350 degrees. Bake uncovered 35 to 40 minutes. Serves 6. ■

Karen Farr, Warsaw, Mo.

Autumn Dinner With Herbs

Fresh from the garden or dried from your pantry—use herbs to punch up the flavor of any meal.

By Barbra Annino

Shown on this page, from the top: Lemon Thyme Zucchini Bake (page 178), Rosemary Roasted Potatoes (page 178) and Grecian Chicken (page 177).

Herbs have been seasoning dishes for thousands of years. A handful of fresh herbs can add a punch of citrus, spicy, sweet or savory flavor to anything from appetizers to aperitifs. Easy to grow and maintain, most herbs require only sun (4 to 6 hours daily) and a weekly watering to thrive. Pick in the morning, after the dew has dried, for the strongest flavor.

If you prefer the jarred varieties, remember that dried herbs are more potent than fresh, and whole leaves will last longer than crushed. Figure on a teaspoon of dried to a tablespoon of fresh herbs.

Grecian Chicken

The sun-kissed flavors of the Greek Isles burst with every bite in this dish. Use dried herbs.

½ teaspoon oregano
½ teaspoon rosemary
½ teaspoon thyme
½ teaspoon garlic powder
½ teaspoon mint
½ teaspoon lemon zest
1 frying chicken, cut up
Salt and pepper to taste
¼ cup olive oil

Preheat oven to 400 degrees. Mix oregano, rosemary, thyme, garlic powder, mint and lemon zest in a small dish. Set aside.

Rinse chicken and pat dry. Place in a 13 x 9-inch dish, skin side up. Season ▸

with salt and pepper. Brush with olive oil. Lift skin and rub spice mixture onto each chicken piece, distributing equally. Roast for 1 hour or until juices run clear. Serves 4 to 6.

Quick Tip If you cannot find lemon thyme, substitute 1 teaspoon thyme and 2 teaspoons lemon juice for the 1 teaspoon of lemon thyme.

Lemon Thyme Zucchini Bake

Use lemon thyme to add a sweet, citrus flavor to everything from poultry to vegetables.

¼ cup seasoned bread crumbs
¼ cup Parmesan cheese
1 teaspoon dried lemon thyme
2 large zucchinis, thinly sliced
1 large Vidalia onion, thinly sliced
4 tablespoons butter, melted

Preheat oven to 425 degrees.
Mix bread crumbs, cheese, and lemon thyme. In a round casserole dish, layer ½ of the zucchini and ½ of the onion slices. Baste with butter. Add half the bread crumb mixture. Repeat layers and bake, covered, for 20 minutes. Serves 4 to 6.

Rosemary Roasted Potatoes

Rosemary stimulates the senses and is said to enhance memory function. Victorian brides presented sprigs of this herb to guests, symbolizing they would never be forgotten.

2 pounds red potatoes, quartered
1 teaspoon minced garlic
2 tablespoons rosemary
Salt and pepper to taste

2 tablespoons olive oil
2 tablespoons butter

Preheat oven to 425 degrees.
Place potatoes in a large roasting pan. Sprinkle garlic, rosemary, salt, pepper and olive oil over potatoes and toss to coat. Dot with butter. Roast for 30 to 40 minutes, stirring occasionally. Serves 4 to 6.

Cheddar Chive Biscuits

Herbs add a unique flavor to all kinds of breads. You can substitute rosemary, thyme or anise hyssop for the chives in this recipe.

2 cups buttermilk baking mix
⅔ cup milk
½ cup shredded cheddar cheese
¼ cup fresh-snipped chives

Preheat oven to 425 degrees.
Combine baking mix, milk and cheddar cheese in mixing bowl. Carefully blend in chives. Drop dough by spoonfuls onto ungreased cookie sheet. Bake 8 to 10 minutes or until golden brown. Makes 10.

Tomato-Basil Pita Pizza

This dish can be a quick midweek supper or an easy appetizer.

3 Roma tomatoes, sliced
3 whole pita breads
1 handful of fresh basil
Olive oil
Parmesan cheese

Scatter tomato slices over pita bread. Tear or chop basil leaves into thin strips and toss over tomatoes. Drizzle with olive

oil and sprinkle with Parmesan cheese. Broil pizzas for 3 to 5 minutes. Slice with pizza cutter and serve. Serves 3 as a main dish and 9 if used as an appetizer.

Spearmint Sundaes

Did you know that mint comes in dozens of flavors? Orange, chocolate, apple and pineapple mint grace many a garden, but peppermint and spearmint are still the most popular.

4 cups spearmint leaves,
    loosely packed
Water
Sugar
Green food coloring

Place leaves in saucepan and cover with water. Simmer for 30 minutes. Strain mixture through coffee filter or cheesecloth. Discard leaves and rinse pan. Return strained liquid to saucepan and add 1 cup of sugar per cup of liquid. Simmer 15 minutes. Add food coloring. Chill for 2 hours before serving over ice cream. Serves 6. ∎

Easy Fruit Favorites

Tasty Banana Bundt Cake

1 (18.25 ounces) yellow cake mix
1¼ cups banana slices
2 eggs
1 cup buttermilk
¼ cup cold coffee
Whipped cream

Preheat oven to 350 degrees. Grease and flour 12-cup bundt pan.

Combine cake mix, banana slices, eggs, buttermilk and coffee in mixing bowl. Beat at low speed until blended. Beat at medium-high speed for 2 minutes. Pour into prepared bundt pan.

Bake for 50 to 65 minutes or until tested done. Cool in pan on wire rack for 45 minutes. Invert onto serving plate. Garnish with whipped cream and additional banana slices just before serving. Serves 10 to 12.

Denise Hansen, Jackson, Minn.

Little Apple Turnovers

1 (21-ounce) can apple pie filling
3 tablespoons dried currants
1 teaspoon apple pie spice
2 (12-ounce) tubes refrigerated buttermilk biscuits
1 tablespoon milk
1 tablespoon sugar

Preheat oven to 400 degrees. Put pie filling in a small mixing bowl. Using a pastry blender or a knife, cut apple slices into bite-size pieces. Stir in currants and spice. Set aside.

With rolling pin or hand, flatten each biscuit to about ⅛-inch thickness and 4½ inches in diameter. Place 1 slightly rounded tablespoonful of apple mixture in the center of each flattened biscuit. Moisten edges with milk and fold in half. Crimp edges with fork and prick tops two times. Place on ungreased cookie sheet. Sprinkle with sugar.

Bake for 10 minutes or until golden brown. Serve warm or cold. Makes 10 turnovers. ■

Melinda Sprunger, Monroe, Ind.

Harvest Vegetables

Celebrate a bounty of tastes and textures with our collection of comfort food—vegetable style—guaranteed to satisfy straight through the holidays.

With corn, zucchini and tomatoes still at their peak and winter squash just coming into season, it's easy to see why right now is "prime time" for vegetables. So, if you're ready to move beyond corn on the cob and plain, sliced tomatoes into something that tastes a bit more comfy—this assortment, including a velvety soup, irresistible small bites and earthy casseroles, will do the trick! Corn treats include classic succotash with a hearty twist and melt-in-your-mouth fritters. Plus, we offer recipes that use squash in every size and color—sliced, shredded, stuffed and even frozen for last-minute ease! Big on flavor and easy on the cook, each dish is sure to delight both friends and family.

Butternut Squash Soup

We add tart apples to this silky-smooth soup to complement the natural sweetness of the squash. Serve as a first course or a light supper with a tossed salad and warm crusty bread.

- **6 cups (about 3 pounds) butternut squash**
- **1 tart green apple, peeled and coarsely chopped**
- **1 cup chopped onion**
- **4½ cups chicken broth**
- **1 teaspoon salt**
- **¼ teaspoon pepper**
- **¼ cup heavy cream or half-and-half**
- **Chopped fresh parsley for garnish**

Peel squash and seed it. Cut into chunks. Combine squash, apple, onion, chicken broth, salt and pepper. Bring to a boil and simmer, uncovered, 45 minutes.

Puree soup in blender. Return mixture to saucepan and bring to boiling point. Reduce heat. Before serving, add cream and sprinkle with parsley. Makes 2 quarts.

Harvest Zucchini Pie

This crustless quiche, chock-full of chopped zucchini, gets its crunch from a scattering of croutons on the top. If you can't find chopped fresh basil for the filling, substitute fresh parsley or a good pinch of dried basil.

- **4 cups peeled, chopped zucchini**
- **1 small onion, finely chopped**
- **¼ teaspoon salt**
- **¼ teaspoon pepper**
- **½ teaspoon coarsely chopped fresh basil**
- **¼ teaspoon nutmeg**
- **2 eggs, beaten**
- **1 cup homemade or prepared croutons**

Preheat oven to 350 degrees. Grease 9-inch pie plate.

Combine zucchini, onion, salt, pepper, basil, nutmeg and eggs. Press into prepared pie plate. Scatter croutons across top. Bake for 12 minutes, or until done.

To serve, cut into wedges. Serve hot or at room temperature. Serves 8.

Gwen Campbell, Sterling, Va. ▶

Curried Squash

This quick skillet dish takes advantage of convenient frozen squash and cauliflower. Curry powder can range from mild to hot, so we suggest adding it gradually according to your taste.

- **½ cup butter**
- **1 to 2 tablespoons curry powder**
- **1 teaspoon garlic powder**
- **½ cup chopped onions**
- **1 (10-ounce) package frozen squash**
- **1 (10-ounce) package frozen cauliflower**
- **1 cup diced celery**
- **1 large unpeeled potato, diced**
- **1 cup unpeeled, diced apples**
- **1½ cups prepared chicken bouillon**
- **1 tablespoon poultry seasoning**
- **Salt and pepper to taste**
- **2 cups hot cooked rice**
- **½ cup golden raisins**

In large saucepan, melt butter. Add curry powder, garlic powder and onions. Simmer and stir until onions are lightly browned. Add squash and cauliflower. Add celery, potato and apples. Pour bouillon over all. Sprinkle on poultry seasoning. Season with salt and pepper. Cover and simmer over very low heat for 15 to 20 minutes, or until vegetables are done.

Serve over hot cooked rice. Sprinkle golden raisins on top. Serves 6.

Corn Fritters

You'll find plenty of golden kernels in every bite of these crisp southern-style fritters. Serve with roast chicken and sautéed greens or alongside steaming bowls of chili.

- **½ cup finely ground yellow cornmeal**
- **½ cup flour**
- **½ teaspoon baking soda**
- **¾ teaspoon salt**
- **½ teaspoon pepper**
- **1 egg yolk, lightly beaten**
- **4 large ears corn, kernels cut from cob**
- **2 tablespoons butter, melted**
- **½ cup buttermilk**
- **½ cup oil, divided**

Combine cornmeal, flour, baking soda, salt and pepper in large bowl. Make a well in center. Add egg yolk, corn, butter and buttermilk.

Heat ¼ cup of oil in large, heavy skillet. Spoon dollops of batter into skillet, pressing with a spatula to flatten. Fry for 1 to 2 minutes on each side, or until golden brown. Use remaining oil as needed. Remove fritters to paper towels to drain. Serves 8.

Succotash

How do you turn this corn and lima bean classic into a family favorite? Add mashed potatoes! If you can't find fresh lima beans, use frozen and reduce the cooking time to about 10 minutes, or until heated through. Then add the corn and proceed with the recipe as directed.

- **1 tablespoon butter**
- **2 green onions, chopped**
- **2 tomatoes, seeded and chopped**
- **1 cup water**
- **1 cup mashed potatoes (about 2 potatoes)**

1 cup fresh lima beans
7 large ears corn, kernels
cut from cob
1 teaspoon salt
¼ teaspoon pepper

Heat butter in large skillet over medium heat. Add green onions. Sauté for 1 minute. Add tomatoes, water, mashed potatoes and lima beans. Cover and gently simmer for 30 minutes, or until beans are tender. Add corn during last 5 to 10 minutes of cooking time. Add salt and pepper. (If mixture becomes too dry, add a little more water. The succotash should be thick, but not dry.) Serve warm. Serves 6.

Baked Acorn Squash With Apple Stuffing

Acorn squash halves are perfect for individual servings, and this savory apple stuffing couldn't be easier to do. For an extra dose of harvest flavor, sprinkle each serving with toasted chopped pecans or walnuts.

2 small acorn squash (1½ pounds), halved and seeded
1 large or 2 small apples, peeled and diced
2 tablespoons diced celery
2 tablespoons finely chopped onion
2 teaspoons butter, melted
2 tablespoons water
Pinch of salt
Pinch of freshly ground pepper

Preheat oven to 400 degrees. Prepare a 10 x 10 x 2-inch baking pan with cooking spray.

Place squash cut side down in baking pan. Bake 20 minutes.

While squash is baking, combine apples, celery, onion, butter and water in a medium bowl; mix well. Turn squash cut sides up. Sprinkle with salt and pepper. Divide apple mixture to fill cavities of the squash. Bake stuffed squash halves, covered with foil, 30 minutes or more. Serve hot. Makes 4 servings.

Carrot-Stuffed Squash

This yummy squash dish with carrot-and-honey-kissed stuffing would make a scrumptious addition to your Thanksgiving menu. It can be completely assembled ahead then broiled just before serving.

4 large crookneck squash
4 large carrots, peeled and cut into 1-inch pieces
2 tablespoons butter, divided
1 cup chopped onion
1 teaspoon honey
½ teaspoon cinnamon
Salt to taste
Freshly grated Parmesan cheese

Preheat broiler.

Cook squash in large saucepan of boiling water until tender, about 8 minutes. Using slotted spoon, remove and drain. Halve lengthwise and scoop seeds from centers. Place halves on broiler pan. Set aside.

Cook carrots in same saucepan of boiling water until soft, about 15 minutes.

Meanwhile, melt 1 tablespoon butter in medium skillet over medium heat. Add onion and stir until golden and beginning to brown, about 10 minutes. Set aside.

Drain carrots. Transfer to food processor or blender. Add onion, remaining butter, honey, cinnamon and salt. Puree. Mound mixture in squash. Top with Parmesan cheese.

Broil until golden, about 5 minutes. Serves 8. ■

You can eat smart and still enjoy great flavor.

Oven Roasting: Salmon & More!

Crumb-Topped Salmon Fillets

- 1½ cups soft bread crumbs
- 2 tablespoons dried parsley flakes
- 1 tablespoon dried thyme
- 1 tablespoon ground dill weed
- 2 cloves garlic, minced
- 1 teaspoon grated lemon zest
- 2 teaspoons fresh lemon juice
- ½ teaspoon salt
- ¼ teaspoon lemon pepper or black pepper
- 4 (4-ounce) salmon fillets
- 4 teaspoons butter
- ¼ teaspoon paprika

Preheat oven to 350 degrees. Grease a 13 x 9 x 2-inch baking pan.

In a bowl, combine bread crumbs, parsley flakes, thyme, dill weed, garlic, lemon zest, lemon juice, salt and lemon pepper; set aside.

Place salmon, skin side down, in prepared pan. Cover salmon with the crumb mixture; gently pat crumbs evenly over the salmon fillets. Dot each serving with 1 teaspoon butter. Sprinkle liberally with paprika. Bake 15 to 20 minutes or until fish flakes easily with a fork. Serves 4.

Per serving: 241 calories, 27g protein, 11g carbohydrates, 10g fat,

3g saturated fat, 75mg cholesterol, 469mg sodium, 1g fiber

Gwen Campbell, Sterling, Va.

Roasted Dijon Potatoes
Spread potatoes evenly for best browning.

- **½ cup Dijon or honey mustard**
- **1 tablespoon olive oil**
- **3 pounds baking potatoes, cubed (1 to 1½ inches)**
- **2 medium onions, sliced**

Preheat oven to 400 degrees.

In a small bowl, combine mustard and olive oil. In a large bowl, toss potatoes and onions with mustard mixture.

Spread in 15 x 10-inch baking pan. Bake 45 to 50 minutes, until potatoes are tender and crispy. Stir once about halfway through roasting to ensure potatoes brown and crisp evenly. Serves 6.

Per serving: 223 calories, 6g protein, 43g carbohydrates, 3g fat, 1g saturated fat, 0mg cholesterol, 524mg sodium, 5g fiber

Margy Mann, St. Louis, Mo.

Stuffed Eggplant
Just 2 grams of fat per serving!

- **1 large or 2 small eggplant**
- **2 tablespoons minced onion**
- **1 teaspoon olive oil**
- **1 cup canned tomatoes or 4 fresh tomatoes, peeled and chopped**
- **1 cup soft bread crumbs**
- **1 teaspoon salt**

Preheat oven to 375 degrees.

Wash eggplant and cut in half. Scoop out pulp to ½ inch of skin. Dice pulp. In nonstick skillet, brown onion in olive oil; add eggplant pulp, tomatoes, bread crumbs and salt. Mix well and fill eggplant shells with mixture. Bake until brown, 30 minutes. Serves 4.

Per serving: 82 calories, 3g protein, 15g carbohydrates, 2g fat, 0g saturated fat, 0mg cholesterol, 729mg sodium, 4g fiber ■

Louise M. Krieger, Youngtown, Ariz.

Planning Great Meals

Here's our all-new collection of recipes! Plus we're offering these menu suggestions to help you plan great meals.

Easy Entertaining
Baked Chicken
Amandine, 193
Potato Pudding, 191
Steamed broccoli
Chocolate Caramel Pecan Pie, 195

Easy Baked Fish, 194
Mediterranean Beans
in Tomato Shells, 191
Old Southern Hominy
Casserole, 192

Make-Ahead Dinner With Friends
Tarragon Chicken Casserole, 192
Refrigerator Slaw, 188
Glazed Citrus Cake, 196

Speedy Weeknight Supper
Meal in Bread, 193
Creamy Fruit Salad, 189
Sugar Cream Pie, 195

Peggy's Chicken, 192
Bread or rolls
Pumpkin Custards, 195

Viva Italiano!
Chicken Spaghetti, 192
Garlic bread
Fresh Peach Cobbler, 197

Kid-Friendly
Tortilla Pizzas, 194
Peanut Butter S'More Tarts, 196

Recipe Contest Winners

You all did yourselves proud. We thought an everyday necessity like a quick-and-easy one-dish meal would strike a chord with home cooks and it did. We narrowed down the stacks and had the cook-off for the final 12, three in each of the four categories. We will publish more of them in future.

The winners had to truly be a one-dish meal—not served over rice or pasta, unless it was cooked as part of the dish. Because we wanted the dishes to be quick and easy, we stuck by the rules and eliminated any recipes with more than 10 ingredients or an ingredient that was difficult to find in a regular grocery store.

We have our winners. Of the four, only Miranda Smith's Tamale Pie bakes in the oven. We think you'll like it as much as our judges did.

Nothing says comfort food like Edie Despain's Chicken & Dumplings. Pat Swart's Veggie & Lentil Stew was thick and hearty and sure to please the vegetarian in your life. New England Fisherman's Skillet from Margy Mann is a quick, satisfying fish and potato recipe.

Tamale Pie

Miranda Smith, Brookwood, Ala.

Corn bread (6-ounce) mix
2 pounds ground beef
1 medium onion, cut up
Seasoning salt
2 (14-ounce) cans corn, drained
**2 (14.5-ounce) cans diced
  tomatoes, ½ drained**
2 (1.25-ounce) packages chili mix
½ cup cheese

Preheat oven to 350 degrees. Mix corn bread in bowl according to package directions and set aside.

Cook ground beef with onion and a little seasoning salt; drain. Mix corn, tomatoes, beef mixture and chili mix; pour in casserole dish. Pour corn bread mixture over meat mixture.

Bake 35 minutes. Pull out, sprinkle with cheese. Bake 10 minutes more. Let rest 15 minutes before serving. Serves 6 to 8.

Veggie & Lentil Stew

Pat Swart, Bridgeton, N.J.

4 cups tomato or vegetable juice
**2 (14½-ounce) cans stewed
  tomatoes**
**1 (16-ounce) can kidney beans,
  drained**
2 medium carrots, sliced
2 medium potatoes, cubed
1 large onion, chopped (optional)
1 cup lentils
2 tablespoons dried parsley
2 teaspoons dried basil
1 teaspoon garlic powder

In a Dutch oven, combine juice, tomatoes, kidney beans, carrots, potatoes, onion, lentils, parsley, basil and garlic powder. Bring to a boil and reduce heat. Cover and simmer for 35 to 40 minutes until lentils and veggies are tender. Cook on medium for 4 hours. Serves 6 to 8.

Add a dollop of sour cream or yogurt to each serving for a garnish if desired. ▶

Quick Chicken & Dumplings

Edie Despain, Logan, Utah

1½ cups milk
1 cup frozen peas and carrots
1 cup cut-up cooked chicken
1 (10¾-ounce) can condensed
    cream of chicken or mushroom
    soup
1 cup biscuit baking mix
⅓ cup milk
Paprika

Heat 1½ cups milk, peas and carrots, chicken and soup to a boil in 3-quart saucepan, stirring frequently.

Mix biscuit baking mix and ⅓ cup milk until soft dough forms. Drop dough by 8 spoonfuls onto chicken mixture (do not drop directly into liquid). Sprinkle with paprika.

Cook, uncovered, over low heat 10 minutes. Cover and cook 10 minutes longer. Makes 4 servings.

New England Fisherman's Skillet

Margy Mann, St. Louis, Mo.

4 small red potatoes, diced
1 onion, chopped
1 tablespoon olive oil
2 stalks celery, chopped
2 cloves garlic, minced
½ teaspoon crushed thyme
1 (14½-ounce) can original-style
    tomatoes
1 pound firm white fish (halibut,
    snapper or cod)
Salt and pepper to taste

In skillet, brown potatoes and onion in oil over medium-high heat; stirring occasionally. Stir in celery, garlic and thyme; cook 4 minutes. Add tomatoes; bring to a boil. Cook 4 minutes or until thickened. Add fish, cover and cook over medium heat 5 to 8 minutes, or until fish flakes easily with fork. ∎

Recipes From Our Readers

Home cooks share their favorite recipes—quick-to-prepare comfort foods, good for family, friends and special occasions.

Refrigerator Slaw

Floy Franks, Amarillo, Texas

3 pounds cabbage, shredded
2 medium onions, diced
2 green peppers, diced
¼ cup pimientos, diced
1 cup vinegar
1 cup sugar
1 cup salad oil
2 tablespoons salt
3 tablespoons prepared mustard
2 teaspoons celery seed (optional)

Put cabbage, onions, peppers and pimientos in a very large bowl.

Combine vinegar, sugar, salad oil, salt, mustard, and celery seed, if desired, and bring to a boil. Pour over cabbage mixture and mix thoroughly. Refrigerate overnight to blend flavors. This slaw keeps well. Yields about 1 gallon.

Spaghetti Salad

Floy Franks, Amarillo, Texas

1 (12-ounce) package thin spaghetti
1 (8-ounce) bottle Italian dressing
1 green pepper, chopped
1 red pepper, chopped
1 cucumber, chopped
1 large tomato, chopped
1 teaspoon salad supreme
    seasoning blend

Cook spaghetti; drain and rinse with cold water. Pour Italian dressing over spaghetti. Combine green pepper, red pepper, cucumber, tomato and salad

supreme. Mix with spaghetti. Marinate 12 hours or overnight in refrigerator before serving. Serves 8.

Three Bean Salad

Helen Harlos, Ethel, Miss.

 1 (16-ounce) can garbanzo beans
 1 (16-ounce) can pinto beans
 1 (16-ounce) can cut green beans
 1 small onion, sliced
 ½ cup green pepper, chopped
 1 or 2 jalapeno peppers, finely
  minced
 ¼ cup sugar
 ¼ cup oil
 ½ cup plus 2 tablespoons vinegar
 Salt and pepper to taste

Drain and combine garbanzo beans, pinto beans and green beans. Add onion and green pepper. Mix jalapeno peppers, sugar, oil and vinegar. Pour over beans. Stir well. Season with salt

and pepper to taste. Refrigerate several hours before serving. Serves 6 to 8.

Creamy Fruit Salad

Helen Harlos, Ethel, Miss.

 3 large peaches, sliced
 3 large bananas, sliced
 1 (15-ounce) can pears, sliced and
  drained
 1 (20-ounce) can pineapple
  chunks, drained, reserve juice
  (6 to 8 ounces)
 1 (5.1-ounce) instant vanilla
pudding
 2 tablespoons sweetened orange
  drink mix

Combine peaches, bananas, pears and pineapple. Mix together pudding, reserved juice, and drink mix. Pour over fruit. Mix well. Chill before serving. Serves 8 to 10.

Sugar Baby Muffins

Gwen Campbell, Sterling, Vir.

 1 cup dark brown sugar, firmly
  packed
 1 cup milk, sweet or buttermilk
 ½ cup canola oil
 ½ cup applesauce
 1 large egg
 2 teaspoons vanilla
 2 cups flour
 1 teaspoon baking soda
 1 teaspoon salt
 ¼ teaspoon ground mace
 ½ cup finely chopped pecans
 Confectioners' sugar

Preheat oven to 375 degrees. Lightly grease, or spray with nonstick cooking spray, a 12-muffin tin.

Mix brown sugar, milk, canola oil, applesauce, egg and vanilla.

Combine flour, baking soda, salt and mace. Stir in nuts. Add milk mixture and stir just until combined.

Sprinkle confectioners' sugar over top of each muffin. Bake 18 to 23 minutes. Serves 12.

Pumpkin Patch Bread

Arlene Ranney, Eureka, Calif.

 1½ cups sugar
 1 cup canned pumpkin
 ½ cup oil
 2 eggs
 ½ cup water
 1⅔ cups flour
 1 teaspoon baking soda
 ¾ teaspoon salt
 ¼ teaspoon baking powder
 ½ teaspoon ground cloves
 ½ teaspoon cinnamon
 ½ teaspoon nutmeg
 ½ cup chopped pecans

Preheat oven to 350 degrees. Grease a 9 x 5 x 3-inch loaf pan.

In large mixing bowl, combine sugar, pumpkin, oil, eggs and water. Combine flour, baking soda, salt, baking powder, cloves, cinnamon and nutmeg. Gradually add to pumpkin mixture and mix well. Fold in pecans.

Pour into prepared pan. Bake 70 to 80 minutes or until toothpick inserted near center comes out clean. Cool 10 minutes before removing from pan to wire rack to cool. Makes 1 loaf.

Pineapple Banana Bread

Nancy Foust, Stoneboro, Pa.

1 cup butter, softened
2⅔ cups sugar
¼ cup honey
3 eggs
1 tablespoon vanilla
4 ripe bananas, mashed
1 (20-ounce) can crushed
   pineapple
4½ cups flour
1 cup chopped walnuts
2 teaspoons cinnamon
1½ teaspoons baking soda
½ teaspoon salt

Preheat oven to 350 degrees. Grease 3 (8 x 5 x 3-inch) large loaf pans.

In a large bowl, beat butter with sugar and honey; beat in eggs and vanilla. Mix well. Stir in bananas and pineapple. Stir in flour, walnuts,

cinnamon, baking soda and salt until moistened. Pour into prepared loaf pans. Bake for 1 hour or until toothpick inserted in center comes out clean. Cool 10 minutes. Remove from pan. Makes 3 loaves.

Peanut Butter Oat Muffins

Arlene Ranney, Eureka, Calif.

1¼ cups flour
¾ cups quick-cooking oats
¾ cups brown sugar, firmly
   packed
3 teaspoons baking powder
½ teaspoon salt
Dash ground cinnamon
1 egg
¼ cup peanut butter
1¼ cups milk
½ cup peanuts, chopped
Whipped topping and additional
   peanuts (optional)

Preheat oven to 375 degrees. Grease a muffin tin or line with paper cups.

Combine flour, oats, brown sugar, baking powder, salt and cinnamon.

In another bowl, beat egg, peanut butter and milk until smooth. Stir in dry ingredients until moistened. Fold in peanuts.

Fill muffin cups ¾ full. Bake 15 to 18 minutes or until toothpick inserted into center comes out clean. Cool 5 minutes before removing from pan. Serve with whipped cream and nuts, if desired. Serves 12.

Potato Pudding

Kit Rollins, Cedarburg, Wis.

- **½ pound bacon, diced**
- **2 medium onions, finely diced, divided**
- **1 (30-ounce) package hash brown potatoes, thawed**
- **4 eggs, slightly beaten**
- **1 (12-ounce) can evaporated milk**
- **1 teaspoon salt**
- **⅓ teaspoon pepper**

Preheat oven to 375 degrees.

Cook bacon until done but not crisp; place in 13 x 9-inch baking pan. Sauté 1 onion in drippings. Mix onion with bacon and 1 tablespoon drippings. Mix potatoes, remaining onion, eggs, evaporated milk, salt and pepper. Pour mixture over bacon and onion. Bake 30 minutes. Lower heat to 350 degrees and bake 30 minutes more or until golden brown. Serves 8 to 10.

Can-Can Chinese Casserole

Gwen Campbell, Sterling, Vir.

- **2 (15.5-ounce) cans French-cut green beans, drained**
- **1 (8-ounce) can bean sprouts, drained**
- **1 (5-ounce) can water chestnuts, drained**
- **1 small onion, chopped**
- **3 tablespoons dark soy sauce**
- **1 (10¾-ounce) can cream of mushroom soup**
- **½ cup milk**
- **½ cup Parmesan cheese**
- **1 (3.5-ounce) can French-fried onions**

Preheat oven to 350 degrees. Grease a 2-quart casserole.

Combine green beans, bean sprouts and water chestnuts in prepared casserole; add onion and soy sauce.

Dilute mushroom soup with milk; pour over vegetables. Sprinkle Parmesan cheese over the top. Bake for 20 minutes. Toss French-fried onions over the top. Continue baking 10 minutes. Serves 6.

Mediterranean Beans in Tomato Shells

Eleanor Craycraft, Sequim, Wash.

- **6 large, firm tomatoes**
- **2 tablespoons lemon juice**
- **2 tablespoons olive oil**
- **½ cup black olives, sliced**
- **Garlic salt to taste**
- **Dried oregano to taste**
- **2 (16-ounce) packages French-cut green beans, cooked**

Preheat oven to 350 degrees. Fill shallow, 13 x 9-inch baking dish with ¼ inch of water.

Cut thin slice from top of each tomato; also cut thin slices from bottoms, if necessary, to prevent tipping when standing upright. Carefully remove pulp (a grapefruit spoon is good for this), leaving a ¼-inch shell. Set upside-down on paper towels to drain.

In a small saucepan, mix together the lemon juice, olive oil, olives, garlic salt and oregano; simmer 1 to 2 minutes. Pour hot mixture over hot green beans.

Place tomato shells in prepared baking dish. Fill shells with green bean mixture. Cover pan with aluminum foil and bake for 10 to 15 minutes until hot throughout. Serves 6.

Old Southern Hominy Casserole

Helen Harlos, Ethel, Miss.

> 3 tablespoons butter
> ½ cup chopped green pepper
> 1 small onion, grated
> 3 tablespoons flour
> ½ teaspoon dry mustard
> 1½ cups milk
> Salt and pepper to taste
> ½ cup grated cheese
> 1 (15-ounce) can hominy
> 1 cup chopped ripe olives
> Bread or cracker crumbs for topping
> 1 (3-ounce) can sliced mushrooms (optional)

Preheat oven to 350 degrees. Grease a casserole dish.

Melt butter. Sauté green pepper and onion in butter. Add flour, mustard, milk, salt and pepper. Cook and stir until thickened. Add cheese, hominy, olives and mushrooms (optional). Put in prepared casserole dish. Top with crumbs. Bake 30 minutes. Serves 4 to 6.

Chicken Spaghetti

Helen Harlos, Ethel, Miss.

> 1 (3-pound) chicken
> 1 onion, chopped
> 1 green pepper, chopped

> 1 cup celery, chopped
> 1 pound uncooked spaghetti
> 1 (10¾-ounce) can condensed cream of mushroom soup
> 1 (10¾-ounce) can condensed cream of chicken soup
> 1 pound processed cheese, cubed
> 1 cup cheddar cheese, grated
> Salt and pepper to taste

Preheat oven to 350 degrees. Grease 13 x 9 x 2-inch casserole.

Boil chicken and debone. Reserve liquid. Add onion, green pepper and celery. Cook until tender. Add spaghetti. Continue cooking until tender. Add mushroom soup, chicken soup and processed cheese. Cook until the processed cheese melts. Add salt and pepper to taste. Pour into prepared casserole. At this point, the prepared dish may be frozen.

When ready to bake, top with grated cheddar cheese. Bake 30 minutes. Serves 8 to 10.

Peggy's Chicken

> 4 to 6 skinless chicken breast halves
> Salt and pepper to taste
> 1 can condensed cream of chicken soup
> 2 tablespoons dry onion soup mix
> ½ cup sour cream
> Parmesan cheese

Preheat oven to 350 degrees.

Salt and pepper the chicken breasts. Mix together the soup, soup mixes and sour cream.

Place the chicken breasts into a shallow 2-quart baking dish. Pour soup mixture over the top and sprinkle with Parmesan cheese.

Bake 35 to 40 minutes, or until chicken is cooked through. Serves 4.

Tarragon Chicken Casserole

Eleanor Craycraft, Sequim, Wash.

> 3 ribs celery, thinly sliced
> 1 tablespoon butter
> 1 (10¾-ounce) can condensed cream of chicken soup
> 1 cup half-and-half
> 2 teaspoons dried tarragon, crushed between the palms of your hands
> ⅛ teaspoon pepper

1 (8-ounce) package small bow
   tie pasta, cooked and drained
3 cups cooked chicken, diced
⅓ cup grated Parmesan cheese

Preheat oven to 350 degrees.

In a skillet, cook the celery in butter until tender. Set aside briefly.

In a large bowl, combine soup, half-and-half, tarragon and pepper. Stir in the pasta, chicken and cooked celery. Transfer to an ungreased 2-quart baking dish and sprinkle with Parmesan cheese. Bake, uncovered, 30 minutes or until bubbly and golden. Makes 6 servings.

Baked Chicken Amandine

Margy Mann, St. Louis, Mo.

½ cup flour
2 teaspoons salt
¼ teaspoon pepper
¼ teaspoon poultry seasoning
¼ teaspoon thyme
⅛ teaspoon powdered sage
1 cut-up frying chicken (about 3
   pounds)
3 tablespoons butter
1 (10½-ounce) can condensed
   cream of mushroom soup
1 cup milk
2 tablespoons white dinner wine
   (optional)
⅓ cup slivered almonds, lightly
   toasted

Preheat oven to 325 degrees.

Mix flour, salt, pepper, poultry seasoning, thyme and sage. Roll chicken pieces in flour mixture. Melt butter in skillet; add chicken and brown slowly

until golden. Place in 1½-quart baking dish or casserole. Blend soup and milk in skillet with chicken drippings; add wine, if desired, and pour mixture over chicken. Cover and bake 45 minutes or until chicken is tender. Remove cover last 10 minutes of baking time and sprinkle chicken with almonds. Serves 8.

Meal in Bread

Carol Mentze, San Marcos, Calif.

1 pound ground beef
1 small onion, chopped
1 (16-ounce) package frozen
   vegetable mixture
1 loaf frozen bread dough, thawed
Butter
12 ounces cheese of choice

Preheat oven to 375 degrees.

Brown beef with onion. Cool. Cook vegetables, drain, then cool. Cut bread dough in half and roll out both halves to ¼-inch thick rectangles. Brush with melted butter.

Put half of the meat mixture on each rectangle. Put half of the vegetable mixture on each rectangle. Add cheese. Roll up so all is enclosed in bread. Pinch shut. Put sealed edges down on cookie sheet. Brush top with melted butter. Cut 3 slits on top for steam to escape. Bake for 20 to 25 minutes. Serves 4 to 6. ▶

Spicy Black-Eyed Peas

Lisa Langston, Conroe, Texas

- **1 pound lean ground beef**
- **1 onion, chopped**
- **½ cup chopped celery**
- **½ bell pepper, chopped**
- **1 can tomatoes**
- **2 (14.5-ounce) cans black-eyed peas, rinsed and drained**
- **1 (2.25-ounce) can chopped black olives, optional**
- **1 teaspoon salt**
- **1 teaspoon black pepper**
- **Cooked rice, optional**

Cook ground beef, onion, celery and bell pepper until done. Drain any fat. Combine ground beef mixture, tomatoes, black-eyed peas, olives, salt and pepper in large pot. Bring to boil. Lower heat to medium and cook 30 minutes. Serve with rice, if desired. Serves 6 to 8.

Tortilla Pizzas

Even the kids can make this Mexican-inspired pizza.

- **4 (10-inch) flour tortillas**
- **¾ pound ground beef**
- **1 small sweet red pepper, diced small**
- **½ teaspoon ground cumin**
- **1 cup salsa**
- **1⅔ cups shredded Monterey Jack and Cheddar cheese mix**
- **4 green onions, sliced**
- **¼ cup chopped cilantro**
- **2 tablespoons grated Parmesan cheese**

Preheat oven to 450 degrees.
Place tortillas in one layer on baking sheet that has been sprayed with non-stick coating.
Brown ground beef and red pepper over medium heat in nonstick skillet for 8 minutes or until beef is no longer pink. Drain excess liquid from skillet. Stir in cumin and salsa.
Spread ½ cup cheese mix on each tortilla. Divide beef mixture equally and spread over cheese on each tortilla. Sprinkle with green onions and cilantro. Top each with remaining cheese mixture and Parmesan cheese.
Bake in lower part of oven for 8 to 10 minutes or until cheese is bubbly. Serves 4.

Easy Baked Fish

Margy Mann, St. Louis, Mo.

- **1 pound fish fillets or steaks (¾ to 1½ inches thick) such as cod or halibut, cut into serving-size pieces**
- **2 tablespoons cornmeal**
- **2 tablespoons flour**
- **¼ teaspoon paprika**
- **Dash of salt**
- **Dash of pepper**
- **1 tablespoon oil**
- **1 tablespoon grated Parmesan cheese**

Preheat oven to 425 degrees.
Pat fish dry with paper towels. Combine cornmeal, flour, paprika, salt and pepper in flat dish. Place oil in baking dish; heat in oven for 1 minute.
Dredge fish in cornmeal mixture; shake off excess. Place in 13 x 9-inch baking dish and turn to coat with oil. Arrange fish pieces 1 inch apart. Sprinkle with Parmesan cheese. Bake in preheated oven, allowing 10 minutes per inch thickness, measured at thickest part. When done, fish should flake when tested with a fork. Serves 4.

Pumpkin Custards

Galelah Dowell, Fairland, Okla.

   3 eggs, slightly beaten
   1 (15-ounce) can pumpkin
   1½ cups whipping cream, half-
     and-half, or light cream
   ⅔ cup packed brown sugar
   1 teaspoon pumpkin pie spice
   ½ teaspoon salt
   ⅔ cup coarsely chopped pecans,
     toasted
   ¼ cup maple syrup

Preheat oven to 350 degrees.

In a large mixing bowl combine eggs, pumpkin, cream, brown sugar, pumpkin pie spice and salt. Mix well with a whisk. Divide mixture among 8 (6-ounce) custard cups. Place in a roasting pan. Pour hot water into pan around custard cups to a depth of 1 inch. Bake for 45 to 55 minutes or until set. Remove cups from water. Cool slightly on a wire rack.

In a small bowl, combine chopped, toasted pecans and maple syrup; spoon on top of warm custards. Serve warm or chilled. Serves 8.

Chocolate Caramel Pecan Pie

Galelah Dowell, Fairland, Okla.

   3 cups pecan pieces, divided
   ¼ cup sugar
   ¼ cup butter, melted
   1 (14-ounce) package caramels
   ⅔ cup whipping cream, divided
   1 (18-square) package semisweet
     baking chocolate
   ¼ cup confectioners' sugar
   ½ teaspoon vanilla

Preheat oven to 350 degrees.

Place 2 cups pecan pieces in food processor; cover. Process until finely ground, using pulsing action. Mix with sugar and butter. Press into 9-inch pie plate. Bake 12 minutes or until lightly browned. Cool completely.

Microwave caramels and ⅓ cup whipping cream in a microwavable bowl on high for 3 minutes or until caramels are melted, stirring after each minute. Pour into crust. Chop remaining 1 cup pecans and sprinkle over pie.

Place chocolate, remaining whipping cream, confectioners' sugar and vanilla in saucepan. Cook and stir on low heat just until chocolate is melted. Pour over pie and gently spread. Refrigerate at least 2 hours. Serves 10.

Sugar Cream Pie

Joye Gardenour, Bluffton, Ind.

   1 (9-inch) pie crust (unbaked)
   1 cup sugar
   ½ cup brown sugar
   ½ cup flour
   2 tablespoons butter
   1 cup boiling water
   ½ pint whipping cream
   Cinnamon
   Nutmeg

Preheat oven to 450 degrees.

Mix sugar, brown sugar and flour. Chop butter and put in sugar mixture. Pour boiling water over mixture and mix until butter is melted. Blend in cream.

Pour into unbaked pie shell and sprinkle with cinnamon and nutmeg. Bake for 10 minutes. Reduce heat to 350 degrees and bake for 30 minutes more. Serves 8.

Cinnamon Roll Pudding

Carolyn Hayes, Johnston City, Ill.

2 to 3 large cinnamon rolls (torn
   to make 3 cups)
2 large eggs, slightly beaten
1½ cups milk
¾ cup sugar
1 teaspoon vanilla extract
¼ cup butter, melted
2 tablespoons honey
Caramel ice cream topping

Preheat oven to 300 degrees.
Lightly grease a 1-quart baking dish.
   Spread torn rolls into prepared dish.
   Combine eggs and milk. Stir in
sugar and vanilla extract, then pour
over rolls.
   Combine butter and honey. Pour
over roll mixture. Bake for 1 hour or
until golden. Serve with caramel ice
cream topping. Serves 4 to 6.

Crackerjack Cookies

Linda Nichols, Steubenville, Ohio

1 cup butter
1 cup sugar
1 cup brown sugar
2 eggs
2 teaspoons vanilla

2 cups crisp rice cereal
2 cups rolled oats
1½ cups flour
1 cup coconut
1 teaspoon baking powder
1 teaspoon baking soda

Preheat oven to 350 degrees.
Cream butter. Add sugar, brown
sugar, eggs and vanilla and cream well.
   Combine cereal, oats, flour, coconut, baking powder and baking soda
and add to wet mixture. Drop by teaspoonfuls onto greased cookie sheets.
   Bake for 10 to 12 minutes until
nicely browned. Makes about 6 dozen
cookies.

Glazed Citrus Cake
Cake

1 (18.25-ounce) yellow cake mix
¾ cup oil
¾ cup water
1 (3.4-ounce) package instant
   lemon pudding mix
4 eggs

Glaze

2 cups confectioners' sugar
⅓ cup orange juice
2 tablespoons melted butter
2 tablespoons water

Preheat oven to 350 degrees. Grease
and flour bundt pan.
   Combine cake mix, oil, ¾ cup water
and pudding mix; beat 2 minutes. Add
eggs 1 at a time. Beat thoroughly. Pour
into prepared pan.
   Bake 40 minutes. While still warm,
prick entire top with a toothpick.
   For glaze, combine confectioners'
sugar, orange juice, butter and water.
Pour glaze over top of entire cake.
Serves 12.

Peanut Butter S'More Tarts

Karen Farr, Warsaw, Mo.

1 cup (6 ounces) semisweet
   chocolate pieces
½ cup peanut butter
1½ cups tiny marshmallows
½ cup chopped peanuts
1 (4-ounce) package graham
   cracker tart shells (6 per
   package)

In small saucepan, melt chocolate
pieces over low heat, stirring constantly.

Remove from heat. Stir in peanut butter until smooth. Stir in marshmallows and peanuts. Spoon into tart shells. Cover; chill at least 2 hours or up to 24 hours. Let stand at room temperature for 30 minutes before serving. Serves 6.

Fresh Peach Cobbler

Arlene Ranney, Eureka, Calif.

- **4 peaches with peel, pitted and thinly sliced**
- **3 tablespoons sugar**
- **2 teaspoons cornstarch**
- **½ teaspoon cinnamon**
- **½ cup cold water**
- **½ cup multigrain pancake and waffle mix**
- **1 tablespoon peanut oil**
- **1 tablespoon honey**
- **2 tablespoons water**

Preheat oven to 400 degrees. Arrange peach slices in an 8 x 8 x 2-inch baking pan. Set aside.

In small saucepan, combine sugar, cornstarch and cinnamon. Stir until blended. Stir in ½ cup water until cornstarch is dissolved. Bring to boil over medium heat and cook, stirring constantly, for about 2 minutes or until thick. Pour over peaches.

In small bowl, combine pancake mix, oil, honey, and 2 tablespoons water. Stir just until blended. Crumble topping over peaches to form 4 biscuits. Bake 15 to 20 minutes or until crisp and browned. Serve warm or at room temperature. Serves 4. ■

Speedy Beef 'n' Bean Supper

To get this meal on the table in under 30 minutes, follow these easy steps:

1. Preheat the oven to 450 degrees.

2. Section grapefruit and slice avocado; combine and set aside.

3. Make Speedy Beef & Beans and let simmer while you complete meal.

4. Make Baking Powder Biscuits.

5. Remove biscuits from oven, toss Avocado Salad and serve dinner.

Avocado Salad
Light and refreshing, citrus and avocado go well together.

Assorted greens
1 grapefruit, sectioned
1 avocado, sliced, dipped in lemon or grapefruit juice and salted
½ sweet onion, thinly sliced, separated into rings
French dressing to taste
Thyme

Toss greens, grapefruit sections, avocado slices and sweet onion with French dressing. Sprinkle a small amount of thyme over salad. Serves 4.

Joseph Kurtz, Reading, Pa.

Speedy Beef & Beans
From start to finish, this satisfying entrée can be on the table in 15 minutes.

½ to 1 pound hamburger
1 small onion, diced
1 (15-ounce) can pork and beans
¼ to ½ cup ketchup
¼ cup brown sugar

Brown hamburger and onion. Drain excess fat, if necessary. Add pork and beans, ketchup and brown sugar to meat and onions. Heat thoroughly. Serves 4.

Dorothy Brummer, Albert City, Iowa

Baking Powder Biscuits
Light and fluffy—these biscuits are as speedy as using a mix and, oh, so good.

2 cups sifted flour
4 teaspoons shortening
5 teaspoons baking powder
½ teaspoon salt
1 cup milk

Preheat oven to 450 degrees.
Mix together flour, shortening, baking powder, salt and milk; beat well. Roll out on a floured board and cut out with a small biscuit cutter. Bake for 11 minutes. Makes 12 biscuits. ■

Louise M. Krieger, Youngtown, Ariz.

Busy Day Beef Dinners

Slow Cooker Sloppy Joes

- 2 pounds hamburger
- 1 large onion, chopped
- 2 tablespoons chili powder
- 2 (15½-ounce) cans regular or Mexican-style canned sloppy joe sauce (if using Mexican style, omit chili powder)

Brown hamburger; drain. Put cooked hamburger, onion, chili powder and sloppy joe sauce into slow cooker. Cook 3 to 4 hours on low heat. Serves 8 to 10.

Joseph Kurtz, Reading, Pa.

Country Stew

- 2 pounds stew meat, cut in 1-inch cubes
- 1 (17-ounce) can peas
- 1 (10-ounce) can tomato soup, undiluted
- 1 cup carrots, sliced
- 1 large potato, cubed
- 2 onions, sliced
- 1⅓ cups water
- 1 bay leaf
- 1 teaspoon salt
- Dash of pepper

Combine meat, peas, tomato soup, carrots, potato, onions, water, bay leaf, salt and pepper in a slow cooker. Cover and cook on low setting 8 to 10 hours. Serves 6 to 8. ■

Dottie Luttrell, Enid, Miss.

Helpful Tips

- It's important to brown and thoroughly cook ground beef before putting in a slow cooker; otherwise, you're inviting bacterial growth.
- Save on cleanup time by spraying the inner container of the slow cooker with non-stick cooking spray before adding any ingredients.

Shown on this page, clockwise from the top; Meatballs in a Garden Vegetable Sauce (page 203), Spinach, Parsley & Pecan Pesto (page 201) and Red Onion Relish (page 203).

Harvest Your Herb Garden

Imagine the fragrant aromas of sauce bubbling when snow falls and winds howl. It will be a sweet reminder of summer.

By Pat Eby

In September, when nights are a tad nippy and the days crisp, think about stocking the freezer with savory spaghetti sauces, relishes and pestos. Harvesting your herb garden before first frost provides just the right incentive to get cooking.

Don't worry if you didn't grow your own. Fresh basils, parsley, thyme, oregano and chives are readily available. I like to use dried herbs, too, like rosemary, marjoram and fennel for taste and convenience. Garlic, harvested in July, is firm and fresh in fall. Bushels of tomatoes, peppers of all colors, onions and summer squashes wait at farmers' markets and roadside stands for good cooks to put by.

Fall is the time to plant garlic for next summer. A single clove develops into a full head of garlic by June. However, planting cloves from the grocery store won't yield good results. Buy garlic from a reputable nursery or by mail order for best results. Maybe you will want to plan an herb garden for next spring.

Here are some tips for successful herb culture. Locate your herb garden in a sunny, well-drained spot. Like most people, herbs don't like wet feet. Think about a location close to your kitchen door. A spot close to the house helps some herbs over-winter to the following spring. And fresh herb flavors are just a short walk from the door.

Spinach, Parsley & Pecan Pesto

The clean taste of spinach and parsley shines through in this variation of classic pesto. Unlike basil leaves, which can turn dark in the freezer, the spinach retains its green color when thawed.

**3 cups spinach leaves (stem and
  devein large leaves)**
**1 cup fresh flat-leaf Italian
  parsley leaves**
6 cloves Roasted Garlic
1 cup coarsely chopped pecans
1 cup grated Parmesan cheese
¾ cup extra-virgin olive oil

Toss spinach, parsley, garlic, pecans and Parmesan cheese together in a mixing bowl.

Blend mixed ingredients to a coarse paste in a food processor.

Remove paste from food processor to mixing bowl.

Using a wooden spoon, add olive oil and mix. Makes 1 quart.

To freeze: Pack the pesto in small screw-top jars. Pour a thin layer of olive oil on top to keep it from drying out. Seal jars and refrigerate for up to 4 days or freeze for up to 1 month.

See serving suggestions on page 202. ▶

Roasted Garlic

This is the ultimate dish for the garlic lover. Used as a flavoring in sauces, it has a milder flavor than garlic sautéed in a pan.

**6 to 8 whole, firm heads
  of garlic**
¼ cup olive oil
**½ cup low-sodium canned
  chicken broth**
**½ teaspoon ground black
  pepper**
½ teaspoon kosher salt

Preheat oven to 350 degrees.
Starting at the center of the garlic head, remove as much as you can of the papery skin. The head will look like a flower of cloves.

Arrange the heads in a small ovenproof baking dish. They can be touching.

If the dish has a lid, use it. If not, use aluminum foil to cover.

Baste the garlic with the broth and oil mixture every 15 minutes. Bake for 1 hour or until the garlic cloves are soft.

Let cool before handling. The fragrant cloves can be squeezed from their skins. Spread directly on bread, or use roasted garlic for a milder flavor in any of the sauces. Serves 12.

Pesto Serving Suggestions:

Pesto Pasta: Toss pesto with hot pasta. Add a little of the pasta cooking water to moisten, if needed.

Herbed Butter: Mix a spoonful of pesto into softened butter. Great tossed with green beans or spread on warm bread.

Vegetable Soup: Add a spoonful of pesto to each bowl.

Quick Olive Oil, Garlic & Pine Nut Sauce

Try this pasta and sauce for a quick weekday-dinner main dish or for a superb side dish with chicken picatta.

¼ cup olive oil, extra-virgin or light
6 cloves Roasted Garlic, mashed
1 cup low-sodium chicken broth
½ cup pine nuts
½ cup finely chopped flat-leaf Italian parsley
1 teaspoon crushed red pepper flakes
Capellini or angel hair pasta
Parmesan cheese, coarsely grated
Salt and white pepper to taste

Heat olive oil over medium heat in 8-inch nonstick skillet.

Add roasted garlic and chicken broth. Stir to mix. Bring to a low boil.

Add pine nuts, parsley and red pepper flakes. Reduce heat to low and simmer 15 minutes.

Meanwhile, cook pasta, then drain.

Toss together pasta and sauce. Add Parmesan cheese, salt and pepper to taste. Serve in warmed pasta bowls. Makes 8 servings.

Note: *This sauce is best made fresh and served immediately.*

Basic Tomato Sauce

This simple sauce can be ready in a little over an hour. It's especially speedy when you use canned tomatoes. Multiply the recipe and keep plenty on hand in the freezer to use in the recipes on pages 202 and 203.

¼ cup olive oil
4 medium sweet white onions, coarsely chopped
6 cloves of Roasted Garlic, mashed
3 pounds fresh plum tomatoes or 2 (28-ounce) cans tomatoes
1 cup dry red wine or 1 cup low-sodium beef broth
1 tablespoon sugar
2 tablespoons butter
Salt and pepper to taste

Heat olive oil in a large heavy pot over medium-high heat. Cook onion for 15 minutes, until translucent. Add garlic and cook for 10 minutes.

Meanwhile, peel, seed and coarsely chop the plum tomatoes, reserving the juices (or coarsely chop the canned tomatoes, reserving juices).

To onions, add tomatoes with juices, wine or broth, and sugar. Simmer for 30 to 40 minutes.

Stir in butter. Add salt and pepper. Makes 2 quarts.

To freeze: Cool sauce completely. Pack in pint or quart-size freezer containers. Freeze up to 10 to 12 months.

Variation

Almost anything can be added to this great basic sauce. Here is one idea to try:

Hearty Ham

Add ½ pound ham or Canadian bacon, cut into ½-inch cubes, along with the garlic.

Sausage & Garbanzo Sauce

Classic Italian additions take the simple sauce from tasty to wow!

1 pound Italian sausage, casings removed
1 cup drained, canned garbanzo beans
1 cup chopped flat-leaf Italian parsley
1 teaspoon fennel seeds
Basic Tomato Sauce

Brown sausage in a nonstick 8-inch skillet, using a spatula to break meat into coarse crumbles. Add sausage, garbanzo

beans, parsley and fennel seeds to the cooked Basic Tomato Sauce. Simmer 10 minutes longer. Serve this sauce over hearty pasta like rigatoni, penne or bow ties. Serves 6 to 8.

Meatballs in a Garden Vegetable Sauce

A healthy, nutritious dish disguised as comfort food, these spicy meatballs in a tomato-y vegetable sauce bring good taste and good nutrition to the table.

Meatballs
    1 pound lean ground beef
    1 pound ground pork, veal or turkey
    1 cup bread crumbs
    1 medium yellow onion, finely chopped
    1 egg
    ½ cup milk
    1 tablespoon dried parsley
    1 teaspoon dried oregano
    1 teaspoon dried basil
    1 teaspoon dried marjoram
    1 teaspoon salt
    ½ teaspoon garlic powder
    ½ teaspoon pepper

Vegetable Sauce
    2 tablespoons olive oil
    1 green pepper, chopped in ½-inch pieces
    1 small eggplant, peeled, seeded and cubed in ½-inch pieces
    1 medium zucchini, cut in half lengthwise then sliced into ⅜-inch pieces
    5 cups Basic Tomato Sauce

For meatballs, preheat oven to 350 degrees.

Combine meats, bread crumbs, onion, egg, milk, parsley, oregano, basil, marjoram, salt, garlic powder and pepper in a large mixing bowl; mix thoroughly.

Shape into balls 2 inches in diameter. Brown lightly in a nonstick skillet.

Place meatballs in 13 x 9-inch pan. Bake for 35 minutes, until well done.

Meanwhile, start cooking sauce. Heat oil in a 4-quart pot over medium-high heat. Add green pepper, eggplant and zucchini. Cook, stirring, for 5 to 10 minutes. Add tomato sauce and simmer over medium-low heat for 15 minutes.

Add meatballs and simmer for 10 to 15 minutes. Serves 6 to 8.

Serve over spaghetti or macaroni. Serve 6 to 8.

Jumbo Spinach & Cheese-Stuffed Shells
Spinach makes these shells healthful and pleasing to your family.

    1 (10-ounce) package frozen chopped spinach, thawed and drained
    2 cups reduced-fat ricotta cheese
    2 cups shredded mozzarella cheese
    2 shallots or 4 green onions, chopped
    ¼ cup chopped parsley
    1 tablespoon dried basil
    1 tablespoon marjoram
    ¼ teaspoon nutmeg (optional)
    1½ cups coarsely grated Parmesan cheese, divided

    24 jumbo pasta shells, cooked and drained
    5 cups Basic Tomato Sauce

Preheat oven to 350 degrees. Butter a 13 x 9-inch ovenproof baking dish.

Mix spinach, ricotta, mozzarella cheese, shallots or green onion, parsley, basil, marjoram, nutmeg and 1 cup of the Parmesan cheese. Stuff cooked shells with 3 to 4 rounded tablespoons of the cheese mixture.

Arrange shells in prepared dish, cheese side up.

Pour sauce over shells. Sprinkle with remaining ½ cup Parmesan cheese. Bake for 35 to 50 minutes. Serves 12.

Red Onion Relish
This versatile relish can be a side dish or used as a topping on pizza, bruschetta or focaccia.

    4 tablespoons olive oil
    2 tablespoons unsalted butter
    3 large red onions, cut in julienne slivers
    2 tablespoons raspberry vinegar
    1 teaspoon sugar
    ½ teaspoon salt
    ⅛ teaspoon ground black pepper
    Zest of one orange (optional)

Heat olive oil and butter in a 3-quart saucepan over low heat. Add onions and cook until they are translucent and wilted, about 45 minutes, stirring occasionally.

Add the raspberry vinegar, sugar, salt and pepper. Cook 10 minutes.

Add orange zest, if desired, and cook 5 minutes longer. Makes 2½ to 3 cups. ■

Baked Pasta, Please!

Macaroni Mousse Casserole

- **2 cups macaroni, cooked**
- **1 cup bread crumbs**
- **¼ cup melted butter**
- **3 eggs, beaten**
- **1 tablespoon chopped onion**
- **1 tablespoon chopped bell pepper**
- **1 tablespoon snipped parsley**
- **1½ cups grated sharp cheddar cheese**
- **Salt and pepper to taste**
- **⅛ teaspoon red pepper**
- **¼ cup crushed cornflakes or extra bread crumbs, for topping**

Preheat oven to 350 degrees. Grease a glass 8 x 8-inch baking dish.

Mix together macaroni, bread crumbs, butter, eggs, onion, bell pepper, parsley, cheese, salt, pepper and red pepper. Pour into prepared dish. Sprinkle with cornflakes.

Place baking dish into a large baking pan. Pour boiling water about 1½ inches deep into outer pan. Bake for 1 hour. Serves 4. ■

Rita Kitsteiner, Tucson, Ariz.

How to Save on Food

Bypass those expensive packages of shredded cheddar and choose a big block of store-brand cheese instead. The savings are substantial—and it takes only a minute to shred the cheese with a box grater. Store leftover cheese in a resealable plastic bag; it should keep for several weeks. For even longer storage, wrap cheese in a paper towel dampened with vinegar (which inhibits mold) before placing in the bag.

Halloween Fun!

Devil Dogs
Cookie

- ½ cup shortening
- 1 cup sugar
- ½ cup unsweetened cocoa powder
- 2 cups flour
- 1½ teaspoons baking powder
- 1 cup milk
- 1 teaspoon vanilla

Filling

- ½ cup butter
- ½ teaspoon vanilla
- 1⅓ cups confectioners' sugar
- ½ (7-ounce) jar marshmallow créme
- Red and yellow food coloring
- Halloween nonpareils (optional)

Preheat oven to 425 degrees.

Cream together shortening and sugar. Add cocoa powder; beat well.

Sift together flour and baking powder. Add to cocoa powder mixture alternately with milk. Mix well. Add vanilla. Drop by teaspoonfuls onto a greased cookie sheet. Flatten a little. Bake for 5 to 7 minutes.

For filling, beat together butter, vanilla, confectioners' sugar and marshmallow créme. Tint filling orange using red and yellow food coloring. Spread on cookie. Top with another cookie. Decorate edges with optional nonpareils.

Kathy Rooney, Point Pleasant, N.J.

Pumpkin Cookies

- 1 cup sugar
- 1 cup shortening
- 1 cup pumpkin
- 1 egg
- 1 teaspoon vanilla
- 2 cups flour
- 1 teaspoon baking soda
- 1 teaspoon baking powder
- 1 teaspoon salt
- 2 teaspoons cinnamon
- ½ cup chopped raisins
- Orange and brown frosting (optional)

Preheat oven to 350 degrees.

Cream sugar and shortening. Add pumpkin, egg and vanilla. Sift together flour, baking soda, baking powder, salt and cinnamon. Add to mixture. Stir in raisins. Drop by teaspoonfuls onto greased cookie sheet, 2 inches apart. Bake 10 to 12 minutes. May be frosted with orange and brown frosting to make Halloween pumpkins. Makes 2 dozen. ■

Louise M. Krieger, Youngtown, Ariz.

After-School Snacks

Everyone needs an energy boost now and then. Hooray for tasty snacks!

Shown on this page: Pizza Muffins (page 206) and Sugar & Spice Raisin Popcorn (page 206).

Active kids with fast metabolisms and small-size tummies need a between-meal pick-me-up. It can be up to six hours between school lunch and the time the family sits down to dinner. Active kids need a snack to give them energy for after-school activities, homework and having fun.

It's easy to equate snacking with junk food, but it doesn't have to be that way. If all the choices you give them are reasonably nutritious, then everybody's happy!

Get them involved in the cooking. Turn eating into an interactive experience. These are just some of the snacks our readers have contributed over the years.

Sugar & Spice Raisin Popcorn

This sweet and spicy popcorn is as good as the store-bought kind!

- ¼ cup butter
- 1 tablespoon brown sugar
- 1 teaspoon cinnamon
- 1 teaspoon nutmeg
- 1½ cups golden or dark raisins
- ¼ cup walnuts
- ¼ cup salted peanuts
- 8 cups popped corn

In small saucepan over low heat, melt butter with brown sugar, cinnamon and nutmeg.

In large bowl, combine raisins, walnuts and peanuts. Toss with butter mixture. Add popped corn. Toss to coat evenly. Makes 10 cups.

Hazel Hullinger, Decatur, Ill.

Pizza Muffins

Imagine a savory muffin that tastes like pizza!

- 2 tablespoons olive oil
- ¼ cup chopped onions
- 1 clove garlic, minced
- 1 egg, beaten
- 1 cup tomato juice
- 2 cups flour
- 2¾ teaspoons baking powder
- ¾ teaspoon salt
- 1 teaspoon dried oregano
- 1 cup finely diced mozzarella cheese
- ¼ cup finely diced pepperoni
- ½ cup grated Parmesan cheese or Romano cheese

Preheat oven to 400 degrees. Oil bottoms of muffin cups.

Heat olive oil in skillet. Sauté onions and garlic until soft. In bowl, combine onion mixture, egg and tomato juice. In another bowl, combine flour, baking powder, salt, oregano, mozzarella cheese and pepperoni.

Quickly stir wet ingredients into dry ingredients, just until moistened. Spoon into prepared cups. Sprinkle Parmesan or Romano cheese on top. Bake for 20 minutes or until done. Serve hot. Makes 1½ to 2 dozen.

Arlene Ranney, Eureka, Calif.

Apple Wraps

Get the kids involved in dipping and folding the biscuits for this delicious apple treat.

  ½ cup sugar
  1 teaspoon cinnamon
  1 (10-count) tube buttermilk
    biscuit dough
  3 tablespoons butter, melted
  2 apples, peeled and thinly sliced
  ½ cup orange juice

Preheat oven to 350 degrees. Grease 8 x 8 x 2-inch baking pan.

Combine sugar and cinnamon. Mix well. Dip biscuits into butter. Coat with cinnamon-sugar mixture. Arrange 3 apple slices in center of each biscuit Fold to enclose filling. Seal edges. Arrange in prepared pan. Sprinkle remaining cinnamon-sugar mixture over biscuits. Drizzle orange juice over top. Bake for 30 minutes, or until done. Serve warm. Makes 10 wraps.

Denise Hansen, Jackson, Minn.

Butterscotch Brownies

Everyone likes a little dessert, and these brownies deliver.

Brownies

  ¼ cup butter
  ¾ cup brown sugar
  2 eggs
  1 teaspoon vanilla
  ¾ cup flour
  1 teaspoon baking powder
  ½ teaspoon salt
  ½ cup walnuts

Topping

  ¼ cup butter
  ½ cup brown sugar
  1 cup flaked coconut

Preheat oven to 350 degrees. Grease 8 x 8 x 2-inch baking pan.

For brownies, melt butter. Add brown sugar. Add eggs and vanilla. Add flour, baking powder, salt and walnuts. Mix well. Pour into prepared pan. Bake for 30 minutes or until done.

For topping, set oven to broil Melt butter. Add brown sugar and coconut. Spread over top of brownies. Broil 3 inches from heat for 1½ minutes. Makes 16.

Jane Weimann, Woodstock, Conn.

Yummy Snack Mix

Keep this on hand for any time you get the munchies!

  4 cups rice cereal squares
  2 cups small pretzels or corn
    chips
  1 cup candy-coated chocolate
    pieces
  1 cup dark raisins
  1 cup golden raisins
  1 cup dried banana chips

In large bowl, combine cereal, pretzels, chocolate pieces, raisins and banana chips. Mix well. Makes 10 cups.

Linda Nichols, Steubenville, Ohio

Chewy Cereal Squares

Breakfast cereal never tasted so good. Eat it for an on-the-go breakfast.

  5 cups cornflakes
  3 cups crisp rice cereal
  1 cup salted peanuts
  1 cup flaked coconut
  ½ cup butter
  1 cup sugar
  1 cup light corn syrup
  ½ cup half-and-half

Grease 15 x 10 x 1-inch jelly-roll pan.

In large bowl, combine cornflakes, rice cereal, peanuts and coconut.

In medium saucepan, melt butter. Stir in sugar, corn syrup and half-and-half. Cook over medium heat to soft-ball stage (234 degrees), stirring occasionally. Pour over cornflake mixture. Toss until well coated. Spread in prepared pan. Cool completely. Cut into squares. Makes 3 dozen. ∎

Sue Wadsworth, Lufkin, Texas

For Meat & Potato Lovers

MENU

"My Own" Meat Loaves

Garlic Potatoes

Baked Asparagus

Butterscotch Nut Squares

"My Own" Meat Loaves

½ pound ground chuck

⅓ cup fine dry bread crumbs

1 tablespoon finely chopped onion

¼ teaspoon salt

Dash of pepper

3 tablespoons milk

¼ cup favorite barbecue sauce

Preheat oven to 400 degrees. Grease a broiler pan.

Combine ground chuck, bread crumbs, onion, salt, pepper and milk; stir until mixture is well blended. Shape into 2 loaves and place on rack of greased broiler pan. Spoon barbecue sauce on top.

Bake for 25 to 30 minutes. Serve hot. Makes 2 loaves.

Edna Askins, Greenville, Texas

Garlic Potatoes

2 large baking potatoes, peeled and cubed
1 stalk celery, finely chopped
½ small onion
1 to 2 cloves garlic, minced
¼ cup butter, melted
1½ tablespoons chopped fresh parsley
¼ teaspoon salt
¼ teaspoon pepper

Preheat oven to 400 degrees. Lightly grease a 12 x 8 x 2-inch baking dish.

Combine potatoes, celery, onion, garlic, butter, parsley, salt and pepper. Place in prepared dish. Bake 45 to 50 minutes or until tender.

Baked Asparagus

16 to 20 asparagus spears
2 slices bacon
Salt and pepper to taste
Extra-virgin olive oil, as needed
Chives, as needed

Preheat oven to 400 degrees.
Remove hard ends from asparagus. Make into bundles of 8 to 10 spears. Wrap bacon around bundles from ends up. Put on grill pan. Season with salt and pepper. Sprinkle with olive oil. Bake for 20 minutes. Sprinkle with chopped chives when served.

Carolyn Hayes. Elba, N.Y.

Butterscotch Nut Squares

These cakelike treats are excellent made with black walnuts.

¼ cup butter
1 cup brown sugar
½ teaspoon vanilla
1 large egg
½ cup flour
½ teaspoon baking powder
¼ teaspoon salt
½ cup chopped black walnuts or pecans

Preheat oven to 350 degrees. Line an 8 x 8 x 2-inch pan with foil.

Easy Serving

When making bar cookies, lining the pan with foil not only makes cleanup easier, it makes serving a snap! Use enough foil so that some extends beyond two opposite sides of the pan. After you've removed the baked treats from the oven and the pan has cooled for a few minutes, you can easily lift out the cookies using the foil "handles" Then simply turn over onto a cutting board, remove the foil and cut into squares.

In a medium saucepan, melt butter over low heat. Add brown sugar and stir to mix; remove from heat.

Stir in vanilla; add egg and beat well with a fork. Add flour, baking powder, salt and walnuts; mix until flour disappears.

Spread in prepared pan. Bake until set, 20 to 25 minutes. Cool slightly in pan on rack before serving. ■

November/December 2005

Savory Holiday Side Dishes

Turkey Dressing

Our holiday tradition always includes "dressing" rather than stuffing. Part of our family loves oysters; part hates them, so we have two kinds of dressing. The recipes follow. Hope they help "dress up" your next holiday function.

1 loaf white bread
2 tablespoons butter
1 onion, chopped
1 cup chopped celery
4 to 5 cups chicken or turkey
  broth, depending on how moist
  you like the dressing
2 large eggs, beaten
2 teaspoons poultry seasoning

The day before: Tear bread into approximately 3 x 3-inch pieces and put in a large bowl or pan to dry out. Stir throughout the day to get even drying.

The day of use: Preheat oven to 350 degrees. Grease a 13 x 9-inch pan.

Melt butter in medium sauté pan. Sauté onions and celery until soft. Set aside.

Bring broth to a boil. Add to dried bread 1 cup at a time and stir. Add onions, celery, beaten eggs, and poultry seasoning to bread mixture. Put in prepared pan and bake uncovered for 35 to 45 minutes. Serves 8 to 10.

Larrinda Bass, Acworth, Ga.

Broccoli Casserole

We are a family of vegetable lovers; however, we like them in a variety of ways. This Broccoli Casserole has been a highlight of family gatherings for years. Even the little ones like it!

2 (16-ounce) packages frozen
  chopped broccoli
1 (16-ounce) package frozen
  lima beans
1 can sliced water chestnuts
1 can cream of mushroom soup
1 package dry onion soup mix
1 (8-ounce) container sour cream
½ cup butter or margarine,
  melted
2 cups crisp rice cereal

Preheat oven to 350 degrees.

Cook broccoli and lima beans according to package directions. Place in a 2½-quart baking dish. Layer water chestnuts on top of vegetables. In a separate bowl, combine mushroom soup, onion soup mix, and sour cream. Spread on top of water chestnuts. Melt butter; combine with rice cereal. Place on top of soup mixture. Bake for 30 minutes. Serves 8 to 10. ■

Larrinda Bass, Acworth, Ga.

Thanksgiving Feast

It's the trimmings that make the turkey—and this Thanksgiving we've gathered all your favorites!

With offerings like Festive Cranberry Stuffing, Root Vegetable Medley, and Apple Pecan Tart, you could say some holiday traditions get better with time. And while golden roast turkey is still the centerpiece of the feast, it's the side dishes that truly showcase the talents of the cook. Our collection of easy casseroles and simple sweets are all you'll need to set a lavish spread on Turkey Day. So whether you grace the bird with Sweet Potato Pone or whipped Potato Casserole, or indulge friends and family with Pumpkin Cake with fluffy cream cheese icing, these delightful recipes will make your holiday dinner nothing less than memorable.

Sweet Potato Pone

This easy one-bowl casserole gets its inspiration from the Southern classic corn pone. Grated sweet potatoes and chopped pecans replace the usual cornmeal.

- **2½ cups grated raw sweet potato**
- **1 cup sugar**
- **2 eggs, well beaten**
- **1 teaspoon nutmeg**
- **1 cup finely chopped pecans**
- **½ teaspoon cinnamon**
- **¾ cup milk**
- **2 tablespoons butter**

Preheat oven to 350 degrees.
Blend sweet potatoes, sugar, eggs, nutmeg, pecans, cinnamon and milk. Place in a 2-quart baking dish. Top with butter. Bake 45 minutes. Serves 6.

Jane Gregg, Bluffton, Ind.

Potato Casserole

Three kinds of cheese transform ordinary mashed potatoes into a scrumptious side dish that's sure to be a hit with the kids. Chopped green onions, bacon bits or diced ham are optional stir-ins—so add any or all of them depending on the rest of your menu.

- **8 to 9 medium potatoes**
- **½ cup milk**
- **¼ cup butter**
- **Garlic powder to taste**
- **Salt and pepper to taste**
- **4 ounces mozzarella cheese, shredded**
- **4 ounces cheddar cheese, shredded**
- **¼ cup chopped green onions (optional)**
- **Bacon bits (optional)**
- **Ham, diced (optional)**
- **½ cup grated Parmesan cheese**

Preheat oven to 350 degrees.
Peel, cut, cook, drain and mash potatoes. Add milk, butter, garlic powder, salt, pepper, mozzarella cheese, cheddar cheese and optional ingredients, if desired. Mix well. Place in 2-quart casserole. Sprinkle top of casserole with Parmesan cheese. Bake until lightly browned. Serves 6 to 8.

Karen Farr, Warsaw, Mo.

Festive Cranberry Stuffing

Ruby-red cranberries don't just make a tasty sauce or relish! They're also a great way to perk up the flavor of dried stuffing mix.

- **1 (14-ounce) can chicken broth (1¾ cups)**
- **Generous dash pepper**
- **1 stalk celery, coarsely chopped (about ½ cup)**
- **½ cup fresh or frozen cranberries**
- **1 small onion, coarsely chopped (about ¼ cup)**
- **4 cups herb-seasoned stuffing mix**

Mix broth, pepper, celery, cranberries and onion in medium saucepan over high heat. Bring to a boil. Cover and cook over low heat 5 minutes or until vegetables are tender. Add stuffing mix. Mix lightly. Serves 5.

Galelah Dowell, Fairland, Okla.

Clockwise from the top; Turkey, Potato Casserole (page 212), Root Vegetable Medley (page 214), Easy Cranberry-Orange Relish (page 214), Festive Cranberry Stuffing (page 212), Sweet Potato Pone (page 212).

Easy Cranberry-Orange Relish

Pleasantly citrus-y and not too sweet, this zesty relish gets its crunch from chopped pecans. It can be refrigerated in an airtight container for up to one week.

¾ cup sugar
1 cup orange juice
1 (12-ounce) package cranberries
1 teaspoon orange zest
½ teaspoon cinnamon, cloves or ginger
½ cup chopped pecans

Mix sugar and orange juice in a medium saucepan; stir to dissolve sugar. Add cranberries. Return to boil and reduce heat; boil gently about 10 minutes until cranberries begin to pop, stirring occasionally.

Remove from heat and stir in orange zest, preferred spice and chopped pecans. Cool completely and refrigerate. Makes 2¼ cups.

Root Vegetable Medley

Two kinds of potatoes, turnip, parsley, parsnip and carrots cook with lemon, olive oil and garlic until tender. Then the veggies are popped under the broiler—caramelizing their natural sugars so they become wonderfully sweet.

1 sweet potato, cubed
1 turnip, cubed
1 parsnip, cubed
1 to 2 potatoes, cubed
2 carrots, cubed
2 to 3 tablespoons olive oil
Juice of half a lemon
1 tablespoon thyme
2 cloves garlic, minced (or 2 teaspoons minced garlic in jar)
½ teaspoon ground black pepper
Sprinkle of kosher salt

Preheat oven to 350 degrees.

In nonmetal bowl or dish, mix sweet potato, turnip, parsnip, potatoes, carrots, olive oil, lemon juice, thyme, garlic, pepper and salt and let sit at room temperature for 15 minutes, stirring occasionally. Toss into skillet and sauté until desired tenderness (10 to 15 minutes, or longer if you like them braised a little). Broil 15 minutes, turning frequently. Serves 4 to 6.

Leslie VanOverberghe, North Liberty, Ind.

Pumpkin Cake

Pumpkin pie lovers will love this subtly spiced cake with cream cheese icing. Better yet, this recipe can be made into bars or a sheet cake, depending on the baking pan you select.

2 cups sugar
4 eggs
1 (15-ounce) can pumpkin
1 cup oil
2 cups flour
2 teaspoons baking powder
1 teaspoon baking soda
½ teaspoon cinnamon
½ teaspoon pumpkin pie spice
Dash of salt

Icing

1 (3-ounce) package cream cheese
¾ stick butter
1 teaspoon vanilla
3 cups confectioners' sugar

Preheat oven to 325 degrees for bars and 350 degrees for cake.

Combine sugar, eggs, pumpkin and oil; mix well. Gradually add flour, baking powder, baking soda, cinnamon, pumpkin pie spice and salt. Pour into prepared jelly roll pan for bars or 13 x 9-inch pan for cake. Bake 30 minutes for bars and 25 to 30 minutes for cake.

For icing, combine cream cheese, butter and vanilla. Gradually add confectioners' sugar.

Cool cake completely and top with cream cheese icing. Serves 12.

Brittany Kitt, Bluffton, Ind.

Apple Pecan Tart

This gorgeous rustic tart is sure to impress guests (but only you need to know that it's even easier to assemble than a typical apple pie)! Dark or light corn syrup can be used, although dark syrup will give you a rich molasses flavor.

1 unbaked pie crust
½ cup sugar
½ cup corn syrup
2 eggs, well beaten
1 teaspoon butter, melted
1 cup chopped pecans

1½ teaspoons vanilla
2 large cooking apples, cored,
  peeled and chopped.
1 teaspoon lemon juice

Preheat oven to 350 degrees.
Place pie crust in a 9-inch tart pan and leave the sides long and free-form.
Combine sugar and corn syrup.

Add eggs and beat until smooth. Add melted butter and continue to beat. Add pecans and vanilla and mix well. Set aside.

Toss apples with lemon juice. Spread apples on bottom of pie crust and pour pecan mixture over apples.

Fold edges of pie crust over filling.

Bake pie until set, about 45 to 50 minutes. Serves 8. ■

Roasting the Perfect Turkey

Whether you are hosting your first Thanksgiving dinner or are a seasoned veteran, the thought of roasting a turkey can be intimidating.

Follow these simple steps and you should have a bird worthy of praise:

1. Thaw your turkey for several days in the refrigerator—plan on one day for every four pounds of turkey.
2. Place a rack under the turkey to keep it from sitting in the greasy drippings.
3. Brush the turkey with oil or rub with seasoned butter to keep the skin from drying out.
4. Roast your turkey at 325 degrees for about 12 minutes per pound.
5. Shield the turkey with foil during the last hour of cooking to keep the skin from overbrowning.
6. Insert a meat thermometer into the thigh to check for doneness. Avoid touching the bone. Turkey is done when the internal temperature reaches 180 degrees in the thigh or 170 degrees in the breast.
7. Check the temperature about 30 minutes before you think the turkey should be done.
8. When finished, let the turkey stand 15 to 20 minutes before carving.

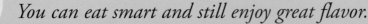

Satisfy Your Sweet Tooth

Chocolate Meringue Drops

   4 large egg whites
   2½ cups confectioners' sugar
   **½ cup unsweetened cocoa
      powder**
   2 tablespoons flour
   **2 teaspoons very finely ground
      fresh coffee (or powdered
      instant coffee)**
   1 tablespoon water
   ¾ cup finely chopped hazelnuts

Preheat oven to 350 degrees. Line 2 baking sheets with parchment paper.

Using an electric mixer, beat egg whites until frothy. Add confectioners' sugar, cocoa powder, flour, coffee and water. Beat on low until combined, turn mixer to high, and beat 3 to 4 minutes until mixture resembles marshmallow topping. Using a rubber spatula, fold in hazelnuts. Drop by heaping teaspoonfuls onto cookie sheets; bake 15 to 18 minutes, or until tops crack. Makes 48 drop cookies.

40 calories, 1 g protein, 7 g carbohydrates, 1 g fat, 0 g saturated fat, 0 mg cholesterol, 1 g fiber, 5 mg sodium.

Fresh Fruit Smoothie

   1 large ripe banana
   ½ cup cubed mango fruit
   ½ cup crushed ice
   2 tablespoons orange juice

Place banana, fruit mango, ice and orange juice in a blender. Blend until smooth. Serves 1.

193 calories, 2 g protein, 49 g carbohydrates, 1 g fat, 0 g saturated fat, 0 mg cholesterol, 5 g fiber, 3 mg sodium. ■

Sweet & Savory Extras

Pumpkin-Pecan Crumble Pie

- 1 (15-ounce) can pumpkin
- 1 (12-ounce) can evaporated milk
- 3 eggs
- 1 cup sugar
- 1 tablespoon pumpkin pie spice
- 1 (18¾-ounce) white or yellow cake mix
- 2 cups chopped pecans
- ½ cup butter, melted

Heat oven to 350 degrees. Grease 13 x 9 x 2-inch baking pan.

Stir together the pumpkin, evaporated milk, eggs, sugar and pumpkin pie spice until smooth. Pour into prepared pan. Scatter dry cake mix over pumpkin mixture. Sprinkle with pecans. Pour melted butter evenly over top.

Bake 50 to 60 minutes or until it tests done. Cool completely and refrigerate. Serves 12.

Swiss Onion Loaf

- 1 cup (4 ounces) shredded Swiss cheese
- 2 tablespoons minced dried onion
- 1 (16-ounce) package hot-roll mix
- 1 tablespoon butter, melted

Preheat oven to 375 degrees.

In a bowl combine cheese and minced onion with dry ingredients of hot-roll mix.

Prepare mix according to package directions. Turn onto a floured surface; knead until smooth and elastic (6 to 8 minutes). Shape into a 5-inch ball and place on a greased baking sheet. Cover and let rise in a warm place for 30 minutes or until doubled. Bake for 25 to 30 minutes or until golden brown. Brush with butter. Remove to a wire rack to cool. Makes 1 loaf.

Galelah Dowell, Fairland, Okla.

Clockwise from top left : Whole-Wheat
Bread dough rising, Whole-Wheat
Bread (page 219), Whole-Wheat Bread
and Provencal Cheese & Herb Bread,
Provencal Cheese & Herb Bread (page
219), Butterball Biscuits (page 220),
Honey Raisin Bran Muffins (page 221),
Holiday Pumpkin Bread (page 221) and
New Orleans French Bread (page 220)

Breads That Rise to the Occasion

Any way you slice it, this collection of hearty loaves and quick breads will make any baker feel proud!

Whole-Wheat Bread

Not too dense but full of whole-grain flavor, it's the blend of whole-wheat and white flours that sets this light-textured loaf apart from other recipes you may have tried. Corn syrup adds a touch of sweetness, or you can use honey or light molasses.

2 packages, or 1½ teaspoons instant, yeast
1¼ cups milk, divided
¼ cup butter
1 teaspoon salt
2 tablespoons corn syrup or honey
2⅓ cups whole-wheat flour
1½ cups flour

Crumble yeast in large bowl and dissolve in a few tablespoons of the milk. Melt butter over low heat. Remove from heat and add remaining milk and yeast mixture. Pour this lukewarm mixture into bowl. Add salt, corn syrup and whole-wheat flour. Gradually add flour.

Beat dough until smooth and beginning to leave sides of bowl. Sprinkle about 1 tablespoon flour on top, cover and let rise until doubled in size. 30 minutes to 1 hour, depending on the temperature of the room.

Preheat oven to 400 degrees. Grease loaf pan

Punch down dough, turn onto lightly floured board, and knead until smooth. Roll into an even loaf and put in the prepared pan. Let rise until doubled in bulk. Cook 40 minutes or until done. Brush the hot bread quickly with cold water. Let cool a few minutes, remove from pan, wrap in kitchen towel and allow to cool. Makes 1 loaf.

Arlene Ranney, Eureka. Calif.

Provencal Cheese & Herb Bread

Stuffed with flecks of Mediterranean herbs, pepper and shredded cheddar cheese, you only need to serve a simple salad with this hearty loaf for a satisfying supper.

1 package active dry yeast
1¼ cups warm water, divided
2 teaspoons sugar, divided
3¾ to 4 cups flour, divided
2 teaspoons salt
1 teaspoon dried rosemary
½ teaspoon dried thyme
½ teaspoon dried basil
½ teaspoon dried oregano
¼ teaspoon dried sage
¼ teaspoon black pepper
2 tablespoons extra-virgin olive oil
1 cup shredded sharp cheddar cheese, divided
1 egg, beaten with 1 tablespoon water

Preheat oven to 400 degrees.
Sprinkle yeast over ¼ cup of the warm water (105 degrees) in a glass measuring cup; stir in 1 teaspoon of sugar. Let stand for 10 minutes; mixture will be foamy.

In a large bowl, stir together 3¼ cups of the flour, salt, rosemary, thyme, basil, oregano, sage, pepper and remaining 1 teaspoon sugar.

Pour yeast mixture into flour mixture. Add remaining 1 cup warm water and the olive oil; stir to form a ball. Mix in ¾ cup of the shredded cheddar cheese. ▶

Turn onto a well-floured surface. Knead for 10 minutes, adding additional flour as needed until dough is smooth and elastic.

Grease a large bowl with a little additional olive oil. Place dough in bowl and turn to coat. Cover with plastic wrap. Let rise in a warm place for 1½ hours, until doubled in size. Punch dough down.

Roll out dough into a 20 x 8-inch rectangle on a lightly floured surface. Roll up from a short side. Fold ends under loaf and place seam side down in a greased 8½ x 4½ x 2⅝-inch loaf pan. Loosely cover with plastic wrap and let rise in a warm place for an additional hour.

Brush top of loaf with the egg wash. Sprinkle with the remaining ¼ cup cheese. Bake for 35 minutes or until loaf sounds hollow when tapped. Remove from pan to rack. Cool. Makes 1 loaf.

Galelah Dowell, Fairland, Okla.

Butterball Biscuits

It's the double dose of butter that makes these old-fashioned biscuits tender and flaky inside, crisp and golden outside.

½ cup butter
2 cups flour
3 teaspoons baking powder
1 teaspoon salt
⅓ cup soft butter
¾ cup milk

Preheat oven to 450 degrees.

Melt ½ cup butter or margarine; put 1 teaspoon into each of 12 (2½-inch) muffin pan cups; reserve remainder.

Sift flour, baking powder, and salt into mixing bowl. Add ⅓ cup soft butter or margarine; cut in with pastry blender until mixture resembles cornmeal. Stir in milk with fork.

Fill each prepared muffin cup nearly to the top with dough. Bake 10 minutes. Spoon 1 teaspoon melted butter or margarine over each biscuit. Bake 10 minutes longer. Serves 12.

Sharon Crider, Lebanon, Mo.

New Orleans French Bread

If you've never tried to make a traditional French baguette—it's easier than you think. This recipe makes 4 loaves, perfect for freezing extra bread to accompany future meals all winter long.

1 package dry yeast
2½ cups warm water (105 to 115 degrees)
2 tablespoons sugar, divided
1 tablespoon salt
6½ to 7 cups flour, divided
1 egg white, slightly beaten

Preheat oven to 450 degrees.

Combine yeast, water and 1 teaspoon sugar in a large bowl, stirring until dissolved. Stir in remaining sugar, salt and 6 cups flour to form a stiff dough.

Turn dough onto a surface sprinkled with remaining flour; knead dough for 8 minutes or until smooth and elastic. Place dough in a greased bowl, turning to grease top. Cover and let rise in a warm place (85 degrees), free from drafts, 1½ hours or until doubled in bulk. Turn dough out onto a lightly floured surface. Cover and let rest 15 minutes. Knead 3 to 4 times.

Divide dough into 4 equal portions; roll each portion into a 13 x 7-inch rectangle. Roll up each rectangle, jelly-roll fashion, starting at a long end. Pinch seams and ends together to seal. Place loaves, seam side down, in 4 heavily greased baguette pans or on baking sheets.

Cut 3 or 4 diagonal slashes, ¾ inch deep, in top of each loaf. Cover and repeat rising procedure 1 hour or until doubled in bulk. Brush loaves with egg white. Bake 15 minutes; reduce heat to 350 degrees and bake 30 minutes or until loaves sound hollow when tapped. Remove bread from pans or baking sheets immediately; cool on wire racks. Makes 4 loaves.

Patricia Cook, Detroit, Mich.

Holiday Pumpkin Bread

No mixer is required to whip up these scrumptious quick breads! Vegetable oil and canned pumpkin make them super moist, so they'll keep tightly wrapped at room temperature up to one week or frozen up to two months. For a more kid-friendly option, omit half the pecans in one of the loaves if desired.

3 cups sugar
2 cups flour
1 teaspoon cinnamon
1 teaspoon nutmeg
1 teaspoon allspice
½ teaspoon baking powder
½ teaspoon baking soda
½ teaspoon salt
3 eggs
1 (15-ounce) can solid-packed pumpkin
1 cup oil
1 teaspoon vanilla extract
1½ cups pecans, chopped

Preheat oven to 350 degrees. Grease and flour 2 (8 x 4 x 2-inch) pans.

In bowl, combine sugar, flour, cinnamon, nutmeg, allspice, baking powder, baking soda and salt.

In another bowl, combine eggs, pumpkin, oil and vanilla; mix well. Stir into dry ingredients just until moistened; fold in pecans.

Spoon into prepared pans. Bake 65 to 75 minutes or until toothpick inserted near center comes out clean. Cool 5 minutes before removing from pans to cool on a rack. Makes 2 loaves.

Arlene Ranney, Eureka, Calif.

Honey Raisin Bran Muffins

1¾ cup flour
1 tablespoon baking powder
¼ teaspoon salt
2 tablespoons sugar
2½ cups raisin bran cereal
1¼ cups skim milk

Preheat oven to 400 degrees. Coat muffin pan with nonstick cooking spray.

Stir together flour, baking powder, salt, and sugar.

In large bowl, stir together cereal, milk, and honey. Let stand 3 minutes or until cereal softens. Add egg and oil. Beat well. Add flour mixture, stirring only until combined.

Spoon batter evenly into prepared muffin cups. Bake 20 minutes or until lightly browned. Serve warm. Yields 12 muffins. ■

Margy Mann, St. Louis, Mo.

Easy Entrees for Busy Weeknights

Delicious Spinach Lasagna

- 1 pound ricotta cheese
- 2 cups shredded mozzarella cheese, divided
- 1 egg
- 1 package frozen chopped spinach, thawed and drained
- ½ teaspoon salt
- 1 teaspoon oregano
- Dash pepper
- 1 zucchini, thinly sliced
- 1 carrot, shredded
- 32 ounces spaghetti sauce, divided
- 12 lasagna noodles, uncooked (or enough to fill pan in layers)
- 1 cup water

Grease a 9 x 13 x 3-inch pan.

In a large bowl, mix ricotta cheese, 1 cup mozzarella cheese, egg, spinach, salt, oregano and pepper. In a separate bowl, combine zucchini, carrots and 1 cup sauce.

In prepared pan, layer 1 cup sauce, 3 of the noodles and half of the ricotta cheese mixture. Add 3 more noodles and the zucchini/carrot/sauce mixture. Continue with 3 more noodles and remaining ricotta cheese mixture. Top with remaining noodles and sauce. Sprinkle with remaining 1 cup mozzarella cheese. Pour water around the edges of the pan. Cover tightly with foil and refrigerate overnight.

To prepare, preheat oven to 350 degrees. Bake, covered, for 60 to 70 minutes. Let stand 10 to 15 minutes. Serves 12.

Suzan Wiener, Spring Hill, Fla.

Chicken Casserole

- 1 (6-ounce) package long-grain and wild rice mix
- 4¼ cups chicken broth
- ¼ cup butter
- 1 (8-ounce) package sliced mushrooms
- ½ cup chopped green onions
- 2 cups cooked chicken or turkey
- ½ cup sour cream
- 1 (10¾-ounce) can cream of mushroom soup
- ⅔ cup crushed round butter-flavored crackers
- ½ (6-ounce) can French-fried onions, crushed
- 2 tablespoons butter, melted
- ¼ teaspoon paprika
- ⅛ teaspoon garlic powder

Spray a 3-quart casserole with non-stick cooking spray.

Cook rice according to package directions, substituting 4¼ cups chicken broth for water and omitting butter and salt.

Melt ¼ cup butter in a skillet over medium heat; add mushrooms and green onions; sauté until tender, about 10 minutes. Stir in rice, chicken, sour cream and soup. Spoon mixture into prepared casserole dish.

Stir together crushed crackers and fried onions. Stir in 2 tablespoons melted butter, paprika and garlic powder. Sprinkle casserole evenly with cracker mixture. Cover with foil. May be frozen for up to 1 month.

To prepare, thaw overnight in refrigerator.

Preheat oven to 350 degrees. Bake 20 to 30 minutes. Uncover and bake 5 to 10 minutes more or until bubbly. Serves 6 to 8. ■

Festive Fruit-Filled Favorites

Chocolate-Covered-Cherries Treat

- 6 (1-ounce) squares semisweet chocolate
- ¼ teaspoon almond extract
- 1 cup flour
- ½ cup dark brown sugar
- ½ cup butter
- ½ teaspoon salt
- 18 maraschino cherries, drained and halved

Preheat oven to 350 degrees.

Melt chocolate in double boiler; stir in almond extract; set aside.

Combine the flour and brown sugar. Cut the butter and salt into the flour mixture until the consistency of pie dough. Press the dough mixture into the bottom of an 8 x 8 x 2-inch baking pan; smooth the dough.

Bake 20 minutes. Cut into 36 small squares while still warm. Cool; place squares on a large plate or baking pan lined with waxed or parchment paper. Place a cherry half on each square; cover each with a spoonful of melted chocolate. Chill until the chocolate hardens; place separately on a candy dish. Makes 36 small squares.

Gwen Campbell, Sterling, Va.

Cranberry Oatmeal Cookies

- 2 cups flour
- 2 teaspoons baking powder
- 1 teaspoon baking soda
- 1 teaspoon salt
- 1 cup shortening
- 1½ cups brown sugar firmly packed
- 2 eggs
- 1 tablespoon water
- 1½ cups uncooked quick oats
- 1⅓ cups white chocolate chips
- ⅔ cup chopped dried cranberries
- 1 teaspoon orange juice concentrate

Preheat oven to 375 degrees.

In small bowl, combine flour, baking powder, baking soda and salt; set aside.

In a large bowl, combine shortening, brown sugar, eggs and water; beat until creamy. Gradually add flour mixture. Stir in oats, white chocolate chips, cranberries, and orange juice concentrate.

Drop in round balls onto greased cookie sheets. Bake for 10 to 12 minutes. Makes about 4 dozen. ■

Sue Wadsworth, Lufkin, Texas

Gifts From the Kitchen

Few things say you care more than a gift made by your own hands!

As temperatures drop and the holidays approach, keep a supply of these homemade treats in your pantry to ensure you never have to drop by someone's home empty-handed.

Homemade gifts, especially those of food, are always special to those we love. Take a little time to prepare these mixes and biscotti, all of which keep well for long periods of time.

Try packaging the biscotti in colorful celephane bags tied with pretty ribbons. Any of the drink mixes, added to the biscotti would make a great care package for your favorite college students as they prepare for semester finals. They will know you are thinking of them while they enjoy saving their cash

by not having to buy expensive coffeehouse drinks. Maybe they'll even call home!

Chai Latte Mix

This popular drink is smooth and spicy. It is simple to make and to alter the spices to suit your tastes.

- **2 cups nonfat dry milk powder**
- **⅓ cup brown sugar**
- **2 tablespoons ground cinnamon**
- **1 teaspoon ground nutmeg**
- **½ teaspoon ground cardamom**
- **1½ teaspoons ground ginger**
- **¼ teaspoon ground allspice**
- **⅛ teaspoon ground cloves**
- **⅛ teaspoon white pepper (optional)**

- **2 cups nondairy powdered coffee creamer**
- **2 cups confectioners' sugar**
- **2 cups instant tea, unsweetened**
- **1 (3.4-ounce) package instant vanilla pudding mix**

Mix 1 cup nonfat dry milk with brown sugar, cinnamon, nutmeg, cardamom, ginger, allspice, cloves, and white pepper, if desired; blend in the blender or food processor to get the lumps out of the brown sugar.

Combine with remaining 1 cup nonfat dry milk, nondairy creamer, confectioners' sugar, instant tea and vanilla pudding; mix well.

Start with 2 rounded tablespoons of mix to an 8-ounce cup of hot water; stir.

Store mix in a covered container. Serves 35.

Carol Forcum, Marion, Ill.

Brownie Biscotti

- **⅓ cup butter**
- **⅔ cup sugar**
- **2 teaspoons baking powder**
- **2 eggs**
- **1 teaspoon vanilla**
- **⅓ cup unsweetened cocoa powder**
- **1¾ cups flour, divided**
- **½ cup mini semisweet chocolate chips**
- **¼ cup chopped walnuts**
- **1 tablespoon water**
- **1 egg yolk, beaten**

On opposite page, in center: Cookie Mix (page 226); Top left: Chai Latte Mix (page 224) Center right: Hot Chocolate Mix (page 226); Lower right: Brownie Biscotti (page 224) and Hazelnut Biscotti (page 226); Lower left: Mocha Java and Cinnamon-Spiced Coffee (page 227).

Preheat oven to 375 degrees.

Beat butter until soft; add sugar and baking powder. Beat in eggs and vanilla. Add cocoa powder and as much flour as you can by mixer. Add the remaining flour by hand. Stir in chocolate chips and walnuts.

Divide dough into 2 equal parts. Shape into 9 x 2 x 1-inch loaves. Place on baking sheet 4 inches apart. Brush with mixture of water and egg yolk.

Bake for 25 minutes. Cool on baking sheet for 30 minutes. Cut loaves diagonally into thick slices. Lay cut side down and bake at 235 degrees for 15 minutes. Turn over and bake other side for 10 to 15 minutes until dry. Cool. Store in an airtight container. Makes 2 dozen

Carol Forcum, Marion, Ill.

Cookie Mix

Let your kids help put these colorful jars together—they make great teacher gifts!

Mix

> **1 cup flour**
> **½ teaspoon baking soda**
> **½ teaspoon salt**
> **1 cup mini candy-coated chocolate pieces**
> **1¼ cups old-fashioned oats**
> **¼ cup brown sugar**
> **¼ cup sugar**
> **1 cup peanut butter chips**

Cookies

> **1 jar cookie mix**
> **¾ cup butter, softened**
> **2 large eggs, beaten**
> **1 teaspoon vanilla**

For mix, combine flour, baking soda and salt; place in a 5-cup jar with a tight-fitting lid. Top with layers of candy and oats. Mix sugars; add to jar. Top with chips. Cover; give with recipe card.

For cookies, preheat oven to 350 degrees. Have baking sheets ready.

Empty cookie mix in large bowl, breaking up brown sugar if clumped. Work in butter with rubber spatula. Add eggs and vanilla; stir until well blended. Drop heaping teaspoonsful of mixture 2 inches apart on ungreased baking sheets.

Bake 12 minutes or until golden brown. Cool on sheet on wire rack 2 minutes before removing from sheet to rack to cool completely. Makes 3 dozen cookies.

Arlene Ranney, Eureka, Calif.

Hot Chocolate Mix

Why buy hot chocolate mixes from the store when you can make your own. Change the flavor by using a flavored nondairy creamer in place of the plain.

> **10⅔ cups (8-quart box) dry milk powder**
> **3 cups instant chocolate-flavored drink mix**
> **1 (6-ounce) jar nondairy creamer**
> **2 cups confectioners' sugar**

Combine milk powder, chocolate-flavored drink mix, nondairy creamer and sugar.

To prepare hot chocolate, use ¼ cup mix to ¾ cup hot water. Makes 1 gallon mix or 4 gallons hot cocoa.

Hazelnut Biscotti

> **½ cup butter**
> **⅔ cup sugar**
> **2 eggs**
> **2 teaspoons baking powder**
> **1 teaspoon vanilla**
> **2 cups flour, divided**
> **1½ cups finely chopped hazelnuts**

1 egg yolk mixed with 1 table-spoon milk
1 cup semisweet chocolate pieces melted with 2 tablespoons shortening, optional

Preheat oven to 375 degrees.

Beat butter with electric mixer on medium speed for 30 seconds or until softened. Add sugar, eggs, baking powder, vanilla and 1 cup flour. Beat until combined. Add the remaining flour and nuts. Mix well.

Divide dough in half. Shape each portion into 9 x 2 x 1-inch logs. Place 4 inches apart on a lightly greased sheet. Brush with egg wash to give it a shiny appearance.

Bake for 25 minutes. Cool on cookie sheet. Cut into 1-inch diagonal slices. Lay on ungreased cookie sheet. Lower oven temperature to 325 degrees and bake for 8 to 10 minutes until toasted.

If desired, melt chocolate. Drizzle chocolate over cookies or dip half the cookies into chocolate. Let chocolate set. Makes about 40.

Cecelia Rooney, Point Pleasant, N.J.

Cinnamon-Spiced Coffee

You'll find this mix reminiscent of the costly name brands—and it is so simple to make!

¼ cup instant coffee granules
¼ cup plus 3 tablespoons sugar
½ cup plus 1 tablespoon non-dairy creamer
⅛ teaspoon cinnamon

Grind the instant coffee into powder using a coffee grinder.

Mix coffee, sugar, creamer, and cinnamon in a small bowl. Store in a sealed container.

To make coffee, measure 2 table-spoons powdered mix into a coffee cup. Add 8 ounces (1 cup) boiling water and stir. Makes 9 servings.

Mocha Java Mix

Smooth chocolate flavors this warming winter drink.

¼ cup instant coffee granules
½ cup plus 2 tablespoons sugar
½ cup plus 1 tablespoon nondairy creamer
2 tablespoons unsweetened cocoa powder

Grind the instant coffee into powder using a coffee grinder.

Mix coffee powder, sugar, creamer and cocoa powder in a small bowl. Store in a sealed container.

To make coffee, measure 4 teaspoons of the powdered mix into a coffee cup. Add 8 ounces (1 cup) boiling water and stir. Makes 16 servings. ■

Get Ready to Give

These hot beverage mixes all stay fresh for several months, so keep them on hand for easy gift giving. Stock up on clear or colorful cellophane bags or interesting, inexpensive containers and pretty mugs and you can have a gift for the forgotten teacher or bus driver ready in minutes. Write the serving instructions on pretty gift tags and keep them stored with the bags and mugs.

Planning Great Meals

Here's our all-new collection of recipes! Plus we're offering these menu suggestions to help you plan great meals.

Lunch With Friends
Baked Turkey Salad, 231
Pineapple-Glazed Carrots, 233
Lettuce salad
Frozen Fruit Salad, 236

One-Dish Delights
Turkey & Vegetable Pie, 235
Marshmallow Hash, 236

Speedy Weeknight Supper
Candied Apple Pork Chops, 234
Basil & Pecan Sweet
Potato Bake, 232
Broccoli
Cheesecake With
Gingersnap Crust, 237

Easy Party Finger Foods
Shrimp Crescent Appetizer, 230
Jalapeno Cheese Bites, 230
Stuffed Mushrooms, 231
Oat Cherry Squares, 236
"I Can't Believe
How Easy" Dessert, 237

Easy Entertaining
Phony Abalone, 231
Pineapple/Sweet-
Potato Mounds, 233
Tossed green salad
Dinner rolls

Recipes From Our Readers

Home cooks share their favorite recipes—quick-to-prepare comfort foods, good for family, friends and special occasions.

Czech Bar Cookies

Judy Shaw, Bluffton, Ind.

1½ cups sugar
1½ cups butter
3 egg yolks
3 cups flour
1½ cups chopped pecans
¾ cup strawberry or
    raspberry jam

Preheat oven to 375 degrees. Grease a 13 x 9-inch pan.

Cream sugar and butter. Add egg yolks, beating well. Stir in flour and pecans. Divide dough in half and press half in bottom of pan. Spread jam over dough. Pat out remaining dough and place on top of jam.

Bake 1 hour, until a deep golden brown.

Makes 24 bars.

Mexican Wedding Cakes

Alice Robinson, Berne, Ind.

1 cup butter, softened
½ cup sifted confectioners'
    sugar, plus more for rolling
1 teaspoon vanilla
2¼ cups sifted flour
¼ teaspoon salt
¾ cup finely chopped nuts

Preheat oven to 400 degrees.

Cream together butter, confectioners' sugar and vanilla. Stir in sifted flour and salt to form a soft dough. Add chopped nuts. Form cookies into 1-inch balls and bake on an ungreased cookie sheet for 10 to 12 minutes, until set but not browned. Roll warm cookies in confectioners' sugar. Cool completely and roll in confectioners' sugar a second time.

Makes about 4 dozen cookies.

Sugar Cookies

Martha Coquat, Big Sandy, Texas

½ cup butter
¼ cup shortening
1 cup white sugar
2 eggs
1 teaspoon vanilla extract
2½ cups flour
1 teaspoon baking powder
1 teaspoon salt
colored sugars or sprinkles for
    decoration

In a large bowl, cream together the butter, shortening, and sugar until fluffy. Beat in the eggs one at a time then stir in the vanilla extract.

Combine the flour, baking powder, and salt; gradually blend into the creamed mixture to form soft dough. Gather dough into a ball or disk and ▶

put into plastic wrap or a plastic bag and chill for 1 hour or overnight.

To bake, preheat oven to 400 degrees.

On a floured surface, roll out dough to a ¼ inch thickness. With cookie cutters, cut dough into desired shapes and place on ungreased cookie sheets about 2 inches apart. Decorate with colored sugars or sprinkles. Bake for 6 to 8 minutes, or until very light brown. Immediately transfer cookies with a spatula to a wire rack to cool. Makes about 4 dozen cookies.

Snickerdoodles

Martha Coquat, Big Sandy, Texas

1½ cups plus 2 tablespoons
   sugar, divided
½ cup butter, softened
1 teaspoon vanilla extract
2 eggs
2¾ cups flour
1 teaspoon cream of tartar
½ teaspoon baking soda
¼ teaspoon salt
2 teaspoons cinnamon

Preheat oven to 400 degrees.

Combine 1½ cups sugar, butter, vanilla and eggs. Mix well.

Stir in flour, cream of tartar, baking soda and salt. Blend well. Shape dough into 1 inch balls. Combine 2 tablespoons sugar and 2 teaspoons cinnamon. Roll dough in sugar and cinnamon mixture and place 2 inches apart on ungreased cookie sheets.

Bake 8 to 10 minutes or until set. Immediately remove from cookie sheets.

Spiral Cheese Slices

Galelah Dowell, Fairland, Okla.

1 (8-ounce) tube refrigerated
   crescent rolls
¼ cup chopped green onions
⅛ teaspoon garlic powder
¼ cup shredded cheddar cheese

Preheat oven to 375 degrees.

Remove crescent dough from tube; do not unroll. Cut into 8 slices; place on an ungreased baking sheet. Top with green onions. Sprinkle with garlic powder and cheese; lightly press cheese into slices. Bake for 14 to 16 minutes or until golden brown. Serve warm. Makes 8 servings.

Shrimp Crescent Appetizer

Gwen Campbell, Sterling, Va.

1 (8-ounce) tube refrigerated
   crescent rolls
16 small cooked shrimp
Cocktail sauce to top each crescent

Preheat oven to 350 degrees.

Separate crescent-roll dough into 8 triangles. Cut each triangle in half. Place 1 cooked shrimp in center of each small triangle; top with cocktail sauce. Fold into crescent shape; moisten sides with water; crimp sides in a decorative pattern. Bake for 12 minutes or until golden brown and slightly puffed. Makes 16.

Jalapeño Cheese Bites

Jo Ann Ervin, Glasgow, Ky.

8 ounces cheddar cheese
8 ounces Monterey Jack cheese
5 or 6 jalapeño peppers
6 beaten eggs

Preheat oven to 350 degrees. Lightly spray a 8 x 11-inch baking dish with cooking spray.

Grate cheddar cheese and Monterey Jack cheese and place in prepared dish. Chop peppers and sprinkle

on top of the cheese. Pour beaten eggs over the cheese and peppers. Bake for 30 minutes. Cool for a few minutes and cut into squares. Serves 10.

Stuffed Mushrooms

Cecilia Rooney, Pt. Pleasant, N.J.

- **3 slices whole-wheat bread**
- **¾ cup grated Romano or Parmesan cheese**
- **⅓ cup chopped flat-leaf parsley**
- **2 garlic cloves, minced**
- **½ teaspoon coarse salt**
- **¼ teaspoon ground pepper**
- **40 medium white mushrooms (about 1 pound), stemmed**
- **6 tablespoons butter, melted**
- **4 tablespoons olive oil**

Preheat oven to 375 degrees.

In a food processor, pulse bread until fine crumbs form (should be 1 cup). In a large bowl, toss bread with cheese, parsley and garlic. Season with salt and pepper.

With one hand, dip a mushroom in melted butter to coat completely; transfer to bread crumbs. With other hand, stuff mushrooms with filling, patting some mixture on bottom and sides. Place stemmed sides up on a rimmed

baking sheet. Repeat until all mushrooms are stuffed. Sprinkle with olive oil.

Bake until golden brown. Let cool before transferring to a serving dish. Makes 40.

Phony Abalone

Karen Farr, Warsaw, Mo.

- **5 boneless, skinless chicken breasts**
- **2 teaspoons garlic salt**
- **1½ teaspoons dried parsley**
- **1 bottle clam juice**
- **2½ cups cracker crumbs**
- **3 tablespoons grated Romano cheese**
- **Olive oil**

Pound chicken until thin. Mix garlic salt, parsley and clam juice in medium bowl. Add chicken and cover with a tight lid. Shake to cover all chicken. Refrigerate 24 hours.

Mix cracker crumbs and Romano cheese. Coat chicken with cracker mixture and brown in a skillet with small amount of oil. Serves 5.

Baked Turkey Salad

Arlene Ranney, Eureka, Calif.

- **4 cups leftover turkey, diced**
- **1 cup celery, minced**
- **¾ to 1 cup mayonnaise**

- **¾ cup toasted almonds**
- **½ cup chopped green onions, tops included**
- **¼ cup chopped parsley leaves**
- **3 tablespoons lemon juice**
- **Salt and freshly ground pepper to taste**

Preheat oven to 450 degrees.

Combine turkey, celery, mayonnaise, almonds, onions, parsley leaves, lemon juice, salt and pepper. Divide among 6 generously buttered ramekins and bake 15 minutes. Serves 6.

Quick Tip For variations, an equal amount of water chestnuts or fresh pineapple may be substituted.

Chicken Divine

Mari Roll, Enumclaw, Wash.

1 bunch fresh broccoli, chopped
2 cups cooked chicken
1 cup bread crumbs
2 teaspoons butter
½ cup mayonnaise
1 teaspoon lemon juice
1 can cream of mushroom soup
Grated cheddar cheese

Preheat oven to 350 degrees.

In an 8 x 8-inch pan or 2-quart casserole dish, layer the ingredients as follows:

1st layer: chopped broccoli.

2nd layer: cooked chicken.

3rd layer: bread crumbs mixed with butter.

4th layer: Mix mayonnaise, lemon juice and cream of mushroom soup. Pour on top.

Sprinkle grated cheddar cheese evenly over the top. Bake for 30 minutes. Serves 4 to 6.

Terrific Turkey Creole

Gwen Campbell, Sterling, Va.

½ cup shortening
1 cup flour
1 cup finely chopped celery
1 cup chopped green, red or yellow bell pepper
¼ teaspoon garlic, minced
½ cup shredded green onions

¼ teaspoon poultry seasoning
1 teaspoon salt
1 teaspoon pepper
½ teaspoon ground marjoram
⅛ teaspoon cayenne pepper
1 (28-ounce) can tomatoes
2 cups tomato juice or vegetable juice cocktail
3 cups cooked turkey, cubed
Hot cooked rice, mashed potatoes, pasta or toasted bread points (toasted bread slices cut on the diagonal)

Heat shortening in large skillet; add flour, stirring constantly until smooth and lightly browned. Add celery, bell pepper, garlic, onions, poultry seasoning, salt, pepper, marjoram, cayenne pepper, tomatoes and tomato juice. Simmer 20 minutes, stirring occasionally. Add turkey cubes; simmer 10 minutes. Serve turkey mixture over hot cooked rice, mashed potatoes, pasta, or toasted bread points. Serves 6.

Corn Casserole

Helen Harlos, Ethel, Miss.

1 (14¾-ounce) can cream-style corn
1 (15¼-ounce) can whole-kernel corn.
1 box sweet corn bread mix
1 cup sour cream
1 cup onion, chopped
1 (14½-ounce) can tomatoes
½ cup margarine, melted
½ to ¾ cup grated cheese

Preheat oven to 350 degrees.

Mix together cream-style corn, whole-kernel corn, corn bread mix, sour cream, onion, tomatoes and margarine; put in prepared, shallow 2-quart casserole. Bake 30 minutes. Place cheese on top during the last 10 minutes of baking. Serves 8 to 10.

Basil & Pecan Sweet Potato Bake

Galelah Dowell, Fairland, Okla.

3 (15-ounce) cans sweet potatoes
½ cup half-and-half
2 tablespoons butter, softened
2 tablespoons chopped fresh basil
¼ teaspoon ground cinnamon
¼ teaspoon ground nutmeg
Salt and pepper to taste
½ cup chopped pecans

Preheat oven to 350 degrees. Grease a 9 x 9-inch baking dish.

¼ cup butter, melted
½ cup orange juice
1¼ teaspoons pumpkin
   pie spice
1 teaspoon grated orange peel
¼ cup chopped pecans
½ cup dark or golden raisins
1 (20-ounce) can sliced pineapple,
   reserve ¾ cup juice
2 tablespoons cornstarch
Miniature marshmallows to top
   sweet potatoes

In medium mixing bowl, combine sweet potatoes, half-and-half, butter, basil, cinnamon, nutmeg, salt and pepper; blend with an electric mixer or in a food processor. Transfer mixture to prepared dish and smooth the surface. Top with chopped pecans. Cover and bake 20 minutes; remove cover and bake an additional 10 minutes. Serves 5 to 7.

Pineapple-Sweet Potato Mounds

Gwen Campbell, Sterling, Va.

  2 cups cooked, mashed sweet
    potatoes
  ⅔ cup dark brown sugar, firmly
    packed

Preheat oven to 400 degrees.

In a bowl, combine sweet potatoes, brown sugar, butter, orange juice, pumpkin pie spice, orange peel, pecans and raisins. Mix well.

Drain pineapple and place in a baking dish.

Mix together cornstarch and pineapple juice; stir well to combine. Mound ⅓ cup of the sweet potato mixture on top of each pineapple slice. Pour cornstarch mixture around each mound. Bake 20 minutes. Top each sweet potato mound with marshmallows and bake for 5 minutes longer, until marshmallows soften and are golden-tipped. Serves 10.

Pineapple-Glazed Carrots

Galelah Dowell, Fairland, Okla.

  3 cups baby carrots or quartered
    medium carrots
  ½ cup pineapple spreadable fruit
  2 tablespoons honey
  2 tablespoons butter or margarine

Place carrots and a small amount of water in a saucepan; bring to a boil. Reduce heat; cover and simmer for 10 to 15 minutes or until crisp-tender. Drain. Set aside and keep warm.

In another saucepan, bring the fruit, honey and butter to a boil. Drizzle over carrots; toss to coat. Serves 4.

Pecan-Crusted Salmon

Arlene Ranney, Eureka, Calif.

  4 salmon fillets (about 6 ounces
    each)
  2 cups milk
  1 cup finely chopped pecans
  ½ cup flour
  ¼ cup brown sugar, packed
  2 teaspoons seasoned salt
  2 teaspoons pepper
  3 tablespoons oil

▶

Preheat oven to 400 degrees.

Place fillets in large resealable plastic bag; add milk. Let stand 10 minutes; drain. In shallow bowl, combine pecans, flour, brown sugar, seasoned salt and pepper. Coat fillets with pecan mixture, gently pressing into fish.

In large nonstick skillet, heat oil and brown salmon. Transfer to baking sheet. Bake for 8 to 10 minutes or until fish flakes easily with fork. Serves 4.

Steak & Potato Pasties

Helen Harlos, Ethel, Miss.

- **1 cup uncooked, tenderized round steak, cut into bite-sized pieces**
- **3 strips bacon, cut up**
- **2½ cups finely diced potatoes**
- **3 tablespoons parsley flakes**
- **2 tablespoons finely chopped onion**
- **1 (16-ounce) can cut green beans, drained**
- **3 tablespoons water**

Salt and pepper to taste
2 deep-dish pie crusts
2 tablespoons butter

Preheat oven to 400 degrees.

Mix steak pieces, bacon, potatoes, parsley flakes, onion, green beans, water, salt and pepper; put in pie shell. Dot with butter. Roll out top crust; place on pie. Cut slits for vents. Bake 15 minutes. Lower heat to 350 degrees. Continue baking for 50 minutes. Serves 6.

Candied Apple Pork Chops

Dottie Luttrell, Enid, Miss.

- **2 medium red apples**
- **4 boneless pork loin chops**
- **2 tablespoons brown sugar**
- **⅛ teaspoon nutmeg**
- **⅛ teaspoon cinnamon**
- **Salt and pepper to taste**
- **2 tablespoons butter**
- **3 tablespoons pecans, chopped**

Core and slice apples. Heat skillet, brush pork chops with cooking oil, and cook until brown. Combine brown sugar, nutmeg, cinnamon, and salt and pepper. Add butter to skillet and stir in brown sugar mixture and apples. Cook until apples are tender. Remove apples with slotted spoon and arrange on top of chops. Continue cooking sauce until it thickens. Spoon sauce over apples and chops. Top with pecans. Serves 4.

Spaghetti With Sausage & Spinach

Cecelia Rooney, Pt. Pleasant, N.J.

- **2 teaspoons olive oil**
- **1 pound sweet Italian sausage, cut into ½-inch slices**
- **1 large onion, chopped**
- **2 large garlic cloves, chopped**
- **2 (14-ounce) cans chicken broth**
- **¼ cup water**
- **½ pound thin spaghetti, broken into halves**
- **2 (10-ounce) packages fresh spinach, coarsely chopped**
- **¼ teaspoon freshly ground pepper**
- **⅓ cup heavy cream**

Heat oil in Dutch oven over medium heat. Add sausage. Cook for 3 to 4 minutes, turning while browning. Add onion and garlic. Cook 2 to 3 minutes. Add broth and water. Cover and bring to a boil. Add spaghetti. Cook 3 minutes, stirring frequently. Add spinach and pepper. Cook and stir for 2 to 3 minutes or until spaghetti is al dente and spinach is wilted. Stir in heavy cream. Serve immediately. Makes 4 to 6 servings.

Fiesta Chicken

Linda Nichols, Steubenville, Ohio

- **4 boneless, skinless chicken breasts,**
- **½ cup sour cream**
- **2 tablespoons taco seasoning mix**
- **Cracker crumbs**
- **1 cup cheddar cheese**

Preheat oven to 350 degrees. Grease baking dish.

Pound chicken breasts slightly to flatten them to a uniform size. Coat chicken breasts with sour cream. Combine cracker crumbs and taco seasoning mix. Dredge chicken in mixture. Place in prepared dish. Sprinkle with cheese. Bake, uncovered, for 30 to 45 minutes. Serves 4.

Chilies Rellenos Bake

1 pound ground beef
½ cup onion
1 teaspoon salt, divided
¼ teaspoon pepper
2 cans whole green chilies, divided
4 eggs, beaten
1½ cups milk
¼ cup flour
1½ cups shredded sharp Cheddar cheese
Taco sauce

Preheat oven to 350 degrees.

Brown beef and onion; drain fat. Add ½ teaspoon salt and pepper. Place half of chilies on bottom of 12 x 8-inch baking dish. Top with meat mixture. Arrange remaining chilies on top. Combine eggs, milk, flour and ½ teaspoon salt until smooth. Pour over chilies. Top with cheese. Bake 45 minutes or until browned and knife inserted just off center comes out clean. Serve with taco sauce. Serves 4 to 6.

Turkey & Vegetable Pie

Carol Faith, Brockton, Mass.

1 onion, chopped
¼ cup chopped green pepper
3 garlic cloves, minced
3 tablespoons oil
1 pound ground turkey
Salt and pepper to taste
1 (10¼-ounce) can brown gravy
½ cup green peas (canned or frozen)
½ cup diced carrots (slice thin or cook slightly)
½ cup green beans (canned or frozen)
Pastry for 2-crust, 9-inch pie

Preheat oven to 350 degrees.

Sauté onion, green pepper and garlic in oil until tender. Brown meat, drain and set aside. Add sautéed vegetables to meat. Stir in salt and pepper, gravy, peas, carrots and green beans. Mix

well. Pour into 9-inch pie crust. Cover with top crust. Seal well. Cut slits in top. Bake for 1 hour, or until top is light brown. Serves 8.

Baked Steak

Karen Farr, Warsaw, Mo.

1 (1½-inch-thick) top round boneless beef steak (about 3 pounds), trimmed of all fat
2 teaspoons oil
Salt and pepper to taste
1 small green bell pepper, cut into ⅛-inch rings
1 small onion, cut into ⅛-inch rings
1 (14-ounce) can Italian stewed tomatoes, drained
½ cup ketchup

Preheat oven to 350 degrees.

In large skillet, brown steak in oil on both sides, cooking about 8 minutes in all. Transfer steak to ovenproof dish or skillet large enough for all ingredients. Season with salt and pepper. Pile bell pepper and onion rings on top of steak. Top with stewed tomatoes. Pour ketchup over all. Bake 60 minutes. Serves 4 to 6.

Marshmallow Hash

Hazel Hullinger, Decatur, Ill.

1 cup evaporated milk
2 cups sugar
⅛ teaspoon salt
2 cups semisweet chocolate bits
1 teaspoon vanilla
1½ cups miniature marshmallows
1 cup chopped nuts

Combine evaporated milk, sugar and salt in saucepan. Cook over medium heat until mixture boils; boil 2 minutes, stirring constantly. Remove from heat; add chocolate and vanilla. Stir until melted. Pour half of mixture in waxed-paper-lined 8 x 8-inch dish. Press marshmallows into chocolate. Cover with nuts then top with remaining chocolate mixture. Cool and cut into squares. Makes 2 pounds.

Oat Cherry Squares

Arlene Ranney, Eureka, Calif.

1 cup whole-wheat flour
1 cup quick-cooking oats
⅔ cup brown sugar, packed
½ teaspoon baking soda
¼ teaspoon salt
⅓ cup butter, melted
1 (10-ounce) jar 100 percent cherry, strawberry or raspberry spreadable fruit

Preheat oven to 350 degrees. Spray a 9 x 9-inch pan with cooking spray.

In large bowl combine flour, oats, brown sugar, baking soda and salt; stir in butter. Reserve ¾ cup for topping. Pat remaining oat mixture into prepared pan. Bake 5 to 7 minutes. Top with spreadable fruit. Sprinkle with reserved crumb topping. Bake 25 to 30 minutes or until edges are light brown. Cool on wire rack. Serves 16.

Fruitcake Supreme

Bobby Langley, Rocky Mount, N.C.

8 ounces candied pineapple
8 ounces candied cherries
1 (8-ounce) bag chopped dates
3 cups pecans
2 (3½-ounce) cans coconut
1 (14-ounce) can sweetened condensed milk
2 ounces rum, brandy, or your favorite wine

Preheat oven to 225 degrees. Line a bread pan or other ovenproof dish with heavy-duty or nonstick aluminum foil.

In a large bowl, stir pineapple, cherries, dates, pecans, coconut, sweetened condensed milk, and rum, brandy or wine. Pack mixture down firmly in prepared pan; bake for one hour. Let cool and place in refrigerator overnight to set before removing foil and slicing. Keeps for weeks in a tin. Serves 10 to 12.

Note: *1 ounce of rum and 1 ounce of brandy may be mixed for this recipe for a great taste, but do not exceed the 2 ounces of any liquor or wine you choose. The alcohol will evaporate during cooking.*

Frozen Fruit Salad

1 (3-ounce) package cream cheese
2 tablespoons cream
⅓ cup mayonnaise
2 tablespoons lemon juice
1 (1 pound, 13-ounce) can fruit cocktail, drained
½ cup pitted Bing cherries
½ cup chopped pecans
2 tablespoons sugar
1 cup whipping cream, whipped

Mix cream cheese and cream. Blend in mayonnaise and lemon

juice. Combine fruit cocktail, cherries, pecans and sugar. Stir cream cheese mixture into fruits. Fold fruit mixture into whipped cream. Pour into freezing mold. Freeze in refrigerator freezing compartment without stirring. Serve on lettuce garnished with Bing cherry halves or pecan halves. Serves 8 to 12.

Raisin Pudding

Hazel Hullinger, Decatur, Ill.

1 cup flour
½ cup sugar
2 teaspoons baking powder
1 cup raisins
½ cup milk
1 cup brown sugar
1 tablespoon butter
2 cups boiling water

Preheat oven to 350 degrees. Grease an 8 x 8-inch baking dish.

Stir together flour, sugar, baking powder, raisins and milk. Pour into prepared dish.

Stir together brown sugar, butter and boiling water. Pour over batter and bake until brown, about 25 to 30 minutes. Serve warm or cold. Serves 6.

Cheesecake With Gingersnap Crust

Catherine Murphy, Eliot, Maine

Crust

¼ cup softened butter
20 gingersnaps, crushed
2½ tablespoons sugar

Filling

1 (8-ounce) package cream cheese, softened
1 (14-ounce) can sweetened condensed milk
⅓ cup lemon juice
1 teaspoon vanilla
1 pint fresh or frozen strawberries (or your favorite fruit)

Preheat oven to 350 degrees.

Combine butter, crushed gingersnaps and sugar. Press crumb mixture with the back of a spoon into a 9-inch pie plate. Bake for 10 minutes. Cool before filling.

In large bowl, beat cream cheese until fluffy. Gradually beat in sweetened condensed milk until smooth. Stir in lemon juice and vanilla; mix well. Spoon mixture into the cool pie crust. Chill 3 hours or until set. Top with fruit before serving. Serves 8.

Chocolate Chip Cheesecake

Denise Hansen, Jackson, Minn.

2 rolls slice-and-bake chocolate chip cookie dough
3 eggs
2 cups sugar
2 (8-ounce) packages cream cheese, softened

Preheat oven to 350 degrees.

Slice one roll of cookie dough into 24 slices and put in the bottom of a 13 x 9-inch pan. Beat eggs until fluffy. Add sugar and cream cheese; beat until smooth. Pour over the sliced cookies. Slice the second roll of cookie dough and put on top of the cream cheese mixture. Bake for 45 to 60 minutes or until cookies turn brown. Cool and refrigerate. Serves 24.

"I Can't Believe How Easy" Dessert

Kit Rollins, Cedarburg, Wis.

8 (½-inch) slices of pound cake
1 (14-ounce) can sweetened condensed milk
1 (7-ounce) package flaked coconut

Preheat oven to broil. Line sheet pan with nonstick foil.

Cut pound cake slices into 3 strips, no crusts. Dip cake strips in milk and roll in coconut. Broil about 4 inches from medium heat, 5 to 8 minutes. Watch carefully. Turn and broil on second side about 3 minutes. Cool before serving. Makes about 24 strips. ■

From the top: Apple-Cranberry Baked French Toast (page 240), Pecan-Apricot Scones (page 240) and Baked Stuffing Cups with Eggs & Bacon (page 240).

Christmas Morning Breakfast

Make Christmas morning even more special with these delicious, easy-to-prepare breakfast treats.

By Suzanne Caithamer

Pumpkin, cranberries, dates, apricots, eggnot, gingerbread and stuffing—all these good foods and flavors conjure up images of traditional, loved holiday dishes. Perhaps baking gingerbread cookies and pumpkin pies is a tradition at your house, or the holiday meal isn't complete without eggnog to sip, cranberry sauce for the turkey, and a big casserole dish of Grandma's stuffing.

With all this preparation for the main meal of the day, it's no surprise that breakfast often gets overlooked. You don't have to settle for coffee and a packaged doughnut; breakfast can be a special meal too, and it's a meal that lends itself to holiday flavors just like Thanksgiving or Christmas dinner. It doesn't have to be complicated or strenuous—many of these dishes can be made or prepped ahead so that morning fuss is kept to a minimum. Make your holiday meals special right from the start with these delicious breakfast and brunch ideas!

Cranberry-Date Granola

This delicious, whole-grain cereal, full of dried cranberries and dates, is also a wonderful gift to give. Package in cellophane bags, and tie with a ribbon.

- 4 cups old-fashioned oats
- ½ cup sliced almonds
- 1 teaspoon cinnamon
- ¼ teaspoon salt
- ½ cup honey

- 2 tablespoons molasses
- ⅓ cup oil
- 2 teaspoons vanilla
- ½ cup toasted coconut
- 1 cup chopped pitted dates
- 1 cup dried cranberries

Preheat oven to 300 degrees. Lightly grease a jelly-roll pan.

In a large bowl, combine oats, almonds, cinnamon and salt. In a medium saucepan, combine honey, molasses, oil and vanilla. Bring to a boil. Pour over oat mixture and combine well.

Spread oat mixture onto prepared jelly-roll pan. Bake 40 minutes, stirring after every 10 minutes. Let cool; mix in coconut, dates and cranberries. Store in an airtight container. Makes 6 cups Serves 12.

Gingerbread Waffles

Who says gingerbread is just cookies or cake? Serve these spiced waffles with butter and homemade apple-cider syrup that has a hint of nutmeg.

- 2 eggs, separated
- 1¾ cups buttermilk
- ¼ cup molasses
- 2 cups flour
- 2 teaspoons baking powder
- 1 teaspoon baking soda
- 1½ teaspoons ground ginger
- 1 teaspoon cinnamon
- ¼ teaspoon cloves
- ½ teaspoon salt
- 4 tablespoons butter, melted

Preheat waffle iron.

In a large bowl, mix egg yolks, buttermilk and molasses. In a medium bowl, combine flour, baking powder, baking soda, ginger, cinnamon, cloves and salt. Add to buttermilk mixture, and mix until smooth. Stir in melted butter.

In a small bowl, beat egg whites until soft peaks form; fold into waffle batter. Bake in preheated waffle iron according to manufacturer's directions.

Serve with Apple Cider Syrup. Makes 4 to 6 waffles. ▶

Pecan-Apricot Scones

Toasted pecans add crunch and apricots add a hint of sweetness to these easy-to-make breakfast breads. Add scrambled eggs and bacon for a filling, festive meal.

2½ cups flour
3 tablespoons brown sugar
2 teaspoons baking powder
¼ teaspoon cinnamon
½ teaspoon salt
4 tablespoons chilled butter
¾ cup chopped dried apricots
½ cup chopped toasted pecans
⅔ cup milk, plus 1 tablespoon
**   for glaze**
2 eggs
1 tablespoon confectioners' sugar

Preheat oven to 425 degrees. Lightly grease a large baking sheet.

In a large bowl, stir together flour, brown sugar, baking powder, cinnamon and salt. Cut in butter until mixture resembles coarse crumbs. Stir in apricots and pecans.

In a medium bowl, combine thoroughly ⅔ cup milk and eggs. Pour all at once into dry ingredients, and combine just until moistened.

Turn dough out onto a lightly floured surface and knead about 10 times or until dough comes together and is smooth. Transfer to prepared baking sheet; pat out into a 9-inch round. Cut dough into 8 wedges, but do not separate them.

Brush 1 tablespoon milk over scones for glaze; sprinkle with confectioners' sugar.

Bake for 15 to 20 minutes or until golden brown. Separate scones and serve warm with butter. Makes 8.

Apple-Cranberry Baked French Toast

Perfect for a busy Christmas morning— assemble this dish the night before and refrigerate overnight. Then bake at your leisure for a warm, satisfying breakfast.

1 cup brown sugar
½ cup butter
1 teaspoon cinnamon
2 tablespoons light corn syrup
2 large tart apples, such as
**   Granny Smith, peeled, cored**
**   and thinly sliced**
1 cup dried cranberries
1 (10-ounce) loaf French bread,
**   cut into ¾-inch slices**
5 eggs
1¼ cups milk
1 teaspoon vanilla
½ teaspoon salt

In a medium saucepan, combine brown sugar, butter, cinnamon and corn syrup. Cook over medium heat until butter is melted and sugar is dissolved. Pour into a greased 13 x 9-inch baking dish. Arrange apples and cranberries over sugar mixture. Place bread slices over apple mixture, covering apples completely.

In a large bowl, combine eggs, milk, vanilla and salt. Pour evenly over bread, soaking slices entirely. Cover and refrigerate overnight.

Preheat oven to 350 degrees. Remove French toast from refrigerator 30 minutes prior to baking.

Bake for about 40 to 45 minutes or until puffy and golden brown. Let stand for 5 minutes before serving. Serves 4 to 6.

Baked Stuffing Cups With Eggs & Bacon

What to do with leftover stuffing? Press into muffin cups, fill with eggs and top with cheese and bacon; then bake for a hearty little individual treat.

1½ cups prepared stuffing
6 eggs
Salt and pepper to taste
2 tablespoons shredded cheddar
**   cheese**
2 strips bacon, crumbled

Preheat oven to 350 degrees. Spray 6 cups of a muffin pan with cooking spray.

Place ¼ cup stuffing into each cup, pressing up sides to make a "cup." Carefully crack an egg into each cup. Sprinkle with salt and pepper.

Bake for 20 to 25 minutes or until eggs are set. Sprinkle each with 1 teaspoon cheese; top with crumbled bacon. Bake until cheese is melted, about 2 to 3 more minutes. Remove stuffing cups from pan and serve immediately. Makes 6.

Eggnog Pancakes

Homemade pancakes mix up in a jiffy and are even better with the flavor of eggnog. Serve with sausage links and lots of butter and maple syrup.

    2 eggs
    1¾ cups eggnog
    ¼ cup oil
    1½ teaspoons vanilla
    1¾ cups flour

    1 tablespoon sugar
    4 teaspoons baking powder
    ½ teaspoon salt
    ½ teaspoon nutmeg

In large bowl, combine eggs, eggnog, oil and vanilla. Sift together flour, sugar, baking powder, salt and nutmeg; add to eggnog mixture and mix just until blended. (Add additional eggnog if needed to make batter the proper consistency.) Pour by ¼ cupfuls onto heated griddle; turn when bubbles form around edges of pancakes. Serve warm. Makes about 15 pancakes.

Apple Cider Syrup

    1 cup apple cider
    ½ cup brown sugar
    ¼ teaspoon nutmeg
    Dash cinnamon
    1 teaspoon lemon juice
    1 teaspoon butter

In medium saucepan, combine cider, brown sugar, nutmeg and cinnamon. Cook over medium heat until sugar is dissolved and mixture just comes to a boil, stirring frequently. Reduce heat to low and add lemon juice and butter. Serve warm. Keep leftovers in the refrigerator. Makes about 1 cup. ■

Appetizers for a Busy Buffet

Buffet Meatballs

- **1 cup apple juice**
- **1 cup grape jelly**
- **1 cup ketchup**
- **1 (8-ounce) can tomato sauce**
- **4 pounds frozen Italian-style meatballs**

In a saucepan combine juice, jelly, ketchup and tomato sauce. Cook and stir over medium heat until jelly is melted. Remove from heat.

Place meatballs in 5-quart slow cooker. Pour sauce over top and gently stir to coat. Cover and cook on low 4 hours, until heated through. Makes approximately 11 dozen meatballs.

Arlene Ranney, Eureka, Calif.

Sugar Dogs

- **3 packages hot dogs, cut into thirds**
- **1 pound bacon, each piece cut in half**
- **1 (2-pound) bag brown sugar**

Wrap each piece of hot dog in a bacon strip. Place hot dogs in slow cooker. Pour bag of brown sugar over top. Cook on low until sugar melts. Serve hot. Serves 18 as an appetizer. ■

Karen Farr, Warsaw, Mo.

Helpful Tips

The slow cooker is perfect for making and keeping appetizers, dips and spreads warm for a party. Even if they have not been cooked in the slow cooker, they can be kept warm on low for several hours. The food will need to remain covered for most of the time to maintain their heat.

Soup: Simple, Satisfying Fare

Soup's on! Our soothing, comforting meals in a bowl are so easy they practically cook themselves.

Nothing chases away winter's chill more deliciously than a steaming bowl of homemade soup. And during the busy holiday season, what could be better than a one-dish dinner, generously portioned with plenty for second helpings, that tastes even better when made ahead? Relax on Sunday while a batch of Lazy Day Beef & Vegetable Soup or Snowy Weekend Turkey & Bean Soup simmers on the stove. Or, whip up a pot of Corn Chowder or Pasta & Bean Soup for a last-minute weeknight meal. So celebrate with soup—a glorious food that's always ready and waiting when you are.

Lazy Day Beef & Vegetable Soup

Chunks of beef, chickpeas, pasta and plenty of veggies make this minestrone-style soup truly a meal in a bowl. The soup tastes even better if made and refrigerated a day ahead, but don't add the pasta until you've returned it to a boil, then cook as directed.

- **1 tablespoon olive oil**
- **2½ pounds beef stew meat, cut into ¾-inch pieces**
- **1 teaspoon salt**
- **1 teaspoon dried Italian seasoning**
- **½ teaspoon pepper**
- **2 (14- to 14½-ounce) cans beef broth**
- **1 (15- to 16-ounce) can chickpeas, drained**
- **1 (14½-ounce) can diced tomatoes with garlic and onion, un-drained**
- **1 cup water**
- **2 cups frozen mixed vegetables**
- **1 cup uncooked ditalini or other small pasta**
- **Shredded Romano cheese (optional)**

Heat olive oil in a Dutch oven over medium heat until hot. Brown half of beef; remove from Dutch oven. Repeat with remaining beef. Pour off drippings. Return all beef to Dutch oven; sprinkle with salt, Italian seasoning and pepper. Add broth, chickpeas, tomatoes and water; bring to a boil. Reduce heat; cover tightly and simmer for 1 hour, or until beef is almost tender. Stir in mixed vegetables and pasta. Continue simmering, covered, for 10 to 15 minutes, or until beef and pasta are tender. Stir occasionally. Serve with cheese, if desired. Serves 6 to 8.

Galelah Dowell, Fairland, Okla. ▶

Homemade Vegetable Soup

Because the rich beef broth must be refrigerated overnight, you'll need to plan ahead to prepare this recipe. But after that you can just add the vegetables and forget it—thanks to the slow cooker.

> 3 pounds beef short ribs, cooked, reserving broth
> Water
> 1 large onion, chopped
> 2 to 3 potatoes, cubed
> ¼ head cabbage, thinly sliced
> 1 (28-ounce) can chopped tomatoes
> Salt and pepper to taste
> 1 can beef broth, if needed

Cover meat with water and cook until tender. Separate meat from broth; refrigerate broth overnight. Next morning, dip fat from broth; put broth in a slow cooker. Trim fat from meat and put meat in a slow cooker. Add onion, potatoes, cabbage, tomatoes, salt, pepper and beef broth; cook on high for several hours. Serves 6.

Helen Harlos, Ethel, Miss.

Corn Chowder

Canned cream-style corn helps turn this summer favorite into a warming winter meal. If you want to skip the bacon, cook ¼ pound diced ham with 3 tablespoons oil. Choose smoked or baked ham for maximum flavor.

> ½ pound bacon, diced
> 1 medium onion, chopped
> ½ cup chopped celery with tops
> 2 tablespoons flour
> 4 cups milk
> 1 (17-ounce) can cream-style corn
> 1 cup frozen corn kernels
> 1 (16-ounce) can tiny whole potatoes, diced
> ½ teaspoon salt
> ½ teaspoon pepper
> Snipped parsley
> Paprika

In a large saucepan, fry bacon until crisp; remove bacon and drain all but 3 tablespoons drippings. Add onion and celery to drippings; cook and stir until onion is tender. Remove from heat; blend in flour. Cook over low heat, stirring until mixture is bubbly. Remove from heat. Stir in milk. Heat to boiling,

stirring constantly. Boil and stir for 1 minute. Stir in cream-style corn, corn kernels, potatoes, salt and pepper; heat through. Stir in bacon. Top with snipped parsley and a sprinkling of paprika. Serves 4.

Arlene Ranney, Eureka, Calif.

Tortilla Soup

Call this the Mexican-style chicken soup with beans and tortilla chips! Use canned chicken for speedier prep or leftover Thanksgiving turkey if you have some on hand.

> 1 large chopped onion
> 1 tablespoon oil
> 2 or 3 cups chopped cooked chicken
> 1 (10-ounce) can tomatoes and green chilies
> 2 (15-ounce) cans pinto beans, drained and rinsed
> 1 (13.25-ounce) can cream-style corn
> 1 (14.5-ounce) can chicken broth
> ½ teaspoon pepper
> 1 tablespoon chili powder
> 1 teaspoon sugar
> ½ teaspoon salt
> 2 or three crispy tortilla chips, crushed
> Fresh cilantro
> Dollop of sour cream, chopped avocado, tomato (optional)

In a 4-quart stockpot, sauté the onion in oil until softened. Add the chicken, tomatoes and green chilies, beans, corn, chicken broth, pepper, chili powder, sugar and salt. Heat to boiling

and simmer for 15 minutes. Garnish with crushed chips, cilantro, and optional ingredients, if desired. Makes 10 cups.

Snowy Weekend Turkey & Bean Soup

Although this one-pot wonder calls for turkey sausage, it's also a great way to use any left-over holiday bird. A combination of barley, lentils and split peas, in addition to the beans, makes the soup extra thick and hearty.

- **6 to 8 cups water**
- **2 chicken bouillon cubes**
- **1 (14½-ounce) can diced tomatoes with garlic and onion**
- **3 (15-ounce) cans black, white or pinto beans, drained and rinsed**
- **⅓ cup barley**
- **⅓ cup dried lentils**
- **⅓ cup dried split peas**
- **1 (14-ounce) package cooked turkey sausage, diced, or 2 cups leftover chicken or turkey**
- **Salt and pepper to taste**

Mix water, bouillon cubes, tomatoes, beans, barley, lentils, split peas, cooked meat, salt and pepper; bring to a boil. Simmer 1 to 2 hours. Serves 8.

Judy Ervin, Glasgow, Ky.

Pasta & Bean Soup

Spinach boosts the flavor and nutrients in this speedy version of the Italian classic. Serve with plenty of crusty bread.

- **1 tablespoon olive oil**
- **3 slices bacon, diced**
- **2 carrots, sliced**
- **2 celery ribs, sliced**
- **1 large onion, chopped**
- **1 tablespoon garlic, minced**
- **1 (48-ounce) can chicken broth**
- **2 cups water**
- **¼ teaspoon Italian seasoning**
- **¼ teaspoon black pepper**
- **1 teaspoon salt**
- **1 cup uncooked elbow macaroni**
- **1 can Great Northern beans, drained and rinsed**
- **1 (10-ounce) package frozen spinach, thawed**
- **Parmesan cheese (optional)**

Heat olive oil in large pot. Add bacon; cook 5 minutes or until browned. Remove bacon with slotted spoon. Set aside.

Add carrots, celery, onion and garlic to pot. Cook, stirring often, until veggies are tender.

Add bacon, chicken broth, water, Italian seasoning, pepper and salt. Bring to a boil; reduce heat, cover and simmer 10 minutes.

Add macaroni; cook 8 minutes or until macaroni is slightly underdone. Stir in beans and spinach; return to simmer and cook 2 minutes, or until hot. If desired, serve with Parmesan cheese. Serves 6 to 8. ■

Lisa Langston, Conroe, Texas

Quick & Healthful Trout Dinner

Broccoli With Compound Butter

- **1 cup unsalted butter, softened**
- **1 teaspoon lemon zest**
- **1 teaspoon lemon juice**
- **¾ teaspoon salt, divided**
- **¼ teaspoon pepper**
- **1 bunch broccoli, trimmed and cut into spears**

Mix butter, lemon zest, lemon juice, salt and pepper. Place on waxed paper and form into a log. Chill.

In microwave-safe dish, place 2 tablespoons water, ¼ teaspoon salt and broccoli. Cover and microwave 2 minutes.

Drain water and season with a pat of compound butter.

Serves 4.

Pan-Fried Trout

- **2 tablespoons olive oil**
- **1 tablespoon butter**
- **4 trout filets**
- **Salt and pepper**
- **3 tablespoons flour**
- **Lemon wedges**

Preheat heavy 10-inch skillet with oil and butter over medium-high heat.

Sprinkle both sides of trout with salt and pepper. Dredge in flour and carefully place fish in skillet, skin side up. When crispy, about 5 minutes, turn over and sauté skin-side down for an additional 5 to 7 minutes, until crispy. Serve with lemon wedges. Serves 4.

Couscous Curry

- **1½ cups chicken broth**
- **½ cup raisins**
- **1 tablespoon butter**
- **1 teaspoon curry powder**
- **1 cup couscous, uncooked**

In a medium saucepan, bring chicken broth, raisins, butter and curry powder to a boil. Remove from heat and stir in couscous. Let sit, covered, for 5 minutes. Fluff with a fork and serve. Serves 4. ■

Helpful Tips

Compound butter is butter with herbs and seasoning added to it to give a punch of flavor with very little effort. Vary the seasonings to suit your family's tastes.

Tuna With a Twist

Seaside Shells & Tuna Casserole

- **2 tablespoons butter**
- **2 tablespoons flour**
- **¼ teaspoon salt**
- **2 cups milk**
- **1 cup shredded cheddar or American cheese**
- **1¼ cups small pasta shells, cooked and drained**
- **4 cups broccoli florets, cooked slightly in small saucepan; set aside**
- **2 (6-ounce) cans tuna in water, drained**
- **Buttery Breadcrumb Topping (recipe follows)**

Topping

- **1 cup soft bread crumbs**
- **2 tablespoons butter, melted**

Preheat oven to 350 degrees. Lightly grease a 2-quart ovenproof casserole dish.

Melt butter in a large saucepan over low heat; stir in flour and salt. Cook, stirring constantly, until smooth and bubbling. Remove from heat; gradually stir in milk. Heat to boiling, stirring constantly. Boil and stir 1 minute; stir in cheese; stir until cheese melts.

Mix pasta, broccoli, tuna and cheese sauce in prepared casserole.

Cover; bake 20 minutes, until heated through and bubbling.

For topping, mix bread crumbs and melted butter; sprinkle across top of casserole; return to oven. Bake, uncovered, 5 minutes or until topping is toasted and golden. Serves 4. ■

Gwen Campbell, Sterling, Va.

Pork Chops & Apple Pie!

MENU

Pork Chops & Rice

Spinich Salad With Bacon Dressing

Mini Apple Pie

Pork Chops & Rice

- **2 boneless pork chops**
- **Salt and pepper to taste**
- **1½ cups chicken or beef broth**
- **¾ cup uncooked white rice**
- **1 cup sliced mushrooms**
- **1 green onion, sliced**
- **½ teaspoon tarragon**

Preheat oven to 350 degrees.

Season pork chops with salt and pepper. Combine broth, rice, mushrooms, green onion and tarragon. Add salt and pepper.

Place in a 1-quart baking dish and arrange pork chops on top. Cover tightly with foil and bake for 1 hour. Serves 2.

Spinach Salad With Bacon Dressing

3 cups baby spinach, stems
  removed
3 large mushrooms, sliced
1 hard-cooked egg, sliced
2 slices bacon, chopped
¼ cup balsamic vinegar
2 tablespoons olive oil

Arrange spinach, mushrooms and egg on two plates. Fry bacon in skillet and remove to paper towel to drain.

Wipe grease from skillet and add balsamic vinegar. Bring to a boil, reduce heat and simmer for 1 to 2 minutes until thickened. Remove from heat and whisk in olive oil. Spoon over salads and serve immediately. Serves 2.

Mini Apple Pie

1 (9-inch) ready-made pie crust
2 baking apples, peeled and
  sliced
¼ cup sugar
1 tablespoon flour
½ teaspoon cinnamon
2 tablespoons chopped walnuts
1 teaspoon lemon juice
1 teaspoon butter

Preheat oven to 350 degrees.

Place pie crust on baking sheet. Mix apples, sugar, flour and cinnamon and spread on half of pie crust. Sprinkle walnuts and lemon juice over apples. Dot with butter.

Fold crust in half over apples. Crimp edges and cut a vent slit in top.

Bake for 1 hour or until golden. Serves 2. ∎

Helpful Tip

If you are looking to make someone special a terrific meal without slaving all day in the kitchen, try this easy pork chop dinner. Both the pork chops and rice and the apple pie bake at the same temperature for an hour. The preparation time is minimal—slice up two apples, use a prepared pie crust and pop it on a cookie sheet. There's no need to brown the pork chops and the salad is last minute. Put everything in the oven and put your feet up until dinner is served.

More Planning Great Meals

Here's even more menu suggestions to help you plan great tasting meals!

Hearty Breakfast
Baked Stuffing Cups With Eggs & Bacon, 240
Cinnamon Rolls, 96
Creamy Fruit Salad, 189

Brunch
Spicy Turkey Sausage, 119
Rise & Shine Biscuits, 72
Fruit Platter, 16

Light Summer Luncheon
Southern Sweet Tea, 103
Apricot Chicken Salad, 112
Fresh Tomatoes &
Mozzarella, 150
Pink Angel Summer Cake, 115

Easy Mid-Day Fare
The California Sandwich, 121
Black Bean Salad, 30
Strawberry Dream, 41

Light & Tasty Lunch
California Chicken Salad, 42
Golden Carrot Muffins, 33
Easy Chocolate Fruit Tart, 159

Kid-Pleasing Supper
Pepper Jack Burgers, 134
Unfried Potatoes, 104
Petunia's Coleslaw Salad, 102
Butterfinger Ice Cream, 106

Weeknight Supper
Skillet Pork Chops, 94
Rosemary Roasted Potatoes, 178
Apple Gelatin Mold, 109
Butter Pecan Pound Cake, 11

Heartwarming Supper
Snowy Weekend Turkey & Bean Soup, 244
Whole Wheat Bread, 219
Side salad
Cinnamon Candy-Glazed Baked Apples, 172

Sunday Lunch
Beef Stroganoff, 91
Sesame Broccoli, 31
Sweet & Sour Orange Beets, 94
Cherry-Berry Pie, 122

Family-Pleasing Italian Dinner
Penne Pasta Bake With Meatballs, 80
Butter Dips, 116
Spinach, Strawberry & Pecan Salad With Orange Vinaigrette Dressing, 92
Chocolate Buttermilk Layer Cake, 20

Simple Summer Supper
Marinated Flank Steak, 139
California Sunburst Salad, 162
Butterball Biscuits, 220

Summer Evening Dinner
Grilled Chicken, 148
Garden Delight Salad, 132
Basic Deviled Eggs, 57
Lemon Icebox Cake, 84

Satisfying Soup & Salad
Slow Cooker White Chili, 49
Cornmeal Yeast Rolls, 11
Special Spinach Salad, 45

Kid-Friendly
Violet's Baked Chicken
Tenders, 103
Green beans
Chunky Applesauce, 49
Devil Dogs, 205

Spicy Mexican Meal
Quick & Tasty Tamales, 61
Spanish Rice, 98
Broccoli
Bananas Foster, 117

Company is Coming!
Crumb-Topped Salmon Fillets, 184
Mesclun & Goat Cheese Salad, 121
Pan-Roasted New Potatoes, 92
Chocolate Turtle Cheesecake, 20

Supper with Friends
Great Grilled New York
Strip Steak, 140
Mediterranean Beans in
Tomato Shells, 191
Couscous Curry, 246
Chocolate Meringue Drops, 216

Hearty Dinner
Sam's Salmon Loaf, 117
Oven-Broiled Asparagus, 94
New Potatoes with Sun-Dried, 161
Tomato Dressing, 211

Mostly Make-Ahead
Lump Crab Cakes, 155
Restaurant-Style Cole Slaw, 30
Twice Baked Potatoes, 129
Icebox Turtle Cake, 136

Vegetarian
Spinach Lasagna, 51
Orange Avocado Salad, 70
Garlic bread
Peanut Butter S'more Tarts, 196

Charts & Conversions

INGREDIENT	AMOUNT	SUBSTITUTE
Allspice	1 teaspoon	½ teaspoon cinnamon and ½ teaspoon ground cloves
Baking powder	1 tablespoon	1 teaspoon baking soda and 2 teaspoons cream of tartar
Brown sugar	1 cup	1 cup sugar plus 1 teaspoon molasses
Butter	1 cup	1 cup margarine, or ⅞ cup shortening and ½ teaspoon salt
Buttermilk	1 cup	1 tablespoon vinegar plus enough milk to equal 1 cup (let stand 5 minutes before using)
Chocolate chips, semisweet	1 ounce	1 ounce sweet cooking chocolate, chopped
Chocolate, unsweetened	1 ounce	3 tablespoons cocoa and 1 tablespoon butter or margarine
Cornstarch (for thickening)	1 tablespoon	2 tablespoons all-purpose flour
Cream, heavy	1 cup	¾ cup milk and ⅓ cup butter or margarine (only for use in cooking and baking)
Cream, light	1 cup	¾ cup milk and 3 tablespoons butter or margarine (only for use in cooking and baking) or 1 cup evaporated milk
Flour, cake	1 cup, sifted	1 cup minus 2 tablespoons all-purpose flour
Garlic	1 clove	⅛ to ¼ teaspoon garlic powder
Herbs, fresh	1 tablespoon	1 teaspoon dried herbs
Honey	1 cup	1¼ cups sugar with ¼ cup water
Lemon juice	1 teaspoon	½ teaspoon vinegar
Molasses	1 cup	1 cup honey
Mustard, dry	teaspoon	1 tablespoon prepared mustard
Oil	1 cup	1 cup melted butter, margarine or shortening
Poultry seasoning	teaspoon	1 teaspoon ground thyme plus ¾ teaspoon ground sage
Pumpkin pie spice	teaspoon	½ teaspoon cinnamon plus ¼ teaspoon ginger and 1/8 teaspoon each nutmeg and cloves
Sour cream	1 cup	1 cup plain yogurt
Tomato sauce	1 cup	¾ cup tomato paste plus 1 cup water
Yogurt, plain	1 cup	1 cup cottage cheese blended until smooth or 1 cup buttermilk or 1 cup sour cream

INGREDIENT	AMOUNT	EQUIVALENT
Almonds, whole	2½ ounces	½ cup
Apples	1 pound	3 or 4 medium
Apples	1 medium	1 cup diced or sliced
Bananas	1 medium	1 cup sliced
Butter/Margarine	1 stick	½ cup; 4 ounces
Lasagna, uncooked	16 ounces	16 to 24 noodles
Lemons	1 medium	2 to 3 tablespoons juice 2 to 3 teaspoons grated peel
Macaroni, uncooked	1 cup	2 cups cooked
Marshmallows, miniature	1 cup	80 miniature; 8 regular
Marshmallows, regular	1 regular	10 miniature
Nuts, in shell	1 pound	4 cups chopped
Oats, rolled	1 cup	1¾ cups cooked
Oranges	1 medium	⅓ to ½ cup juice
Popcorn, unpopped	3 tablespoons	4 cups popped
Raisins, seedless	16 ounces	2¾ cups
Shortening	1-pound can	2½ cups
Sugar, brown	1 pound	2¼ cups packed
Sugar, granulated	1 pound	2¼ cups
Tomatoes, fresh	1 pound	2 cups chopped
Tomatoes, canned	1 (28-ounce) can	3 cups undrained
Walnuts, chopped	1 pound	3½ cups

Conversion Chart

3 teaspoons	1 tablespoon
4 tablespoons	¼ cup
16 teaspoons	⅓ cup
1 cup	16 tablespoons
2 cups	1 pint
4 cups	1 quart or 1 liter
16 cups	1 gallon

Cooking Terms

Al dente	Describes the correct degree of doneness when cooking pasta and vegetables. The food should maintain a firm, chewy texture.
Baste	To ladle a liquid (meat drippings, stock, barbecue sauce, melted butter) on food while it cooks to prevent drying out and to add flavor.
Beat	To smoothen a mixture by briskly whipping or stirring.
Blend	To mix or fold two or more ingredients together to obtain equal distribution throughout the mixture.
Cream	To beat shortening, butter or margarine, with or without sugar, until light and fluffy.
Cut in	To work shortening, margarine, or butter into dry ingredients.
Dredge	To coat an item with dry ingredients such as flour and salt.
Fold	To mix gently, using a turning motion with a spatula.
Julienne	To cut into long, very thin strips.
Knead	To mix and work dough into a pliable mass either manually or with a mixer/food processor. When done by hand, you press the dough with the heels of your hands, fold in half, give a quarter turn, and repeat until smooth and elastic.
Lentil	A flat, edible seed of the pea family, generally used in soup.
Mesclun	A combination of young salad greens—often a mix of arugula, dandelion, frisee, mizuma, oak leaf, radicchio and sorrel.
Parboil	To partially cook and boil in water.
Pare	To cut off the outer covering or skin with a knife or other sharp tool.
Popovers	Quick, puffed-up hot bread made of milk, sugar, eggs and flour.
Sauté	To quickly heat meat or vegetables in fat in an open pan.
Simmer	To cook liquid just below the boiling point.
Zest	The thin, brightly colored outer part of the peel of citrus fruits.

Indexes

Recipe Title Index

A

Angel Food Cake With Orange Coconut Frosting, 58
Angel-Hair Pasta With Sesame-Ginger Dressing, 162
Apple Cider Syrup, 241
Apple Cobbler, 63
Apple Crisp, 175
Apple Crisp, 122
Apple Gelatin Mold, 109
Apple Pecan Tart, 214
Apple Spice Muffins, 34
Apple Wraps, 207
Apple-Cranberry Baked French Toast, 240
Applesauce Oatmeal Muffins, 174
Apricot Chicken Salad, 112
Avocado Salad, 198
Avocado Salsa, 70

B

Bacon-Ranch Potato Salad, 152
Baked Acorn Squash With Apple Stuffing, 183
Baked Apple Doughnuts, 48
Baked Asparagus, 209
Baked Chicken Amandine, 193
Baked Ham With Raisin Sauce, 53
Baked Onion Rings, 31
Baked Steak, 235
Baked Stuffing Cups With Eggs & Bacon, 240
Baked Tuna Foldovers, 77
Baked Turkey Salad, 231
Baking Powder Biscuits, 198
Banana Pie Delight, 157
Banana-Rum Pudding, 28
Bananas Foster, 117
Barbecue Meatball Hoagies, 78
Barbecue Sauce, 149
Basic Deviled Eggs, 57
Basic Tomato Sauce, 202
Basil & Pecan Sweet Potato Bake, 232
Bean & Sweet Onion Salad, 132
Beef & Bean Roundup, 75
Beef & Cabbage Rolls, 12

Beef Barley Soup, 19
Beef Enchilada Bake, 74
Beef Stroganof, 91
Beef Tenderloin Steaks With Mushroom Sauce, 128
Berry Buttermilk Pie, 95
Billy Bob's Barbecue, 148
Biscuit Mix Cheeseburger Pie, 77
Black Bean Salad, 30
Blackberry Jam Cake With Ice Cream, 60
Black-Eyed Pea Salad, 14
Blossom's Seasoned Potatoes, 102
Blue Lagoon, 145
Boiled Dinner, 126
Breaded Tomatoes, 112
Breakfast Potato Casserole, 84
Brie in Puff Pastry, 151
Broccoli Casserole, 211
Broccoli Wild Rice Soup, 19
Broccoli With Compound Butter, 246
Broiled Salmon With Cucumber Sauce, 154
Brownie Biscotti, 224
Buffet Meatballs, 242
Bugs on a Bench, 145
Butter Dips, 116
Butter Pecan Pound Cake, 11
Butterball Biscuits, 220
Butterfinger Ice Cream, 106
Buttermilk Fruit Salad, 157
Butternut Squash Soup, 181
Butterscotch Bars, 146
Butterscotch Brownies, 207
Butterscotch Nut Squares, 209

C

Cake Doughnuts, 43
California Chicken Salad, 42
California Sunburst Salad, 162
Can-Can Casserole, 74
Can-Can Chinese Casserole, 191
Candied Apple Pork Chops, 234
Carol's Caramel Coffee, 119
Carrot-Stuffed Squash, 183
Catch of the Day Chowder, 124
Chai Latte Mix, 224

Cheddar Chive Biscuits, 178
Cheese Ball, 151
Cheesecake With Gingersnap Crust, 237
Cheesy Ground Beef & Pasta, 77
Cherry Ice Cream, 106
Cherry-Berry Pie, 122
Chewy Cereal Squares, 207
Chewy Fruit 'n' Flax Cookies, 83
Chicken Casserole, 222
Chicken Divine, 232
Chicken Florentine Soup, 159
Chicken Piccata, 64
Chicken Reuben Casserole, 27
Chicken Spaghetti, 192
Chicken Stir-Fry, 42
Chili Dog Wraps, 111
Chili-Cheese Fingers, 150
Chilies Con Queso, 32
Chilies Rellenos Bake, 235
Chinese Noodle Candy, 156
Chocolate Angel Tea Cake, 60
Chocolate Banana Parfaits, 28
Chocolate Buttermilk Layer Cake, 20
Chocolate Cake Doughnuts, 47
Chocolate Caramel Pecan Pie, 195
Chocolate Cheese Fudge, 26
Chocolate Chip Cheesecake, 237
Chocolate Meringue Drops, 216
Chocolate Muffins With Gooey Centers, 156
Chocolate Nut Revels, 89
Chocolate Snack, 114
Chocolate Toffee Candy, 26
Chocolate Turtle Cheesecake, 20
Chocolate Wows, 146
Chocolate-Covered Cherries Treat, 223
Chocomallow Brownies, 68
Chunky Applesauce, 49
Cinnamon Roll Pudding, 196
Cinnamon Rolls, 96
Cinnamon Candy–Glazed Baked Apples, 172
Cinnamon-Spiced Coffee, 227
Citrus Blast Sherbet, 106
Classic Corn Muffins, 33
Classic Grilled Alaska Salmon, 121

General Recipe Index

Notes

Use these pages for your favorite recipe tips and notes!

Notes

Use these pages for your favorite recipe tips and notes!

Notes

Use these pages for your favorite recipe tips and notes!